Disciplines in the Maki

The organisation of higher education across the world is one of the factors that conspire to create the assumption that our own map of the intellectual disciplines is, broadly speaking, valid cross-culturally. *Disciplines in the Making* challenges this in relation to eight main areas of human endeavour, namely philosophy, mathematics, history, medicine, art, law, religion, and science. Lloyd focuses on historical and cross-cultural data that throw light on the different ways in which these disciplines were constituted and defined in different periods and civilisations, especially in ancient Greece and China, and how the relationships between them were understood, particularly when one or other discipline claimed hegemonic status (as happened, at different times, with philosophy, history, religion, and science). He also explores the role of elites, whether positive (when they foster the professionalisation of a discipline) or negative (when they restrict recruitment to the profession, when they insist on adherence to established norms, concepts, and practices and thereby inhibit further innovation). The issues are relevant to current educational policy in relation to the ever-increasing specialisation we see, especially in the sciences, and to the difficulties encountered in making the most of the opportunities for inter- or trans-disciplinary research.

G. E. R. Lloyd is Emeritus Professor of Ancient Philosophy and Science at the University of Cambridge.

Disciplines in the Making

Cross-Cultural Perspectives on
Elites, Learning, and Innovation

G. E. R. LLOYD

OXFORD
UNIVERSITY PRESS

OXFORD
UNIVERSITY PRESS

Great Clarendon Street, Oxford OX2 6DP

Oxford University Press is a department of the University of Oxford.
It furthers the University's objective of excellence in research, scholarship,
and education by publishing worldwide in

Oxford New York

Auckland Cape Town Dar es Salaam Hong Kong Karachi
Kuala Lumpur Madrid Melbourne Mexico City Nairobi
New Delhi Shanghai Taipei Toronto

With offices in

Argentina Austria Brazil Chile Czech Republic France Greece
Guatemala Hungary Italy Japan Poland Portugal Singapore
South Korea Switzerland Thailand Turkey Ukraine Vietnam

Oxford is a registered trade mark of Oxford University Press
in the UK and in certain other countries

Published in the United States
by Oxford University Press Inc., New York

© G. E. R. Lloyd 2009

The moral rights of the author have been asserted
Database right Oxford University Press (maker)

First published 2009
First published in paperback 2011

British Library Cataloguing in Publication Data
Data available

Library of Congress Cataloging in Publication Data
Data available

Typeset by SPI Publisher Services, Pondicherry, India
Printed in Great Britain
on acid-free paper by
MPG Books Group, Bodmin and King's Lynn

ISBN 978–0–19–956787–4 (Hbk.)
978–0–19–969471–6 (Pbk.)

1 3 5 7 9 10 8 6 4 2

CONTENTS

PREFACE

This book is a sequel to my *Cognitive Variations: Reflections on the Unity and Diversity of the Human Mind* (Oxford, 2007). That work explored the commonalities and the differences in human cognition in relation to such subjects as space, colour, the emotions. But one major recurrent set of issues that I was unable to tackle there, but now take up in this further study, relates to how understanding of the various areas of human experience has been organized, how the various intellectual disciplines emerged, and the institutional contexts in which that happened. Where my earlier book challenged a too swift assumption that the perception of space, for instance, is a cross-cultural universal, this study raises similar questions about the understanding of such disciplines as philosophy, mathematics, history, across different societies at different times. How far is there reason to suppose that these understandings correspond to cognitive ambitions shared by all, or most, humans? Or how far is it the case that each discipline has grown up in quite distinctive forms in different societies? Our modern Western understanding of the matter is enshrined in the faculty structure of our universities. But if that is where my inquiry begins in each case, it ends by pointing to the inadequacies of any such assumption.

In the course of writing this book I have had the enormous good fortune to have had the advice of a large number of friends and colleagues, each of whom has given me the benefit of their expert views on their own special disciplines, Alan Blackwell, Johannes Bronkhorst, Paul Cartledge, Karine Chemla, Serafina Cuomo, Simon Goldhill, Rob Foley, Nick Humphrey, Catherine Osborne, Robin Osborne, Eleanor Robson, Ami Salmond. None of them is, of course, responsible for the ways in which I have used that advice, but it is certainly the case that the book would have been less well informed than it is if they had not had the generosity to offer it.

It remains to thank Peter Momtchiloff and his colleagues and advisers at Oxford University Press for their help both in criticizing earlier drafts and in seeing the eventual final version through the press.

G.E.R.L.

Introduction

THE organization of higher education across the world is one of several factors that conspire to create the assumption that our own map of the intellectual disciplines is, broadly speaking, valid cross-culturally. We seem to have no difficulty in identifying university departments of mathematics, the various natural sciences, medicine, history, even philosophy and religion. There are obvious differences in the actual legal arrangements in place in different societies and in the art that is produced in different parts of the world: but even in those cases we still tend to assume that law and art are disciplines or activities that correspond to well-defined areas of social and human experiences—and both of those fields, too, are generally represented in tertiary education, in universities or art schools, that are responsible for turning out specially qualified practitioners. If we accept that comfortable view, as practitioners ourselves we can get on with the job without too much soul-searching as to *what* we are doing, while as historians of these disciplines we can be confident of their coherence.

This book has as its primary goal to problematize that set of assumptions in relation to the eight areas I have mentioned, namely philosophy, mathematics, history, medicine, art, law, religion, and science. I shall focus especially on historical and cross-cultural data concerning the constitution and definition of learned disciplines, on the varying roles, both positive and negative, of elites in that process, and on how and within what limits innovation occurs. I accept that many features of how these fields are construed today stem from comparatively recent institutional developments in nineteenth-century Europe, the formation of faculties and the endowing of chairs in the universities. But earlier periods and other cultures have their contribution to make to our grasp of the issues. My aim is to explore the insights to be gained from bringing a global perspective to bear on our understanding of those eight areas of human endeavour.

Of course it is impossible to attempt to survey all the data relevant to these problems from different societies, literate and non-literate, ancient and modern. I shall have to be rigorously selective, concentrating on those periods and societies that seem to throw particular light both on the communalities and on the specificities in the ways in which learned disciplines have been classified, established, and maintained. I shall focus particularly on Greece and China both because they are the ancient societies with which I am most familiar and because both happen to offer rich evidence on the issues, enabling us to trace the emergence of widely different understandings of the principal disciplines and of the relations between them. In such a wide-ranging study neat conclusions and crisp definitions are, in any case, out of the question and indeed tend to be misleading. Such positive conclusions as I shall tentatively suggest must then be understood to be subject to qualifications as to their scope though they do, I shall claim, have relevance to current issues in educational policy.

The project faces an immediate methodological objection. If we say that mathematics, for instance, or history, varies in different societies and at different periods, how are we to identify these non-standard varieties, and are they indeed varieties of mathematics, or history, or something else? Do we not have to use our own familiar categories in evaluating deviations from them? Will it not turn out that non-standard varieties will have to be dismissed as not mathematics at all, and so also for history and the rest? That may have the unfortunate consequence that everyone else's intellectual performance will be judged by 'our', Western, criteria.[1] But there have, in any case, been strong tendencies (however much we may deplore them) to identify both 'science' and 'philosophy' at least as essentially Western creations. Just how far learning should be defined in Western terms will, indeed, be one of my recurrent concerns.

---

[1] The problem has sometimes been posed, how can we make any judgements whatsoever other than from 'within' 'our own' conceptual framework. That was at the root of the debate in the 1960s and 1970s concerning the 'apparently irrational beliefs', often reported from 'primitive' societies. While I would not go so far as to say that that was just a pseudo-problem, the terms in which it was discussed certainly suffered both from a frequent radical decontextualization of the reports in question, and from the inflexibility with which the notions of 'our' criteria of intelligibility, 'our' concept of rationality, were applied. I discussed this issue in Lloyd 2004: ch. 1 ('Understanding Ancient Societies') and will return to it briefly in my examination of religion in Ch. 7.

The principal flaw in the methodological objection I have just stated lies in its assumption that we have clear, unequivocal, standard definitions of the major intellectual disciplines ourselves in the first place. But if we take 'philosophy' (the topic of my first chapter) as an example, we can see that, even if we confine ourselves to Western traditions, very different views have been entertained on how that study should be conducted and what it should be held to cover. Once we recognize that there have been those very different understandings in the West, we shall be less inclined to dismiss the idea that non-Western investigations may also count as 'philosophy' out of hand. Where natural science and medicine are concerned, there is an obvious sense in which Western experimental science and biomedicine serve as the dominant current paradigms in twenty-first-century Europe and North America. But again other claims have been and continue to be made—for so-called 'alternative' medicine especially—that need to be studied with some care, not simply ruled out of court for failing to conform to those paradigms.

My tactics throughout are to examine the evidence for the creation of more or less systematic inquiries in different societies and at different periods, to investigate why they were defined or understood in the ways they were, on what basis particular individuals or groups claimed special expertise, and what the effects of a professionalization of the field were when that occurred. I have, to be sure, to start with some points of similarity or contact with the concepts that we are used to, even though in several cases these will turn out to be less clear-cut than may generally be assumed—as I have already argued for 'philosophy'. I shall thus end with expanded notions of what the fields I examine can legitimately be held to cover. In the process I shall identify some of the factors that stimulate or inhibit the growth of inquiries and suggest conclusions in that area that have some bearing on the problems we continue to face today. Discipline boundaries have certain distinctively inhibiting effects—or so I shall argue.

The subjects I have chosen to examine are a mixed bag. The circumstances in which they are practised, and the individuals or cadres who claim special expertise in the domain show wide variation. In some cases, the field answers to a practical need—to restore health, or secure law and order, however 'health' or 'order' is conceived, although that is where some of the chief problems lie. In others, the focus is rather on meeting some demand or quest for understanding.

One added considerable complication comes with the divergent claims made for hegemonic status as between the different disciplines. When religion represents itself as supreme, this may be because all other human activities should be subordinate to the worship of God. History sometimes stakes its claim with the argument that the true account of the past it provides serves as the best guide we have to the future: and science sees its role as revealing the causes of things, how the natural world actually works. To that, religion often responds first by saying that human history is the unfolding of God's purposes, and secondly that while science explains how things are, it has no business saying why, which, on one view, is precisely the province of religion. Adjudicating between such views, some philosophers will argue, is not the work of any one of the disciplines concerned. Rather it is philosophy, as a second-order inquiry, which is supreme, since its task is to answer questions to do with the subject-matter, aims, methods, and criteria of success of the other, first-order studies, and that will include art, law, and mathematics as well. But in no case are the views I have just mentioned the *only* ones that command support even among just the specialists in the field concerned. I shall return briefly to the problems posed by the relations *between* disciplines in my concluding chapter.

All eight subjects *may* be represented in the work of universities or other institutions of advanced education (art schools, or religious seminaries, for instance), but none is confined to such institutions. How and why these subjects come to be viewed as learned disciplines, when that is the case, is one of my recurrent questions and we shall see that the answers that have to be given differ widely in different cases. If we may assume, as I believe we may, that all humans potentially share intellectual, creative, spiritual, ambitions, we have, nevertheless, much to learn from the diversity in the ways in which those ambitions have been implemented, developed, and sometimes thwarted, in societies past and present across the world, and every reason to expand our own horizons beyond the familiarities of our modern Western experience.

1

What is Philosophy?

WHAT counts as 'philosophy' is contentious in the extreme, including, indeed especially, among those who call themselves 'philosophers'. Let me outline my tactics in this chapter. I shall begin with some remarks about the divergent views taken on the principal question still today as between different European and North American traditions. What those traditions owe to Greece will take me to the first of the ancient civilizations I shall consider. The Greeks, of course, coined the term *philosophia*: they had, in other words, a category that looks as if it ought to correspond to ours today. We shall have to test that assumption carefully.

But three other ancient civilizations each pose a distinct set of problems. Can ancient China—without an equivalent actors' category— be thought to have had 'philosophy'? That is a topic to which one of the most reputed sinological journals has recently devoted a whole issue (Cheng 2005, cf. Deleuze and Guattari 1991: 89), where most of the contributors consider, though most reject, the thesis that what China had was not 'philosophy' but 'wisdom'. Indian inquiries, by contrast, seem more readily comparable with Greek, though that too is a view that we shall have to examine critically. Where Arabic investigations are concerned, there is some borrowing from the Greeks and that establishes a certain continuity, though the role that philosophy played in Islam obviously differs from the place it occupied in pagan Graeco-Roman antiquity. The final topic I shall broach takes me even further afield, to the question of whether philosophy can only be said to be practised in literate societies that possess the kinds of institutions and academies in which we think of it as being taught today. Many philosophers wrote nothing: but is philosophy conceivable in essentially non-literate cultures?

Two tensions will punctuate the whole of my discussion. The first is between a restricted and a broad understanding of 'philosophy', where the restricted sets up stringent conditions for what is to pass as such, including explicit concern with most, if not all, of the main areas of academic philosophical investigation, logic, epistemology, ontology and metaphysics, philosophy of mind, aesthetics and ethics. On a much broader view, however, philosophy is an extension of basic human cognitive capacities, a matter of explicit reflection and argument on such subjects as morality and reasoning in particular.

The second tension contrasts two opposing views of the aims of philosophizing. On one, the focus is on what reason reveals has to be the case, and if that yields counter-intuitive conclusions or ones that conflict with ordinary opinions, reason should nevertheless prevail. On the second view, the task of philosophy is rather to 'save the phenomena' in the sense of elucidating and clarifying what is normally believed, removing inconsistencies in those beliefs, and no doubt modifying some of them in the course of clarification. But on that view, if the conclusions are counter-intuitive, that suggests that the arguments should be re-examined, not that ordinary intuitions should be abandoned.

The contrasts are clear and fundamental. But in my view neither is such that we should attempt to resolve the issue by plumping for one option, to the exclusion of the other. Rather, my aim is to do justice to what may be said on either side of the questions.

We have 'philosophy', the French *philosophie*, the Germans *Philosophie*, the Italians *filosofia*. One might have imagined that students enrolling in faculties or departments with those names would be taught according to more or less the same curriculum. In practice, however, the emphasis and even the content of their courses differ to a considerable extent as between different European countries and sometimes even within the same country. Sometimes the emphasis is on so-called analytical philosophy, sometimes on metaphysics in the grand manner, that is in the manner, say, of the German idealists. History of philosophy may be considered fundamental, or it may be largely neglected. In what was called the Moral Sciences Tripos in Cambridge, when I was a student, history of philosophy was not considered to be proper philosophy—but then so-called continental philosophy, phenomenology, existentialism, even Hegel and Nietzsche, hardly figured at all either. The professors who taught the subject were not personally responsible for the label 'Moral Sciences' with its positivist overtones: but in the wake of Wittgenstein and under the influence of A. J. Ayer, the aim was to show that most traditional philosophical problems were based on confusions.

There has been some convergence, in recent years, within European and North American practitioners of 'philosophy'. History of philosophy is now taken seriously at Cambridge, though its aims and methodology remain problematic. To make long-dead philosophers relevant to contemporary debates is (on one view) bound to distort their ideas, but to reconstruct those ideas on their own terms (on the other) is either impossible or irrelevant or both. Nevertheless more attention is paid nowadays to French and German philosophical traditions, even if non-Western ones scarcely figure in the courses taught. Conversely, so-called analytical philosophy in the English-speaking tradition has become accepted, and is practised with distinction, by many French, German, and Italian philosophers.

Yet the debate about what the nature of philosophy itself is, and about what its principal aims, subject-matter, and methods should be, continues, and has indeed intensified in recent decades with the challenges to positivism, and even to any claims to objectivity, mounted by various strands of deconstructionism, post-modernism, feminism, and the 'strong programme' of scientific knowledge. At one end of the spectrum, philosophy is essentially a second-order discipline, where philosophy of science, for instance, investigates the nature of science, its subject-matter, and the basis of the knowledge claims it makes, and similarly, *mutatis mutandis*, for the philosophy of law, of religion, of mathematics, of history, and so on. At the other, philosophy's aim is to reveal the truth about Being. Where ethics and political philosophy are concerned, there is a marked contrast between the view that holds that the philosopher's remit is—at most—the abstract clarification of the issues, and one that goes much further and suggests that the goal should be to offer rational grounds for normative recommendations about how to behave, about how to live a good and happy life, and about how society should best be organized. Where some students are given positive leads on questions of morality and government, more often they are provided with a set of analytical tools and left to work out solutions for themselves. On that view, to make recommendations or even to offer models to follow is unacceptably intrusive.

The divergences within European and American philosophy reflect, to be sure, certain national traditions, and the particular influences of groups and individuals, of the British empiricists, for example, or of Descartes or Kant or Croce, or more recently of Heidegger, Gadamer, Foucault, Derrida, Rorty. But most of those working in European traditions acknowledge some debt to the origins of philosophy in Greece, to the point where to trace the differing views on how that legacy is to be used is to trace the main lines of the development of Western philosophical thinking—a theme well brought out by Bernard Williams (1981). After all, throughout the quarrel between the 'ancients' and the 'moderns', the former were used as stalking horses by the latter, even when their thesis was the need to break away from the influence of the past. Yet it is an illusion to suppose that divergences in views as to the nature of philosophy were any less prominent in Graeco-Roman antiquity than, say, in the twentieth century. It is true that in the Hellenistic period there was general agreement that philosophy should deliver freedom from anxiety, *ataraxia*, and so happiness. It was no mere academic subject, in our terms: the claim that philosophers made was that what they taught was directly relevant to people's well-being.

Yet fundamentally different views were entertained on how to go about that. Both Stoics and Epicureans thought it was essential to have the right answer to the question of the *summum bonum* (virtue for the Stoics, pleasure for the Epicureans), and both those schools considered that to attain peace of mind you needed a correct understanding both of 'physics'—that is of natural phenomena—and of logic and epistemology. But the Sceptics held that speculation about underlying realities and the hidden causes of things was futile. The principle of equipollence they adopted stated that for every positive view on one side of such questions a negative one of equal force on the other could be proposed. The Sceptics derived their peace of mind, not from solving the problems, but from the realization that no solution is possible. It is remarkable that while some philosophers were insisting that doubt had to be removed, if you were to be happy, others contemporary with them were suggesting that, to be happy, you had to recognize that no such removal of doubt was possible.

Those Hellenistic Greek and Roman philosophers had, of course, their own predecessors to look back to, though they disagreed as much on how they should be interpreted as on every other issue. What Socrates stood for, in particular, varied widely, even while different schools of thought adopted him as an iconic figure. Yet there was no more of a consensus about what 'philosophy' is, when that term was first coined, than at later periods (cf. Frede 2004). From Plato onwards, for sure, philosophy had positive overtones. Socrates was not wise, *sophos*, but a lover of wisdom, *philosophos*, the point being that he provided a shining model of the search for truth. Yet in two writers before Plato the terms *philosophos* and *philosophia* were hardly used with approval. Heraclitus uses the former critically in relation to thinkers who claim to know a lot, to be 'polymaths'—while Heraclitus' own idea of the right method was to search oneself. Again the writer of the medical treatise *On Ancient Medicine*, at the end of the fifth or start of the fourth century BCE, associates 'philosophy' with futile speculation. It took an effort on Plato's part, in other words, to secure a positive role for 'philosophy'[1] and in his day that meant driving a wedge between Socrates' genuine aspiration to pursue the truth and what Plato polemically represented as the superficial, and commercialized, learning he associates with the 'sophists'.

While Plato was able to reverse the negative undertones that some of his predecessors had attached to 'lovers of wisdom', he was far from entirely successful in imposing his own positive views on what philosophy consisted in and how it should be practised. Among his contemporaries, Isocrates taught and advocated what he also called 'philosophy', but that consisted principally of education in the skills of public speaking—rhetoric—and in statesmanship. Aristotle, Plato's pupil for twenty years, rejected his basic metaphysical doctrine, the theory of Forms. Where for Plato the ultimate goal of dialectic is the supreme Form, that of the Good, Aristotle criticized that as both confused and useless. For sure, philosophizing was, for Aristotle too, the highest mode of human activity, but both his theoretical analysis of what that chiefly consisted in (the study of being qua being) and his actual practice of inquiry were quite distinctive. In particular, he placed a far greater emphasis on the study of nature, second philosophy, or 'physics', than Plato had done. But while Aristotelians stressed the value and importance of finding out about the world, for other

---

[1] Some of our late sources report that Pythagoras coined the term and used it with approval, but as with most of our evidence for the Pythagoreans this tradition is hard to evaluate. On the one occasion when Plato refers to Pythagoras, however, he suggests that he taught a way of life (*Republic* 600a–b).

Greeks—among the late neo-Platonists for instance—what philosophy was good for was rather training you to cultivate the self (Hadot 1990, cf. Hadot 2002).

The Greeks made important contributions to each of the main areas of philosophy that remain basic to the modern Western academic discipline, namely logic, ontology, epistemology, philosophy of mind, aesthetics, ethics, and political philosophy, but in each they disagreed on the answers to the substantive questions. To mention just a couple of the most striking examples, in philosophy of mind Plato held that body and soul are two distinct types of being, the first corporeal, the other incorporeal. But against that, Aristotle insisted that the soul is the activity of the living body, not a separate kind of entity inhabiting it. In epistemology Parmenides inaugurated the view that reason is the criterion of truth and that sense-perception is fundamentally deceptive. But against that, empiricist epistemologies that reinstate perception were also proposed, not least by Aristotle and both main Hellenistic schools, Stoics and Epicureans. But where the Greeks were generally agreed—and differed from most modern academic philosophers—was that philosophy was important for life, essential for happiness, no mere abstract intellectual discipline.

Thus far I have been discussing Western traditions. But the situation becomes appreciably more complex as soon as we go a little further afield. The very question of whether any non-Western traditions can be accepted as 'philosophy' is a matter of intense dispute. It is worth spending some time analysing the data for China in some detail as it is something of a test case for our inquiry. I mentioned before the view that denies that China has 'philosophy', though conceding that it has 'wisdom'. In classical Chinese thought, from the Warring States to the end of the Han,[2] there is no term that corresponds to Greek *philosophia* or its European descendants. The word in modern Chinese for 'philosophy', namely *zhexue*, is borrowed from the term the Japanese coined when they first encountered European ideas on the subject.

The teachers and writers who generally figure in conventional histories of Chinese thought were known to their contemporaries by

---

[2] The Warring States period is conventionally dated from 480 or 475 to 221 BCE. The Qin dynasty which then unified China lasted only until 206, but the Han which succeeded it, ruled, intermittently, until 221 CE.

a number of titles, especially *shi*₁, *boshi*, and *youshui*. The most generic of these, *shi*₁, underwent a number of shifts in meaning.[3] Originally it designated the well-born, landed gentry but it came to be used more and more of those who were well educated, cultivated, learned in the classics. The binome *boshi*, literally those of broad learning, was applied to the top echelons of such a group. The conventional translation is 'erudite' and we hear of them in many contexts in government and as advisers to rulers. The third term, *youshui*, literally means 'wandering advisers' and aptly describes those who went from court to court offering 'persuasions' to ministers and kings. We shall come back to this point.

The general term for what these figures were learned in is *xue*, study, which covers a wide range and in that is similar to Latin *scientia* or Greek *episteme*. Conventionally a number of schools of thought were distinguished already in the Warring States period, the *ru* (usually translated 'Confucians'), 'Mohists', the 'School of Law' or 'Legalists' (*fa jia*), the 'School of Names' (*ming jia*), 'Daoists' (*dao jia*), and the 'yin-yang school' (*yin yang*), but we must be very much on our guard. That particular sixfold classification appears in the final chapter of the first great Chinese general history, the *Shiji*, composed by Sima Qian, and his father Sima Tan, around 90 BCE.[4] It is specifically attributed to Sima Tan, and it is clear that it reflects his rather idiosyncratic views in one respect, in that with the exception of the 'Mohists', named after Mozi, it uses points of view, or concepts, rather than persons as the criterion. Although I have noted the conventional rendering 'Confucian' for the first group, the *ru*, that term is applied to members of the literate elite more generally. We find wide discrepancies among the views propounded by different *ru*, even by *ru* who did express some sort of allegiance to the teachings of Confucius, Kong Fuzi, himself. One clear example of this is the attack that Xunzi, himself usually classified as a 'Confucian', launched, in the third century BCE, against twelve masters who included direct disciples of Confucius, and indeed the most eminent of these, namely Mencius, Mengzi (*Xunzi* 6, see below p. 13). Again, as I shall be noting in a moment, following the *dao* is an ideal shared by all Chinese thinkers, though what they meant by this differed: so the term 'Daoist' risks

---

[3] Cf. Lloyd and Sivin 2002: 17ff.
[4] I shall be analysing this text in Ch. 3.

becoming so general as to be useless, when not actually confusing (Sivin 1995b).

Three features that are common to much of the activity of the members of these groups stand out, namely the importance of texts, the engagement in debate, and the focus on practical advice especially on government.

First, each group or 'family'[5] tended to be defined by an allegiance to a set of canonical writings, *jing*, that were often attributed to the presumed founder of the group and incorporated his teachings. To be inducted into the family, new recruits had first to memorize such texts: committing the canon to memory came before any ambition to interpret or understand it. Thereafter it was the initiates' duty to hand the text on, in turn, to their pupils and disciples. We cannot tell how much this idea owed to a sense of vulnerability generated by such notorious episodes as the 'burning of the books' ordered by Li Si, in 213 BCE,[6] but it is clear that the preservation of the canons was a preoccupation during the formative period of Chinese thought, even though we now know from the texts excavated from Han tombs that several of these canons existed in different forms or recensions already in Qin–Han times. But after the unification, the curriculum of the Chinese Imperial Academy, founded by Han Wu Di, around 124 BCE, came to be dominated by certain texts, the five so-called Confucian classics, the *Odes* (*Shi*$_2$), the *Documents* (*Shu*$_3$), the *Rites* (*Li*$_1$), the *Book of Changes* (*Yi*$_1$), and the *Spring and Autumn Annals* (*Chunqiu*) (see Nylan 2001). These did not comprise a single intellectual discipline but they constituted the core of the education of the elite who on graduating from the Academy formed the backbone of the cadres on which the increasingly complex but intermittently efficient Chinese bureaucracy depended.

Secondly, debate and disagreement between the schools and within them are well attested in our evidence. Xunzi, as I noted, attacked other masters, including other prominent *ru*. We hear of different followers of Mozi who criticized one another in attempts to appropriate his teaching in support of their own interpretations of it—very

---

[5] The common Chinese term for philosophical or other groups or sects was *jia*, the primary meaning of which is simply 'family'.

[6] Li Si was prime minister to the first emperor, Qin Shi Huang Di, who unified China. The stories of his anti-intellectual moves have undoubtedly been magnified by anti-Qin propaganda under the succeeding dynasty, the Han.

much as happened to Socrates and to Plato in Greece. While face-to-face exchanges are represented in the dialogues Confucius had with his pupils, and in the writings of Zhuangzi,[7] polemic was more often conducted in writings than orally, and it more usually targeted dead masters than living ones who could reply in kind. Although members of the 'School of Names', Hui Shi and Gongsun Long, have regularly been compared to Greek sophists, that is misleading (pace Reding 1985). Although they were frequently accused of paradox-mongering by other Chinese writers, they certainly did not give public lectures which anyone could attend who could pay for their instruction.

The third feature I mentioned takes us to the content of the teaching and instruction on offer. What was at stake in the disputes between leading figures was not so much a matter of the theoretical solutions to abstract problems, as one of how one should behave. The *dao* was not a matter of knowing the answers to theoretical questions, but of knowing what conduced to correct behaviour, indeed not just knowing that, but practising it. Much attention was accordingly paid, by Confucius especially, to the correct observance of ritual, to proper deportment in different contexts (greeting your prince, dealing with superiors, inferiors, guests, family members, and so on) even to the dress you wore. In Xunzi's attacks on the Twelve (*Xunzi* 6: Knoblock 1988–94: i. 228 f.), the way their students dress improperly—their caps bent low over their foreheads, their cap-strings loose and slack—is mentioned as an indication of their untrustworthiness.

Advice about attaining the elusive *dao* is the generic goal of many texts. But more specifically many writers belonging to different schools focused on the advice they should give to rulers about government. Several aspects of this call for comment. First, the interest was not in political constitutions as such. On the contrary, all were agreed that the ideal was the benevolent rule of a wise emperor, monarchy in other words. Monarchic rule did not, to be sure, imply autocracy. The need for the ruler to pay attention not just to his ministers, but also to what his people thought, is given considerable emphasis in a number of texts. But in none of the discussions of good

---

[7] The collection of writings that goes by the name of Zhuangzi is a compilation of different strata dating from the 4th to the 2nd century BCE. His conversations with his friend Hui Shi are products of the literary—and philosophical—imagination rather than historical records.

government do we find alternative political constitutions proposed: that was simply not on the agenda.

The ideal was to secure the welfare of 'all under heaven', *tian xia*. But the problem was, how was this to be attained? Some put the stress on the strictest control of every aspect of social life, including the promulgation of law codes that incorporated extreme punitive measures to be taken against dissidents of any kind. But others thought that the ruler's own interventions should be minimal. In the doctrine of *wu wei*, 'no ado', the idea was that the best rule was when the ruler did nothing. He was to provide a model of calm and wisdom and leave what governing needed to be done to his subordinates.

These and other proposals for good government came from individuals who, in many cases, were close to actual rulers, and sometimes held high office themselves. Confucius failed to find a king who was worthy of receiving his advice, but that was not for want of trying. His chief eventual rivals, the Mohists, made it their business to become experts in defensive warfare, in order to be in a position to advise rulers on military affairs as on other matters. Both Mencius and Xunzi are represented in audience with rulers. Hui Shi served as a minister and composed a law code for the king of Wei in the fourth century BCE, and Gongsun Long too, in the next century, claimed to be concerned with order and good government, despite the criticisms that were levelled at him for wasting his time with paradoxes. Han Fei, one of the most prominent thinkers of what was called the School of Law, was a nobleman and he too acted as adviser to kings.

The pattern continues during and after the unification. One of the first great cosmological syntheses, the *Lüshi chunqiu*, was compiled under the auspices of Lü Buwei, around 240 BCE. While he started as a merchant (so we are told in the hostile biography of him in the *Shiji*), he became prime minister to the man who was to become the first emperor. Around a century later, a second summa, the *Huainanzi*, was put together by Liu An, who was king of Huainan. Of course not all aspiring advisers were successful in obtaining positions of power and influence. Wang Chong, in the first century CE, abandoned the only post he held, that of prefectural clerk, to write his book, the *Lun Heng*, more or less in reclusion as a private teacher.

Thus while some advisers were in no real position to influence those who actually wielded power, many were. While the rewards of success were high, the risks were undeniable. Han Fei, Lü Buwei, and Liu An all ended up being forced to commit suicide when they fell out of favour with rulers. This makes it all the more remarkable that there was a well-established Chinese tradition of the responsibility of advisers to reprimand rulers when they saw their behaviour as not conducive to good government. As I have discussed elsewhere (Lloyd 2005a) there is an extraordinarily rich vocabulary of terms for use by advisers criticizing rulers, reprimanding them, objecting to the way they were behaving, and warning them of the dire consequences of the policies they were pursuing. All of that may sound idealistic, and certainly when we find references to the welfare of 'all under heaven', we should not suppose that that meant all *equally*. But that these advisers were no mere armchair idealists, commenting on the iniquities of the day from the safety of some ivory tower, is clear from the fates they suffered. Many were prepared to continue performing their duty of censure at considerable personal cost to themselves and indeed their families. For if you fell from favour, it was not just you, but your entire clan, who were liable to be punished, by exile, castration, or death.

But where, we must now ask, does that leave our understanding of Chinese 'philosophy' and indeed of what 'philosophy' is? Some areas of what is included in most modern universities are poorly represented in the extant remains for classical Chinese thought, that is before the influence of Buddhism began to be felt. There is little debate on the nature of being, that is on ontology, as such. While such questions as the reliability of hearsay evidence compared with eyewitness reports are discussed,[8] there is no sense that reason and sense-perception or experience pose alternatives between which a choice has to be made, and thus no concern with the epistemological crisis that has beset Western philosophy ever since Parmenides. Unlike many Hellenistic Greek philosophers and some modern thinkers, the Chinese did not generally consider that happiness and well-being depended on a correct understanding of physics and a grasp of logic. Where 'physics' is concerned, texts such as the *Lüshi chunqiu* and *Huainanzi* show an interest in the processes of change and in the resonances between things, and these and many other writings confidently represent the cosmos as a whole, the political state and the

---

[8] Such discussion is reported in our limited evidence for Mohist thought, cf. Graham 1978: 30ff.

human body as all exemplifying the same basic patterns of alternating *yin* and *yang*. But none sets the subject-matter of 'physics' apart as a domain to be investigated according to its own specific methods, and none drives a wedge between physics and 'mathematics', downgrading the former by contrast with the latter's claim to yield knowledge of pure intelligible objects.[9]

Where 'logic' is concerned, the nature of classical Chinese interests is revealing. Those who explored paradox were, as I noted, criticized by others for wasting their time, and there is no doubt that the critics represented a common point of view and the dominant tradition. On the other hand, we find in the *Hanfeizi* for instance a notable interest in the techniques of persuasion. The *shuonan* chapter (12) in that text is devoted to an issue that often confronted Chinese advisers in practice, namely how to get the ruler to agree to your proposals without his seeing that he is being manipulated. The understanding of the psychology of such exchanges is sophisticated, more sophisticated indeed, in my view, than anything we find in Greek writings on rhetoric. But conversely, Aristotle's studies in the formal analysis of rhetorical arguments, and where they differ from dialectical and demonstrative ones, have no parallel in the Chinese texts.[10]

Yet when all these reservations have been expressed, we must return to the central point. With regard to the questions of how humans should behave, of human nature in general, and of how good government is to be achieved, many Chinese consistently exhibit an intense and dedicated interest and engage in sophisticated debates between alternative views.[11] Moreover on those issues, in what we should call ethics and political philosophy, they generally show a far greater personal involvement than most classical Greek philosophers—even though the situation changes, in the West, under Rome, when we find more examples of philosophers not just theorizing in those domains, but attempting to advise rulers (Seneca) or

---

[9] I shall be considering this issue further in Ch. 2.

[10] It is typical that Aristotle should want to distinguish not just the goals of rhetoric and demonstrative reasoning, but also the argument schemata each of them depends on.

[11] In the 4th and 3rd centuries BCE there is a debate between Mencius, Gaozi, and Xunzi on human nature, that is, on whether humans are naturally good (as Mencius held), bad (the position of Xunzi, ch. 23), or neither (the view of Gaozi as reported by Mencius at least, 6 A 6). The issue had important repercussions for education, where Xunzi, for example, insisted that teachers and standards were needed to guide humans towards the good, cf. Graham 1989: 117 ff., 244 ff.

reflecting on how they should themselves rule (Marcus Aurelius).[12] Certainly Chinese writers were generally more actively and riskily engaged in affairs of state and involved in matters of great public concern than most of those who hold chairs of philosophy in modern Western universities.

It is, of course, more important to analyse what Chinese thinkers achieved than to settle the terminological issue of whether that should count as philosophy. On the former question I have done no more than draw attention to some of the salient points. But these have been enough to make some progress on the latter issue—my main concern in this study. It would surely be excessively restrictive to exclude a Chinese claim to title in the matter of an engagement in philosophy. We have, to be sure, to recognize the particular grounds on which it can be made, namely chiefly on their explorations of questions of morality, but we have also to bear in mind the remarks I made at the outset, namely that there is no universal consensus, even today, on the proper aims of philosophy and on its core constituents.

The third great ancient civilization for which we have abundant evidence relevant to our concerns is India, where again we have a variety of different 'schools' locked in debate with one another over a considerable period of time. This applies particularly to the ongoing battles between Buddhism and Hindu Brahmanism and their various branches or sects. But reconstructing the earliest stages of their development is in many cases problematic, given the difficulties of determining the chronology of many of the principal classic texts, the Vedas, Brāhmaṇas, Upaniṣads, and Sūtras.

The problems discussed include ontology, metaphysics, philosophy of mind, and ethics, a range that bears certain obvious similarities to those of Greek philosophy, and in three cases, namely atomism, logical analysis, and the practice of debate, the resemblances are

---

[12] This is not the place to attempt to go into the question of the degree of involvement in political affairs on the part of later European philosophers. But I may note that whereas in the 16th and 17th centuries there were plenty of politically engaged philosophers, Hobbes, Locke, Voltaire, Rousseau, and others, some of whom got into trouble with the authorities for their outspoken views, the trend with the expansion of the universities in the 19th century was rather towards confirming the understanding of philosophy as a theoretical, academic discipline. Not all those who called themselves philosophers thought it part of the job to be politically active, though there were of course notable exceptions, not least Marx himself.

such as to have suggested the possibility of diffusion or of mutual interaction between the two civilizations. Let me first briefly discuss that issue before reviewing some of the major original aspects of Indian philosophizing.

Various forms of atomism appear among the Buddhists (the Sarvāstivāda school), the Jains, and two Brahmanical sects (Nyāya and Vaiśeṣika, founded by the legendary figures Gautama and Kaṇāda respectively). But given the difficulty that none of the reliable sources for Indian atomism clearly dates it before the third century BCE, it is wise to return an open verdict here about possible borrowings from the Greeks.

Nyāya logic also post-dates Aristotelian, let alone Stoic, theories in this area: the Nyāyasūtra is generally dated at the earliest to around 200 BCE. But in this case the Nyāya analysis of sequences of premises and conclusions is sufficiently distinctive[13] to be more likely to be an independent development than one influenced by earlier Greek formal logic.

Then there is the practice of debate, where there is definite early evidence of Buddhist knowledge of Greek activity in the Pali text of late second or early first century BCE known as the Milindapañha, the *Questions of Milinda*.[14] In this a Greek wise man first defeats a number of Indian ones in debate, only to be worsted by the last one he encounters, the Buddhist monk Nagasena. Milinda is the Indian version of the Greek name Menander, ruler of the kingdom of Bactria that was founded by Alexander in the fourth century BCE. Bronkhorst, in particular, has suggested that knowledge of a Greek model may be the key to the development of Indian traditions of rational debate.[15]

However, it is important to note Bronkhorst's qualifications to his thesis. The actual content of the debate reported in the Milindapañha owes nothing to Greek ideas. Rather the borrowing that he suggests may have happened is limited to the possibility of engaging in

---

[13] Cf. Matilal 1971, 1985. I have briefly analysed the similarities and differences between the misnamed Nyāya syllogism and Aristotelian syllogistic in Lloyd 2004: 128–9.

[14] This text came to be widely used in Buddhist proselytizing and it was translated into several languages, into Chinese for instance in the 3rd century CE, and into Korean in the 13th.

[15] 'It is not adventurous to conclude that the Greeks may have exerted an influence on the Sarvāstivāda Buddhists' (Bronkhorst 1999: 22). Bronkhorst points out that that Buddhist sect was active in north-west India which was in intermittent close contact with Bactria, as the influence of Greek art forms on Buddhist art from Gandhāra illustrates.

rational, critical inquiry. Debates between sages are represented in much earlier Upaniṣad texts, but in Bronkhorst's view they lack one ingredient he associates with philosophy, namely the ambition to produce a systematic theory.

Yet maybe the more important difference between Indian and Greek styles of debate, which would dictate caution in the matter of the transmission of influence, lies in the ways in which those debates are resolved. In the Upaniṣads and in the Milindapañha the question of who has won is decided by the participants themselves on the basis of their expert, usually esoteric, knowledge. The winner is the sage who has the last word.[16] The confrontations are certainly serious ones: the party who concedes defeat suffers humiliation (cf. Bronkhorst 2002). At the same time the institutions of debate in India were rather different from those in Greek philosophical or medical schools. When staged as they often were at the courts of rulers, Indian debates were, for the audience, sometimes as much occasions for entertainment as for edification.

But to leave aside now the tricky problems of possible Greek influences, direct or indirect, the most distinctive contributions of Indian thinkers are on such questions as the philosophy of time, the philosophy of language, and the philosophy of the self. In the first case, as Thapar (1996) showed, Indian thought is far more complex than earlier stereotypes that focused on the cyclical view of time supposed. That view was often combined with a linear conception: some schools related time to the reality of change, others emphasized the distinctiveness of the instant to the point of negating tense, while yet others saw time flowing constantly like a river. But the immensity of the Kalpa of 4,320 million years, and the conception of the four Yugas each of only slightly less mind-boggling dimensions, as these ideas were developed in some schools, opened up a cosmological perspective that has important repercussions on the insignificant place of humans in the scheme of things, quite apart from the further connections that were sometimes made with theses of social and moral decline. This was one area where Indian speculation entertained ideas that went far beyond what ordinary experience might suggest.[17]

---

[16] One clear example of this from the Upaniṣads is the debate in which Yājñavalkya reduces his Brahmin interlocutors to silence, where the final topic discussed is the nature of ātman, *Bṛhadāraṇyaka Upaniṣad*.

[17] Indian conceptions of time will also be relevant, of course, to my examination of different notions of history in Ch. 3.

On language, Pāṇini, who is usually dated to the second half of the second century BCE, produced a comprehensive analysis of the rules of grammar in a rational system that served as a model or ideal for classification in other fields. It has been said that while mathematics was the dominant and most prestigious intellectual discipline in Greece, that position was held by linguistics in India, thanks to Pāṇini's pioneering work (cf. Bronkhorst 2001).

But it is especially in reflections on the self—one of the principal preoccupations of Indian philosophizing in general—that both Buddhist and Brahman thought excel. In the Upaniṣads *ātman* (the self) is identified with *brahman*, the ultimate, imperishable, timeless reality and the grounds of the being of everything else, time and space included. The Buddhists, for their part, held that the individual's conscious personality is a false self, to be contrasted with the true Self to be revealed by spiritual exercises. In both schools of thought we have further evidence of the rejection of the superficial appearances of ordinary experience in favour of an underlying, if scarcely accessible, reality, the apprehension of which is the ultimate goal of human endeavour.

Certain contrasts thus stand out between the aims of Indian thought and those that many Greeks and Chinese set themselves. Neither Greek *ataraxia*, nor the Chinese *dao*, involves the transcending of the self of quite the kind that many Indian thinkers sought, for whom well-being depends on a state in which individuals have rid themselves of the delusions of worldly values and experiences and even of the temptations of intellectual understanding. In that form, this is an otherworldliness that is more radical than any of the kinds of that ideal to be found in Greek and Chinese thought.

The reasons that might be conjectured for the particular views and modes of inquiry that came to be cultivated in the ways they did in India raise severe historical problems that are certainly beyond my competence to resolve. This survey has done no more than identify certain striking features in the complex Indian data. But it is enough for us to register that Indian thinkers not only address the same issues we think of as belonging to different areas of philosophy, but can also enlarge our own ideas of the possible answers to the substantive questions that those subject-areas pose.

I shall be even briefer on my next, and final, ancient society, or complex of societies, namely those of Islamic faith. In this instance the influence of Greek thought is incontestable and explicit. At the same time the Arabs transformed what they took over, in two main ways. First in continuing Greek inquiries in each of the principal areas of philosophy, they frequently went beyond them. Secondly, philosophy as a whole—the work of those they called *falāsifa*—had to be set in the context of the Islamic faith, just as in late Graeco-Roman antiquity pagan philosophy had somehow to be accommodated to Christianity, by those, that is, who did not simply reject it out of hand as irrelevant or worse, that is positively distracting. As is well known, the actual incorporation of many pagan Greek ideas into Christian theology took considerable efforts on the part first of Augustine, among others, and then, much later, of Aquinas.

First, then, as to Greek influence, the history of the translation of the works of Aristotle, Euclid, Galen, and the rest, often first into Syriac and then into Arabic, has been well documented. Al-Kindī in the ninth century was one of the first to make extensive use of Aristotle and in the next three centuries one important Muslim thinker after another, al-Fārābī, Ibn Sīnā (Avicenna), Ibn Rushd (Averroes) took Aristotle as their starting-point in their own original, often brilliant, work in logic, philosophy of mind, cosmology, and metaphysics. Ibn Rushd said that Aristotle was 'an example which nature had devised to demonstrate supreme human perfection' (*Commentary on De Anima III*) and in his *Preface to Physics* he declared that Aristotle not only discovered, but also carried to perfection, the three main branches of knowledge, namely logic, natural science, and metaphysics. Of course the reception of Aristotle and other Greeks was not always so favourable. There are sharp and perceptive criticisms of Aristotle's natural philosophy in al-Rāzī (Rhazes) in the twelfth century, especially. But in that and other cases those objections provide a good indication of the perceived importance of the ideas so criticized.

But how was this use of Greek philosophy to be reconciled with Islam, since on all fundamental issues the Ḳur'ān was the supreme authority? Again different points of view were expressed. Most held that if philosophy disagreed with the Ḳur'ān, then philosophy was in the wrong, though the question of whether it did disagree might be debated. But philosophy could be a useful supplement when, as was often the case, the sacred text simply did not broach the problems in question. Philosophy was then the servant of religion. So books were written to show that the two can be reconciled. Sometimes the line of argument was that they conveyed two different sets of truths—the doctrine that was later interpreted by Christians as that of double truth—but sometimes the claim was that they both deliver the same truth though expressing it differently. Ibn Rushd's *Faṣl al-Maḳāl* argued for the agreement between revelation and philosophy, including where the latter dealt with religious matters (Martínez Lorca 1990a: 73) and another slightly earlier twelfth-century Andalusian philosopher, Ibn Ṭufayl, following al-Fārābī, maintained that there is just a single truth that is reached by two different routes (Gómez Nogales 1990: 381). His view was the maybe surprising one that the symbolic expressions of mysticism were more accessible to ordinary people, while philosophy was for the elite.

Yet of course Muslim thinkers did not always persuade their co-religionists that such a reconciliation was possible or correct. Already in the eleventh century al-Ghazāli, in his *Tahāfut al-Falāsifa* (*De-structio philosophorum*, 'The Incoherence of the Philosophers'), launched a vitriolic attack on thinkers such as al-Fārābī and Ibn Sīnā who hoped to incorporate Greek ideas and interests. Their thought was full of inconsistencies and of theses, such as the eternity of the world, that conflicted with what the Ḳur'ān taught. Moves were made to suppress philosophy as a whole and to persecute its practitioners, to ban and burn books in logic and natural science. Two of the most notorious instances were those instigated by al-Manṣūr Bi'llāh (Almanzor) who burnt the library of al-Hakam II at the end of the tenth century and the edicts promulgated by the third Almohad Caliph of Cordoba, Abū Yūsuf Yaᶜḳub al-Mānṣur, in the twelfth. At that time Ibn Rushd himself was disgraced and exiled, though there were political reasons for this over and above the issue of his hetero-doxy: besides he was reinstated before he died. But these hostile moves did not prevent many Muslims continuing the inquiries the Greeks had initiated, not just mathematics, astronomy, and medicine, but also the various branches of philosophy itself. They did so indeed with success and distinction, though there was this major difference, namely that philosophy could not openly be proclaimed to be supreme.

It is not that there is unanimity, of course, on the relations between philosophy and religion even today: I shall be returning to discuss this in Chapter 7. On one view, to be sure, philosophy of religion examines, among other things, the status of discourse about God and the nature of the knowledge claims that can be made in this area. Those who see the primary task of philosophy to be clarification can fit philosophy of religion in as one of the second-order inquiries to be pursued, leaving the question of a commitment to faith to one side. But reconciliation is not sought and is positively rejected in some quarters. The issues to do with God as first cause, as the instigator of the plan of the universe, as responsible for Intelligent Design, have recently re-emerged in the United States as a major controversy in educational policy. It is part of the rhetorical strategy of those who promote those views *not* to invoke God too overtly in case that should be used as an argument to undermine their credentials as secular and rationalist. Yet while their quarrel is as much with science—with Darwinism in particular—as with philosophy, it takes up the refrain of the conflict between reason and faith that dogged Christian thought already in late antiquity and has continued to do so intermittently since Galileo. As with the Muslim faith I have considered in this section, the issue is the sphere of influence of philosophy and the domain over which it has authority.

I turn now to my last and maybe trickiest group of problems. So far I have dealt with the notions and practices of philosophy found in highly literate societies. But how far can there be philosophy in the absence of literacy? Let me first briefly broach the question of whether there can be such a thing as a naive, universal, philosophy, on the model of the naive psychology, naive biology, and naive physics that cognitive scientists have claimed represent the initial beliefs of the young across the world. Developmental psychologists have put it that children everywhere pass through a series of stages in their progress towards an adult comprehension of the world. They do not at first grasp the principles of causation and conservation, for instance. Thus when the same quantity of water is poured from a wide glass into a narrow one and of course reaches a higher level in the latter, they are reported as tending to suppose that the narrower glass contains a greater quantity, even though they have seen the operation of pouring performed in front of them. In naive psychology, the child initially assumes that every kind of object possesses or may possess intentionality.

Yet it is obvious that no such model could be used to support a claim for the universality of philosophy, since the point that most cognitive developmentalists will insist on is that the naive physics we begin with has to be outgrown.[18] There appears to be no candidate for naive philosophical beliefs from which we progress to a mature adult understanding of the issues, and there is, in any event, in philosophy, no equivalent for an adult consensus on what that understanding would amount to.

The topic we need to address is rather whether or how far 'philosophy' depends on written records, and on the types of institutions in which it has generally been taught not just in the modern but also in the ancient world. Some philosophers, as I noted, themselves wrote nothing, though none of the more famous ones, such as Thales and Socrates, lived in societies that had no written texts at all, even if they did not use them to record their teaching. Socrates won his reputation for his insistent probing of the basis of his fellow citizens' beliefs and attitudes. I do not think it is extravagant to suggest a comparison with the situation of individuals in societies where skills in argument are highly prized and explicitly recognized and commended.

One such society is the Barotse, a non-literate society in Southern Africa on which Gluckman reported extensively in the mid-1950s and early 1960s.[19] The Lozi, as the people concerned are called, pride themselves on their talents in argument in general, where the qualities of good speakers are identified and commented on explicitly. There is no question, of course, of their being judged by their ability with truth tables and with well-formed formulae, nor even by whether their arguments are formally valid. But speakers are criticized for inconsistency, for irrelevance, for failing to take objections into account, and so on. Conversely they are praised for sticking to the point, for their ability in classifying different types of affairs, and for their skill in asking searching questions. None of these informal rules is set out in formal guise. Though the vocabulary and the concepts exist to identify virtues and vices in reasoning, they are not the subject of formal instruction, but learnt by practice and experience.

---

[18] This is not, however, the position of all cognitive scientists, since some argue that naive physics, in the sense of the informal views of the layperson, presents an adequate basis for competent adult performance. The first view stems from the work of Piaget (e.g. 1930), the second is represented in the Naive Physics manifesto of Patrick Hayes (1990, originally 1979) and cf. Smith and Casati 1994.

[19] See Gluckman 1965, 1967, 1972.

The point is the obvious one that skills in reasoning—logical skills—exist prior to and independently of any formal institution of logic as a discipline belonging to what we call philosophy. Turning the subject into such a discipline undoubtedly transforms it in various ways: in particular the diagnosis of errors in reasoning becomes easier once they have been subjected to classification and analysis. But while formal logic departs from informal in these and other ways, the ability to reason correctly is a cognitive skill shared—up to a point at least—by members of societies with and without writing, by humans, indeed, at all periods and across the world.

How far do similar arguments—to the effect that informal philosophical skills are widespread—apply to other areas of what we normally recognize as philosophical study? The obvious prime candidate[20] is morality, though the difficulties it presents are equally obvious. Some notion of the contrast between good and evil, between what is approved and what is disapproved, can be claimed, relatively uncontroversially, to underpin the values of any society, even though the way those contrasts are understood differs very considerably from one society to another. But the fact that humans disagree fundamentally on values does not militate against the possibility that the problem that poses may surface in explicit discussion. Rather, if anything, such disagreements may stimulate people to reflect on the issues, on the basis of their own, or others', beliefs, though it takes a Socrates to do so persistently—and he complained, precisely, that his fellow citizens were slow at examining such questions. Yet when these topics do start to be the subject of explicit scrutiny, and people produce arguments for and against different views and question how the truth on the matter is to be reached, is not that the point at which we can see moral philosophy beginning? If so, that does not depend on written texts that give guidance on the subject, nor on academic institutions that proceed to a formal analysis of the strengths and weaknesses of alternative positions. That is to say no more than that the sophisticated moral theories we find in such civilizations as ancient Greece, China, and India *built on* earlier reflections on common attitudes,

---

[20] See e.g. Haidt and Joseph (2004) on 'intuitive ethics'. But Matthews (1984), working with schoolchildren in Scotland, found an interest also in problems to do with other minds, with time, and with the matter of which things are made, in 8- to 11-year-olds.

even when the theories presented themselves as radical departures from earlier beliefs.

Aristotle pointed out that if in moral philosophy one came across a view that was universally accepted, that would constitute the truth. But he did not claim to have found any such agreements other than purely verbal ones, to the effect, for instance, that happiness is the goal—which left the substantive question of what happiness consisted in unresolved. The task of scrutinizing apparently shared beliefs involves technical analyses such as Aristotle himself undertook, but that scrutiny may begin with simple reflections that anyone is capable of.

That does not settle the second of the two issues I noted at the outset—between an a priori and an empirical approach to philosophical questions. The claim that philosophy began with explicit reflections on common beliefs says nothing about where it ends, since the perception of the incoherence of those beliefs may (though it does not necessarily) lead to the adoption of reason and argument, rather than sense-perception and experience, as the criteria.

On the other hand, on the other issue I mentioned, the points I have made may be used to support a broader, rather than a narrower, construal of philosophy, since they suggest that the potential for such explicit reflections may exist anywhere. The fact that critical scrutiny of ordinary beliefs is developed differentially, in different circumstance in different societies, poses problems for the specialist study of each society to tackle, but again that does not affect the argument that a widespread potential for such scrutiny exists.[21]

So the problem of what philosophy is is not one to which a crisp solution can be offered—not without begging the question as between the main contending views. Certainly there have been powerful lobbies advocating one or other restrictive construal of the central concerns and methods of the subject, and some elite groups have been highly exclusive, seeking to impose strict criteria on those whom they are prepared to accept *as* philosophers. That began in ancient Greece and it continues today, particularly among those who see the horizons

[21] In his examination of the 'domestication of the savage mind', Goody (1977) argued that literacy has a marked effect on the development of the capacity for reflective rumination on, and criticism of, ordinary beliefs: but he acknowledged that such reflections are not confined to highly literate societies.

of the subject defined in Western terms. Yet an examination just of Western traditions already brings to light a variety of conceptions of what the subject may comprise and how it should be conducted.

On the broader view I have considered, philosophy is associated with basic human cognitive capacities, and informal reasoning on the issues, in morality for instance, should be included. But on the more restricted and it has to be said more conventional view, philosophy will consist of technical and systematic analyses of well-defined questions in one or other of such areas as epistemology, ethics, philosophy of mind, and metaphysics, and those can only be successfully undertaken by specialists who will certainly need training for the task. On that view, the institutions of higher education that we find not just in modern, but also in some ancient, societies,[22] will be an important, maybe a necessary, factor in the development of the subject, not that the way that has happened shows much uniformity across the world.

But if new ideas generally need some institutional basis if they are not to be stillborn, we have also to recognize that the institutionalization of the subject may stifle innovation, not foster it. As we shall see in our other studies, the growth of elites carries with it the dangers of restrictiveness, even of intolerance towards innovative ideas, let alone towards alternative conceptions of the subject. In the case of philosophy, an inquiry that may start out with an ambition to yield understanding, remove puzzlements, and indeed provide guidance for life, may be turned into a narrow academic, even scholastic, discipline. That tendency remains a danger even today. As an antidote, it would seem that a certain pluralism is desirable, the very openness to alternative views that I have associated with the broader construal of the subject.

---

[22] The record not just in the West, but also in China, in India, and in Islam, shows that important new insights have often depended on a reaction to the work of those seen as intellectual rivals, even when the aim has been to demolish others' systems in their entirety.

2

Mathematics

Two different types of approach may be suggested to the question of what mathematics is or has been for different peoples. On the one hand we might attempt to settle a priori on the criteria for mathematics and then review how far what we find in different cultures measures up to those criteria. Or we could proceed more empirically or inductively by studying those diverse traditions and then deriving an answer to our question on the basis of our findings.

Both approaches are faced with difficulties. On what basis can we decide on the essential characteristics of mathematics? If we thought, commonsensically, to appeal to a dictionary definition, which dictionary are we to follow? There is far from perfect unanimity in what is on offer, nor can it be said that there are obvious, crystal-clear, considerations that would enable us to adjudicate uncontroversially between existing divergent philosophies of mathematics. What mathematics is will be answered quite differently by the Platonist, by the constructivist, by the intuitionist, by the logicist, or by the formalist (to name but some of the divergent views on the twin fundamental questions of *what* mathematics studies, and *what* knowledge it produces).

The converse difficulty that faces the second approach is that we have to have some prior idea of what is to count as 'mathematics' to be able to start our cross-cultural study. Other cultures have other terms and concepts and their interpretation poses delicate problems. Faced with evident divergence and heterogeneity, at what point do we have to say that we are not dealing with a different concept of mathematics, but rather with a concept that has nothing to do with mathematics at all? The past provides ample examples of the dangers involved in legislating that certain practices and ideas fall beyond the boundaries of acceptable disciplines.

Two ancient civilizations, Greece and China, provide particularly rich evidence not just for mathematical practice, but also, precisely, for ideas on what mathematics comprises, and after a brief general introduction to the problems, my discussion here will concentrate on these materials where my analysis will owe more to the second than to the first approach. Of course, to study the ancient Greek or Chinese contributions in this area—their theories and their actual practices— we have to adopt a provisional idea of what can be construed as mathematical, principally how numbers and shapes or figures were conceived and manipulated. But as we explore further their ancient ideas on these topics, we can expect that our own understanding will be subject to modification as we proceed. We join up, as we shall see, with those problems in the philosophy of mathematics I mentioned: so in a sense a combination of both approaches is inevitable.

Before we engage in a detailed analysis of what the Greeks and Chinese had to say on the issues, we need to consider briefly some of the general anthropological background. As usual with ethnographic reports, the outsider needs to be wary. Thus it has often been asserted that many cultures have no concept of number at all. Sometimes this is an inference from the use of numeral classifiers, sometimes from the lack of an extensive number series, but some doubt is in order about what conclusions should be drawn in either case. When the word for two humans differs from that used for two trees, does that suggest the lack of a concept of two, and so *mutatis mutandis* for other numerals and by extension for the notion of number itself? As I have remarked elsewhere, the lack of a concept should not be inferred just from the lack of a term for it. The use of numeral classifiers might indeed be thought to be evidence *for* an implicit notion of number, though not for an explicit one of number as such, as an abstraction from things numbered. The notion of number in play will, of course, not be one of a continuum, including both positive and negative integers, for instance, but rather that of a plurality of discrete units. Meanwhile how children develop a concept of number, at what age they do so, and whether that development happens in precisely the same way in different societies with different uses of number, are highly disputed issues in developmental psychology (see, for example, Gelman and Gallistel 1986).

But what of languages with a limited vocabulary for things numbered? A drastically impoverished conceptual framework has sometimes been mistakenly inferred from an assumption that the language, like the practices, under consideration, will be 'primitive'.

In the moving story of Ishi, the last remaining member of an indigenous tribe that lived in California before they were wiped out by
American settlers in the gold rush, his language had been assumed
to be incapable of expressing numbers beyond 10. Yet Ishi proved to
be perfectly able to count beyond that number when he chose to do so
(Kroeber 1961: 144 f.). When a language is said to distinguish only one,
two, and many, we should be clear that that already implies a basic
contrast between a singleton and a plurality, and we should bear in
mind the possibility that the difficult question of the reasons both for
the extent of an interest, and for a lack of it, in counting the members
of such pluralities, will need specific answers in specific cases.[1]

Yet another instance where assumptions based on our own experience may mislead relates to questions of the comparative advantages
and disadvantages of different notations. These certainly differ widely
across the world, and include cases where numerals are not written,
but physically represented, as with the Peruvian *quipu* used as an
aide-memoire in general as well as for expressing numbers. The
clumsiness of the ancient Greek use of letters of the alphabet to
represent numbers is easily exaggerated by those who have had no
occasion to use them in practice, and so too is the relative disadvantage
of having no way of expressing zero—other than by representing it
with a gap.

Then what of 'geometry'? Again it is all too easy to jump to
conclusions. The lack of terms for straight and curved lines, triangles,
squares, cubes, and so on does not mean that there is no understanding of these two- or three-dimensional figures. Vertical lines are well
understood, in practice, by those who build houses with one or more
upright posts. Right angles, to be sure, are understood by those who
construct rectangular buildings, and circles by those who make circular ones. Of course that does not mean that these geometrical con-
structions are the subject of study in themselves, but again we must
distinguish between the explicit concepts and their implicit practical
use. Geometry as a learned discipline had its history, or rather
histories, since it was developed differently, as we shall see, in different ancient societies. But a practical grasp of some geometrical

---

[1] Compare the contrasting views on the competence of Pirahã speakers in relation to
mathematics in Gordon (2004) and Everett (2005) and in general on this issue, Dehaene
(1997).

concepts is widespread and may even be universal. So if we must admit that mathematics only became a subject of explicit investigation in a number of certain complex, literate, societies, we should not underestimate the mathematical knowledge available in many others.[2]

Turning now to two of those ancient, literate, societies, namely Greece and China, we have not only sophisticated practices, but also reflections on the studies that deal with what we can call mathematical matters. This provides us with an entry into the major problems, though we should notice at the outset that neither society had a concept of 'mathematics' that is the exact equivalent to our own. I shall first discuss the issues as they relate to Greece before turning to the less familiar data from ancient China.

Our term 'mathematics' is, of course, derived from the Greek *mathēmatikē*, but that word comes from the verb *manthanein* which has the quite general meaning of 'to learn'. A *mathēma* can be any branch of learning, anything we have learnt, as when in Herodotus, 1.207, Croesus refers to what he has learnt, his *mathēmata*, from the bitter experiences in his life. So the *mathēmatikos* is, strictly speaking, the person who is fond of learning in general, and it is so used by Plato, for instance, at *Timaeus* 88c, where the point at issue is the need to strike a balance between the cultivation of the intellect (in general) and that of the body—the principle that later became encapsulated in the dictum 'mens sana in corpore sano'. But from the fifth century BCE certain branches of study came to occupy a privileged position as the *mathēmata* par excellence. The terms mostly look familiar enough, *arithmētikē, geōmetrikē, harmonikē, astronomia*, and so on, but that is deceptive. Let me spend a little time explaining first the differences between the ancient Greeks' ideas and our own, and secondly some of the disagreements among Greek authors themselves about the proper subject-matter and methods of certain disciplines.

Arithmētikē is the study of *arithmos*, but that is usually defined in terms of what we would call positive integers greater than one.

<hr>

[2] Cf. Ascher (1991) on what she calls 'ethnomathematics'. Some at least of the cognitive capacities that underlie our mathematical understanding are not confined to human beings, if one thinks of the bees' construction of hexagons that maximize the storage capacity of the cells they make, and of the elaborate concentric webs spun by certain species of spiders. Aristotle already noted the accuracy with which the spider judges the centre of the web it starts to spin (*History of Animals* 623a10).

Although Diophantus who lived at some time in late antiquity, possibly in the third century CE, is a partial exception, the Greeks did not normally think of the number series as an infinitely divisible continuum, but rather as a set of discrete entities. They dealt with what we call fractions as ratios between integers. Negative numbers are not *arithmoi* and do not enter into consideration. Nor is the monad an *arithmos*: it is thought of as neither odd nor even. Plato draws a distinction, in the *Gorgias* 451b–c, between *arithmētikē* and *logistikē*, calculation, derived from the verb *logizesthai*, which is often used of reasoning in general. Both studies focus on the odd and the even, but *logistikē* deals with the pluralities they form, while *arithmētikē* considers them—so Socrates is made to claim—in themselves. That at least is the view Socrates expresses in the course of probing what the sophist Gorgias was prepared to include in what he called the art of rhetoric, though in other contexts the two terms that Socrates thus distinguished were used more or less interchangeably. Meanwhile a different way of contrasting the more abstract and the more practical aspects of the study of *arithmoi* is to be found in Plato's *Philebus* 56d, where Socrates distinguishes the way the many, *hoi polloi*, use them from the way philosophers do. Ordinary people use units that are unequal, speaking of two armies, for instance, or two oxen, while the philosophers deal with units that do not differ from one another in any respect, abstract ones in other words.[3] A gap thus opens up between the mathematical concepts that anyone might be expected to have, and a deeper, more sophisticated, approach, though that is here represented as depending not so much on advanced mathematical skills as on a philosophical grasp of the subject. We shall find other examples, in our study of Greece, where it is the philosophers, as much as mathematicians themselves, who claim superior knowledge in the domain.

At the same time the study of *arithmoi* encompassed much more than we would include under the rubric of arithmetic. Like some other peoples the Greeks represented numbers by letters, where α represents the number 1, β the number 2, γ 3, ι 10, and so on. This means that any proper name could be associated with a number. While some

---

[3] Cf. Asper (2009) who highlights the divergences between practical Greek mathematics and the mathematics of the cultured elite. On the proof techniques in the latter, Netz (1999) is fundamental.

held that such connections were purely fortuitous, others saw them as deeply significant. When in the third century CE the neo-Pythagorean Iamblichus claimed that 'mathematics' is the key to understanding the whole of nature and all its parts, he illustrated that with the symbolic associations of numbers, the patterns they form in magic squares and the like, as well as with more widely accepted examples such as the identification of the main musical concords, the octave, fifth, and fourth, with the ratios 2:1, 3:2, and 4:3. The beginnings of such associations, both symbolic and otherwise, go back to the pre-Platonic Pythagoreans who are said by Aristotle to have held that in some sense 'all things' 'are' or 'imitate' numbers. Yet this is quite unclear, first because we cannot be sure what 'all things' covers, and secondly because of the evident discrepancy between the claim that they *are* numbers and the much weaker one that they merely *imitate* them.

What about 'geometry'? The literal meaning of the components of the Greek word *geōmetria* is the measurement of land. According to a well-known passage in Herodotus, 2.109, the study was supposed to have originated in Egypt in relation, precisely, to land measurement after the flooding of the Nile. Measurement, *metrētikē*, still figures in the account Plato gives in the *Laws* 817e when his spokesman, the Athenian Stranger, specifies the branches of the *mathēmata* that are appropriate for free citizens, though now this is measurement of 'lengths, breadths, and depths', not of land. Similarly in the *Philebus* 56e we again find a contrast between the exact *geōmetria* that is useful for philosophy and the branch of the art of measurement that is appropriate for carpentry or architecture.

Those remarks of Plato already drive a wedge between practical utility—mathematics as securing the needs of everyday life—and a very different mode of usefulness, namely in training the intellect. One classical text that articulates that contrast is a speech that Xenophon puts in the mouth of Socrates in the *Memorabilia*, 4.7.2–5. While Plato's Socrates is adamant that mathematics is useful primarily because it turns the mind away from perceptible things to the study of intelligible entities, in Xenophon Socrates is made to lay stress on the usefulness of geometry for land measurement and on that of the study of the heavens for the calendar and for navigation, and to dismiss as irrelevant the more theoretical aspects of those studies. Similarly Isocrates too (11.22–3, 12.26–8, 15.261–5) distinguishes the practical and the theoretical sides of mathematical studies and in certain circumstances has critical remarks to make about the latter.

The clearest early extant statements of the view privileging the theoretical come not from the mathematicians but from philosophers commenting on mathematics from their own distinctive perspective. What mathematics can achieve that sets it apart from most other modes of reasoning is that it is exact and that it can demonstrate its conclusions. Plato repeatedly contrasts that with the merely persuasive arguments used in the law courts and assemblies where what the audience can be brought to believe may or may not be true, and may or may not be in their best interests. Philosophy, the claim is, is not interested in persuasion but in the truth. Mathematics is repeatedly used as the prime example of a mode of reasoning that can produce certainty: and yet mathematics, in the view Plato develops in the *Republic*, is subordinate to dialectic, the pure study of the intelligible world that represents the highest form of philosophy. Mathematical studies are valued as a propaedeutic, or training, in abstract thought: but they rely on perceptible diagrams and they give no account of their hypotheses, but rather take them to be clear. Philosophy, by contrast, moves from its hypotheses up to a supreme principle that is said to be 'unhypothetical'.

The exact status of that principle, which is identified with the Form of the Good, is highly obscure and much disputed. Likening it to a mathematical axiom immediately runs into difficulties, for what sense does it make to call an axiom 'unaxiomatic'? But Plato was clear that both dialectic and the mathematical sciences deal with independent intelligible entities.

Aristotle contradicted Plato on the philosophical point: mathematics does not study independently existing realities. Rather it studies the mathematical properties of physical objects. But he was more explicit than Plato in offering a clear definition of demonstration itself and in classifying the various indemonstrable primary premises on which it depends. Demonstration, in the strict sense, proceeds by valid deductive argument (Aristotle thought of that in terms of his theory of the syllogism) from premises that must be true, primary, necessary, prior to and explanatory of the conclusions. They must, too, be indemonstrable, to avoid the twin flaws of circular reasoning or an infinite regress. Any premise that can be demonstrated, should be. But there have to be *ultimate* primary premises that are evident in themselves. One of Aristotle's examples is the equality axiom, namely if you take equals from equals, equals remain. That cannot be shown other than by circular arguments, which yield no proof at all, but it is clear in itself.

It is obvious what this model of axiomatic-deductive demonstration owes to mathematics. I have just mentioned Aristotle's citation of the equality axiom, which figures also among Euclid's 'common opinions' (sometimes called 'common notions') and most of the examples of demonstrations that Aristotle gives, in the first book of the *Posterior Analytics*, are mathematical. Yet in the absence of substantial extant texts before Euclid's *Elements* itself (conventionally dated to around 300 BCE) it is difficult, or rather impossible, to say how far mathematicians before Aristotle had progressed towards an explicit notion of an indemonstrable axiom. Proclus, in the fifth century CE, claims to be drawing on the fourth-century BCE historian of mathematics Eudemus, in reporting that Hippocrates of Chios was the first to compose a book of 'Elements', and he further names a number of other figures, Eudoxus, Theodorus, Theaetetus, and Archytas among those who 'increased the number of theorems and progressed towards a more epistemic [that is, systematic] arrangement of them' (*Commentary on Euclid Elements I* 66.7–18).

That is evidently teleological history, as if they had a clear vision of the goal they should set themselves, namely the Euclidean *Elements* as we have it. The two most substantial stretches of mathematical reasoning from the pre-Aristotelian period that we have are Hippocrates' quadratures of lunes and Archytas' determining two mean proportionals (for the sake of solving the problem of the duplication of the cube) by way of a complex kinematic diagram involving the intersection of three surfaces of revolution, namely a right cone, a cylinder, and a torus. Hippocrates' quadratures are reported by Simplicius (*Commentary on Aristotle's Physics* 54.12–69.34), Archytas' work by Eutocius (*Commentary on Archimedes On the Sphere and Cylinder II*, vol. iii, 84.13–88.2), and both early mathematicians show impeccable mastery of the subject-matter in question.[4] Yet neither

---

[4] Archytas Fr. 1 offers some reflections on the relations between the different branches of mathematics, including on its importance for the study of nature, though the problems of interpretation of his views are compounded by the fact that they are transmitted in different versions in our sources (see Huffman 2005).

text confirms, nor even suggests, that these mathematicians had defined the starting-points they required in terms of different types of indemonstrable primary premisses.

Of course the principles set out in Euclid's *Elements* themselves do not tally exactly with the concepts that Aristotle had proposed in his discussion of strict demonstration. Euclid's three types of starting-points include definitions (as in Aristotle) and common opinions (which, as noted, include what Aristotle called the equality axiom) but also postulates (very different from Aristotle's hypotheses). The last included especially the parallel postulate that sets out the fundamental assumption on which Euclidean geometry is based, namely that non-parallel straight lines meet at a point. However, where the philosophers had demanded arguments that could claim to be incontrovertible, Euclid's *Elements* came to be recognized as providing the most impressive sustained exemplification of such a project. It systematically demonstrates most of the known mathematics of the day using especially *reductio* arguments and the misnamed method of exhaustion. Used to determine a curvilinear area such as a circle by inscribing successively larger regular polygons, that method precisely did *not* assume that the circle was 'exhausted', only that the difference between the inscribed rectilinear figure and the circumference of the circle could be made as small as you like. Thereafter the results that the *Elements* set out could be, and were, treated as secure by later mathematicians in their endeavours to expand the subject. Mastery of the *Elements* came to be an essential prerequisite for those seeking to join the ranks of what became an increasingly self-conscious elite.[5]

The impact of this development first on mathematics itself, then further afield, was immense. In statics and hydrostatics, in music theory, in astronomy, the hunt was on to produce axiomatic-deductive demonstrations that basically followed the Euclidean model. But we even find the second-century CE medical writer Galen attempting to set up mathematics as a model for reasoning in medicine—to yield conclusions in certain areas of pathology and physiology that could claim to be incontrovertible (Lloyd 2006). Similarly, Proclus

---

[5] Yet while skill in mathematics came to carry, in certain quarters at least, considerable prestige, the perceived difficulty of the subject made it unpopular in others. While Galen often uses mathematics as a model of method, he recognizes that this was liable to deter readers even among his more educated contemporaries, cf. Lloyd (2006).

attempted an *Elements of Theology* in the fifth century CE, again with the idea of producing results that could be represented as certain.

The ramifications of this development are considerable. Yet three points must be emphasized to put it into perspective. First, for ordinary purposes axiomatics was quite unnecessary. Not just in practical contexts, but in many more theoretical ones, mathematicians and others got on with the business of calculation and of measurement without wondering whether their reasoning needed to be given ultimate axiomatic foundations.[6]

Secondly, it was far from being the case that all Greek work in arithmetic and geometry, let alone in other fields such as harmonics or astronomy, adopted the Euclidean pattern. The three 'traditional' problems, of squaring the circle, the duplication of the cube, and the trisection of an angle were tackled already in the fifth century BCE without any explicit concern for axiomatics (Knorr 1986). Much of the work of a mathematician such as Hero of Alexandria (first century CE) focuses directly on problems of mensuration using methods similar to those in the traditions of Egyptian and Babylonian mathematics by which, indeed, he may have been influenced.[7] While he certainly refers to Archimedes as if he provided a model for demonstration, Hero's own procedures sharply diverge, on occasion, from those of Archimedes.[8] In the *Metrica* for instance he sometimes gives an arithmetized demonstration of geometrical propositions, that is he includes concrete numbers in his exposition. Moreover in the *Pneumatica* he allows exhibiting a result to count as a proof. Further afield I shall be discussing in a minute the disputes in harmonics and the study of the heavens on the aims of the study and the right methods to use.

---

[6] Cuomo (2001) provides an excellent account of the variety of both theoretical and practical concerns among Greek mathematicians at different periods and cf. Fowler (1999).

[7] Cf. Robson (2009), Rossi (2009), and Imhausen (2009).

[8] Tybjerg (2004) argues that Hero set out to eliminate the boundary between Euclidean-Archimedean proof and the methods and practices of practical mathematics. Moreover at two points he distances himself from 'philosophy'. On the problem of the void, he criticizes those who tried to settle the issue by a priori arguments as opposed to empirical tests (*Pneumatica* 1 16.16 ff.). On the subject of peace of mind, the agreed goal of Hellenistic philosophers of all persuasions, he ruefully remarked that this was better able to be secured by the applications of engineering—by better weaponry indeed—than by abstract philosophical reflection (*Belopoeica* 1 71 ff.). As for Archimedes himself, he too sometimes departed from the Euclidean model, especially, for example, in the area we would call combinatorics: cf. Saito (2009) and Netz (2009).

Thirdly, the recurrent problem for the model of axiomatic-deductive demonstration that the *Elements* supplied was always that of securing axioms that would be both self-evident and non-trivial. Moreover it was not enough that an axiom set should be internally consistent: it was generally assumed that they should be true in the sense of a correct representation of reality. Clearly outside mathematics they were indeed hard to come by. Galen, for example, proposed the doctrine that 'opposites are cures for opposites' as one of his indemonstrable principles, but the problem was to say what counted as an 'opposite'. If not trivial, it was contestable, but if trivial, useless. Even in mathematics itself, as the example of the parallel postulate itself most clearly showed, what principles could be claimed as self-evident was intensely controversial. Several commentators on the *Elements* protested that the assumption concerning non-parallel straight lines meeting at a point should be a theorem to be proved and removed from among the postulates. Proclus outlines the controversy (*Commentary on Euclid's Elements I* 191. 21 ff.) and offers his own attempted demonstration as well as reporting one proposed by Ptolemy (365. 5 ff., 371. 10 ff.): yet all such turned out to be circular, a result that has sometimes been taken to confirm Euclid's astuteness in deciding to treat this as a postulate in the first place. In time, however, it was, of course, the attack on the parallel postulate that led to the eventual emergence of non-Euclidean geometries.

These potential difficulties evidently introduce elements of doubt about the ability of mathematics, or of the subjects based on it, to deliver exactly what some writers claimed for it. Nevertheless, to revert to the fundamental point, mathematics, in the view both of some mathematicians and of outsiders, was superior to most other disciplines precisely in that it could outdo the merely persuasive arguments that were common in most other fields of inquiry.

It is particularly striking that Archimedes, the most original, ingenious, and multifaceted mathematician of Greek antiquity, insisted on such strict standards of demonstration that he was at one point led to consider as merely heuristic the method that he invented and set out in his treatise of that name.[9] He there describes how he discovered the

---

[9] He sent this to Eratosthenes on the grounds of his abilities in both 'philosophy' and 'mathematics'—which might suggest that, unlike some of the philosophers, Archimedes himself saw no great gulf between these two disciplines.

truth of the theorem that any segment of a parabola is four-thirds of the triangle that has the same base and equal height. The method relies on two assumptions, first that plane figures may be imagined as balanced against one another around a fulcrum and secondly that such figures may be thought of as composed of a set of line segments indefinitely close together. Both ideas breached common Greek pre-suppositions. It is true that there were precedents both for applying some quasi-mechanical notions to geometrical issues—as when figures are imagined as set in motion—and for objections to such procedures, as when in the *Republic* 527a–b Plato says that the language of mathematicians is absurd when they speak of 'squaring' figures and the like, as if they were doing things with mathematical objects.

But in Archimedes' case, the first objection to the method would be that it involved a category confusion, in that geometrical objects are not the types of item that could be said to have centres of gravity. Moreover Archimedes' second assumption, that a plane figure is composed of its indivisible line segments, clearly breached the Greek geometrical notion of the continuum. The upshot was that he cate-gorized his method as one of discovery only, and he explicitly claimed that its results had thereafter to be demonstrated by the usual method of exhaustion. At this point there appears to be some tension between the preoccupation with the strictest criteria of proof that dominated one tradition of Greek mathematics (though only one) and the other important aim of pushing ahead with the business of discovery.

The issues of the canon of proof, and of whether and how to provide an axiomatic base for work in the various parts of 'mathematics', were not the only subjects of dispute. Let me now illustrate the range of controversy first in harmonics and then in the study of the heavens.

'Music', or rather *mousikē*, was a generic term, used of any art over which one or other of the nine Muses presided. The person who was *mousikos* was one who was well educated and cultured generally. To specify what we mean by 'music' the Greeks usually used the term *harmonikē*, the study of harmonies or musical scales. Once again the variety of ways that study was construed is remarkable and it will be worth exploring this in some detail straight away as a classic illustra-tion of the tension between mathematical analysis and perceptible phenomena. There were those who were engaged in music-making, practical musicians who were interested in producing pleasing sounds, whose claims to special status depended on skill in performance, not on theoretical know-how. But then there were also plenty of theorists who concerned themselves, precisely, with theoretical analyses even though those they developed adopted quite different starting assumptions. One approach, exemplified by Aristoxenus, insisted that the unit of measurement should be something identifiable to perception. Here a tone is defined as the difference between the fifth and the fourth, and in principle the whole of music theory can be built up from these perceptible intervals, namely by ascending and descending fifths and fourths.

But if that approach accepted that musical intervals can be construed on the model of line segments and investigated quasi-geometrically, a rival mode of analysis adopted a more exclusively arithmetical view, where the tone is defined as the difference between sounds whose 'speeds' stand in a ratio of 9:8. In this, the so-called Pythagorean tradition, represented in the work called the *Sectio Canonis* in the Euclidean corpus, musical relations are understood as essentially ratios between numbers, and the task of the harmonic theorist becomes that of deducing various propositions in the mathematics of ratios.

Moreover these quite contrasting modes of analysis were associated with quite different answers to particular musical questions. Are the octave, fifth, and fourth exactly six tones, three and a half, and two and a half tones respectively? If the tone is identified as the ratio of 9 to 8, then you do not get an octave by taking six such intervals. The excess of a fifth over three tones, and of a fourth over two, has to be expressed by the ratio 256 to 243, not by the square root of $^9/_8$.

This dispute in turn spills over into a fundamental epistemological disagreement. Is perception to be the criterion, or reason, or some combination of the two? Some thought that numbers and reason rule. If what we hear appears to conflict with what the mathematics yields by way of an analysis, then too bad for our hearing. We find some theorists who denied that the interval of an octave plus a fourth can be a harmony precisely because the ratio in question (8:3) does not conform to the mathematical patterns that constitute the main concords. Those all have the form of either a multiplicate ratio, as for example 2:1 (expressing the octave) or a superparticular one, as for example 3:2 and 4:3, both of which meet the criterion for a superparticular ratio namely n+1:n.

It was one of the most notable achievements of the *Harmonics* written by Ptolemy in the second century CE to show how the competing criteria could be combined and reconciled (cf. Barker 2000, 2007). First the analysis had to derive what is perceived as tuneful from rational mathematical principles. Why should there be any connection between sounds and ratios, and with the particular ratios that the concords were held to express? What hypotheses should be adopted to give the mathematical underpinning to the analysis? But just to select some principles that would do so was, by itself, not enough. The second task the music theorist must complete is to bring those principles to an empirical test, to confirm that the results arrived at on the basis of the mathematical theory did indeed tally with what was perceived by the ear in practice to be concordant—or discordant—as the case might be.

The study of the heavens was equally contentious, with rival views on its proper subject-matter and methods, and especially on the claims that could be made for the knowledge it yielded. Hesiod is supposed to have written a work entitled *Astronomia*, though to judge from his *Works and Days* his interest in the stars related rather to how they tell the passing of the seasons and can help to regulate the farmer's year. In the *Epinomis* 990a (whether or not this is an authentic work of Plato) Hesiod is associated with the study of the stars' risings and settings—an investigation that is *contrasted* with the study of the planets, sun, and moon. The latter, true astronomy, like the other branches of mathematics when properly construed, is a source not so much of practical know-how as of true wisdom.

Both *astronomia* and *astrologia* are attested in the fifth century BCE and are often used interchangeably, though the second element in the first has *nemo* as its root and that relates to distribution, while *logos*, in the second term, is rather a matter of giving an account. Although genethlialogy, the casting of horoscopes based on geometrical calculations of the positions of the planets at birth, does not become prominent until the third century BCE, the stars were already associated with auspicious and inauspicious phenomena in, for example, Plato's *Symposium* 188b. Certainly by Ptolemy's time (second century CE) an explicit distinction was drawn between predicting the movements of the heavenly bodies themselves (astronomy, in our terms, the subject-matter of the *Syntaxis*), and predicting events on earth on their basis (astrology, as we should say, the topic he tackled in the *Tetrabiblos*, which he explicitly contrasts with the other branch of the study of the heavens). Yet both Greek terms themselves continued to be used for either. Indeed in the Hellenistic period the term *mathēmatikos* was regularly used of the astrologer as well as of the astronomer. However, the extent of the mathematical knowledge the former needed varied considerably. Some extant horoscopes are based on a minimal analysis of the positions of the sun and moon at birth, while others, the deluxe models as Jones (1999) calls them, involve detailed examination of all the heavenly bodies and the relations between them.

Both studies of the heavens, however, remained controversial. The arguments about the validity of astrological prediction are outlined in Cicero's *De Divinatione* for instance: but the Epicureans also dismissed astronomy itself as speculative. On the other hand, there were those who saw theoretical astronomy as one of the most important and successful of the branches of mathematics—not that they agreed on how it was to be pursued.[10] We may leave to one side Plato's provocative remarks in the *Republic* 530a–b that the *astronomikos* should pay no attention to the empirical phenomena—he should 'leave the things in the heavens alone'—and engage in a study of 'quickness and slowness' themselves (529d), since at that point Plato is concerned with what the study of the heavens can contribute to abstract thought. If we want to find out how Plato himself (no practising astronomer, to be sure) viewed the study of the heavens, the *Timaeus* is a surer guide, where indeed the contemplation of the heavenly bodies is again given philosophical importance—such a vision encourages the soul to philosophize—but where the different problems posed by the varying speeds and trajectories of the planets, sun, and moon are recognized each to need its own solution (*Timaeus* 40b–d).

Quite how the chief problems for theoretical astronomy were defined in the fourth century BCE has become controversial in modern scholarship (Bowen 2001, 2002a, 2002b). But it remains clear first that the problem of the planets' 'wandering', as their Greek name ('wanderer') implied, was one that exercised Plato. In his *Timaeus*, 39c–d, their movements are said to be of wondrous complexity, although in his last work, the *Laws* 822a, he came to insist that each of the heavenly bodies moves with a *single* circular motion. The model of concentric spheres that Aristotle in *Metaphysics Lambda* ascribes to

---

[10] That issue has been discussed recently by Mueller 2004 and Bowen 2007, and cf. Vitrac 2005.

Eudoxus, and in a modified form to Callippus, was designed to explain *some* anomalies in the apparent movements of the sun, moon, and planets. Some *geometrical* model was thereafter common ground to much Greek astronomical theorizing, though disputes continued over *which* model was to be preferred (concentric spheres came to be replaced by eccentrics and epicycles). Moreover some studies were purely geometrical in character, offering no comments on how (if at all) the models proposed were to be applied to the physical phenomena. That applies to the books that Autolycus of Pitane wrote *On the Moving Sphere*, and *On Risings and Settings*. Even Aristarchus in the one treatise of his that is extant, *On the Sizes and Distances of the Sun and Moon*, engaged (on the view I favour) in a purely geometrical analysis of how those results could be obtained, without committing himself to concrete conclusions, although in the work in which he adumbrated his famous heliocentric hypothesis, there are no good grounds to believe he was *not* committed to that as a physical solution.

Yet if we ask *why* prominent Greek theorists adopted *geometrical* models to explain the apparent irregularities in the movements of the heavenly bodies, when most other astronomical traditions were content with purely numerical solutions to the patterns of their appearances, the answer takes us back to the ideal of a demonstration that can carry explanatory, deductive force, and to the demands of a teleological account of the universe, that can show that the movements of the heavenly bodies are supremely orderly.

We may note once again that the history of Greek astronomy is not one of uniform or agreed, goals, ideals, and methods. It is striking how influential the contrasts that the philosophers had insisted on, between proof and persuasion, or between demonstration and conjecture, proved to be. In the second century CE Ptolemy uses those contrasts twice over. He first does so in the *Syntaxis* in order to contrast 'mathematics', which here clearly includes the mathematical astronomy that he is about to embark on in that work, with 'physics' and with 'theology'. In a remarkable move that effectively turns the tables on both Plato and Aristotle, each of whom had, in their different ways, subordinated mathematics to dialectic and to first philosophy, Ptolemy claims that both 'physics' and 'theology' are conjectural, the first because of the instability of physical objects, the second because of the obscurity of the subject. 'Mathematics', on the other hand, can secure certainty, thanks to the fact that it uses—so he says—the incontrovertible methods of arithmetic and geometry. In practice, of course, Ptolemy has to admit the difficulties he faces when tackling such subjects as the movements of the planets in latitude: and his actual workings are full of approximations. Yet that is not allowed to diminish the claim he wishes to make for his theoretical study.

Then the second context in which he redeploys the contrast is in the opening chapters of the *Tetrabiblos*, which I have already mentioned for the distinction it draws between two types of prediction. Those that relate to the movements of the heavenly bodies themselves can be shown demonstratively, *apodeiktikōs*, he says: but those that relate to the fortunes of human beings are an *eikastikē*, conjectural, study. Yet while for some to classify a subject as 'conjectural' was drastically to undermine any claims for its credibility, that was not Ptolemy's view here, for he insists that astrology is founded on assumptions that are tried and tested. Like medicine and navigation, it cannot deliver certainty: but it can yield probable conclusions.

Many more illustrations of Greek ideas and practices could be given, but enough has been said for one important and obvious point to emerge in relation to our principal question, of what mathematics was in Greece, namely that generalization is especially difficult in the face of the widespread disagreements and divergences that we find at all periods and in every department of inquiry. Some investigators, to be sure, got on with pursuing their own particular study after their own manner. But the questions of the status and goals of different parts of the study, and of the proper methods by which it should be conducted, were frequently raised both within and outside the circles of those who styled themselves mathematicians. Having convincing positions on those issues was often a crucial factor in justifying pretensions to intellectual leadership and prestige, whether in mathematics itself or in philosophy, where as I have noted, there were considerable disputes as to which could claim hegemonic status and on what grounds. But if no single univocal answer can be given to our initial question of what 'mathematics' covered for the Greeks, we can at least remark the intensity with which the Greeks themselves debated it.

The situation in ancient China is, in some respects, very different, though the similarities are not confined to a fascination with magic squares and the like. The key point is that two common stereotypes about Chinese work are seriously flawed, the first that their concern for practicalities blocked any interest in theoretical issues,[11] and the second that while they were able calculators and arithmeticians, they were weak geometers.

It is true that while the Greek materials we have reviewed may suffer from a deceptive air of familiarity, Chinese ideas and practices are liable to seem exotic to Westerners. Their map or maps of the relevant intellectual disciplines, theoretical or practical and applied, are very different both from those of the Greeks and from our own. One of the two general terms for number or counting, shu_1, has meanings that include 'scolding', 'fate', or 'destiny', 'art' as in 'the art of', and 'deliberations' (Ho 1991). The second general term, *suan*, is used of planning, scheming, and inferring as well as reckoning or counting. The two major treatises that deal with broadly mathematical subjects, that date from a hundred years or so either side of the millennium, both have *suan* in their title: we shall have more to say on each in due course. The *Zhoubi suanjing* is conventionally translated 'Arithmetic Classic of the Zhou Gnomon'. The second treatise is the *Jiuzhang suanshu*, the 'Nine Chapters on Mathematical Procedures'. That draws on an earlier text recently excavated from a tomb sealed in 186 BCE, which has both general terms in its title, namely *Suanshushu*, the 'Book of Mathematical Procedures', as Chemla renders it (Chemla and Guo 2004), or more simply 'Writings on Reckoning' (Cullen 2004). But the *Nine Chapters* goes beyond that treatise, both in presenting the problems it deals with more systematically, and in extending the range of those it tackles, notably by including discussion of *gou gu*, the properties of right-angled triangles (a first indication of those Chinese interests in geometrical questions that have so often been neglected or dismissed). Indeed thanks to the existence of the *Suanshushu* we are in a better position to trace early developments in Chinese mathematics than we are in reconstructing what Euclid's *Elements* owed to its predecessors.

When around the turn of the millennium the Han bibliographers, Liu Xiang, and Liu Xin, catalogued all the books in the imperial library under six generic headings, shu_1 shu_2,—that is, on one view, 'calculations and methods'—appears as one of these. Its six subspecies comprise two that deal with the study of the heavens, namely *tianwen*

---

[11] Cf. Chemla and Guo 2004.

(the patterns in the heavens) and *lipu* (calendars and tables), as well as *wu xing* (the five phases), and a variety of types of divinatory studies. The five phases provided the main framework within which change was discussed. They are named fire, earth, metal, water, and wood, but these are not elements in the sense of the basic physical constituents of things, so much as processes. 'Water' picks out not so much the substance, as the process of 'soaking downwards', as one text (the 'Great Plan', *Hong Fan*, from the *Book of Documents*, the *Shangshu*) puts it, just as 'fire' is not a substance but 'flaming upwards'.

This already indicates that the Chinese did not generally recognize a fundamental contrast between what we call the study of nature (or the Greeks called *physike*) on the one hand and mathematics on the other. Rather, each discipline dealt with the quantitative aspects of the phenomena it covered as and when the need arose. We can illustrate this with harmonic theory, included along with calendar studies in the category *lipu*.

Music was certainly of profound cultural importance in China. We hear of different types of music in different states or kingdoms before China was unified under Qin Shi Huang Di in 221 BCE, some the subject of uniform approval and appreciation, some the topic of critical comment as leading to licentiousness and immorality—very much in the way in which the Greeks saw different modes of their music as conducive to courage or to self-indulgence. Confucius is said to have not tasted meat for three months once he had heard the music of *shao*, in the kingdom of Qi (*Lunyu* 7.14).

But musical sounds were also the subject of theoretical analysis, indeed of several different kinds. On the one hand, as in Greece, a gap opens up between practitioners and theoretical analysts. On the other, there is no explicit Chinese epistemological polemic between rival theorists as to the correct mode of analysis to give of harmonics. We have extensive extant texts dealing with the subject, starting with the *Huainanzi*, a cosmological summa compiled under the auspices of Liu An, king of Huainan, in 136 BCE, and continuing in the musical treatises contained in the first great Chinese universal history, the *Shiji* written by Sima Tan and his son Sima Qian around 90 BCE. Thus *Huainanzi*, chapter 3 sets out a schema correlating the twelve pitch-pipes, that give what we would call the 12-tone scale, with the five notes of the pentatonic scale. Starting from the first pitch-pipe, named Yellow Bell (identified with the first pentatonic note, *gong*), the second and subsequent pitch-pipes are generated by alternate ascents of a fifth and descents of a fourth—very much in the manner in which in Greece the Aristoxenians thought that all musical concords should be so generated. Moreover *Huainanzi* assigns a number to each pitch-pipe. Yellow Bell starts at 81, the second pitch-pipe Forest Bell is 54, that is 81 times $^2/_3$, the next is 72, that is 54 times $^4/_3$, and so on. The system works perfectly for the first five notes, but then complications arise. The number of the sixth note is rounded from $42\,^2/_3$ to 42, and at the next note the sequence of alternate ascents and descents is interrupted by two consecutive descents of a fourth—a necessary adjustment to stay within a single octave.

On the one hand, it is clear that a numerical analysis is sought and achieved, but on the other a price has to be paid. Either approximations must be allowed, or alternatively very large numbers have to be tolerated. The second option is the one taken in a passage in the *Shiji* 25, where the convention of staying within a single octave is abandoned, but at the cost of having to cope with complex ratios such as 32,768 to 59,049. Indeed *Huainanzi* itself in another passage, 3.21a, generates the twelve pitch-pipes by successive multiplications by 3 from unity, which yields the number 177,147 (that is 3^{11}) as the 'Great Number of Yellow Bell'.

That section associates harmonics with the creation of the 'myriad things' from the primal unity. The *dao* comes from the one, and this subdivides into *yin* and *yang*, which between them generate everything else. Since *yin* and *yang* themselves are correlated with even and with odd numbers respectively, the greater and the lesser *yin* being identified as 6 and 8, and the greater and lesser *yang* 9 and 7, the common method of divination, based on the hexagrams set out in such texts as the *Yijing*, the *Book of Changes*, is also given a numerical basis. But interestingly enough the *Book of Changes* was not classified by Liu Xiang and Liu Xin under $shu_1\ shu_2$. Rather it was placed in the group of disciplines that dealt with classic, or canonical, texts. Indeed the patterns of *yin* and *yang* lines generated by the hexagrams were regularly mined, both by ordinary folk and by specialists in the field, for insight into every aspect of human behaviour as well as into the cosmos as a whole. As in Greece, so too in a distinctive way in China, numbers were often construed as the key to deep understanding.

Similarly complex numbers are also required in the Chinese studies of the heavens. One division dealt with 'the patterns of the heavens', *tian wen*, and was chiefly concerned with the interpretation of omens. But the other, *lifa* (included under *lipu*), included the quantitative analysis of periodic cycles, both to establish the calendar and to enable eclipses to be predicted. In one calendrical schema, called the Triple Concordance System, a lunation is $29^{43}/_{81}$ days, a solar year $365^{385}/_{1539}$ days, and in the concordance cycle 1,539 years equals 19,035 lunations and 562,120 days (cf. Sivin 1995a). On the one hand, considerable efforts were expended on carrying out the observations needed to establish the data on which eclipse cycles could be based. On the other, the figures for the concordances were also manipulated mathematically, giving in some cases a spurious air of precision—just as happens in Ptolemy's tables of the movements of the planets in longitude and in anomaly in the *Syntaxis*.

Techniques for handling large-number ratios are common to both Chinese harmonics and to the mathematical aspects of the study of the heavens. But there is also a clear ambition to integrate these two investigations—which both form part of the Han category *lipu*. Thus each pitch-pipe is correlated with one of the twelve positions of the handle of the constellation Big Dipper as it circles the celestial pole during the course of the seasons. Indeed it was claimed that each pitch-pipe resonates spontaneously with the qi_1, of the corresponding season and that that effect could be observed empirically by blown ash at the top of a half-buried pipe, a view that later came to be debunked as mere fantasy (Huang Yilong and Chang Chih-Ch'eng 1996).

While the calendar and eclipse cycles figure prominently in the work of Chinese astronomers, the study of the heavens was not limited to those subjects. In the *Zhoubi suanjing* (23.10ff.) the Master Chenzi is asked by his pupil Rong Fang what his *dao*, his way, achieves, and this provides us with one of the clearest early statements expressing the power and scope of mathematics, at least as studied by experts such as Chenzi himself. The *dao*, he says in reply, is able to determine the height and size of the sun, the area illuminated by its light, the figures for its greatest and least distances, and the length and breadth of heaven, solutions to each of which are then set out. That the earth is flat is assumed throughout, but one key technique on which the results depend is the geometrical analysis of gnomon shadow differences. Among the observational techniques is sighting the sun down a bamboo tube. Using the figure for the distance of the sun obtained in an earlier study, the dimension of the sun can be got

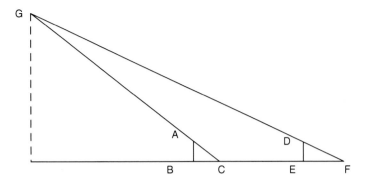

Figure 2.1. Given that the distance between the two gnomons (AB and DE), namely BE, is known, and also that the shadows (BC and EF) also are, then the height of the sun at G can be calculated, assuming a flat earth. The same method can be used to determine the height of any object as observed from two points on the same plane.

from those of the tube by similar triangles. Such a result was just one impressive proof of the power of mathematics (here *suan shu₂*) to arrive at an understanding of apparently obscure phenomena. But it should be noted that although Chenzi eventually explains his methods to his pupil on the whole quite clearly, he first expects him to go away and work out how to get these results on his own. Instead of overwhelming the student with the incontrovertibility of the conclusion *quod erat demonstrandum*, the Chinese master does not rate knowledge unless it has been internalized by the pupil.

The other major classical Chinese mathematical treatise, the *Nine Chapters*, indicates both the range of topics covered and the ambitions of the coverage. Furthermore the earliest extant commentary on that text, by Liu Hui, in the third century CE, provides precious evidence of how he saw the strategic aims of that treatise and of Chinese mathematics as a whole. The *Nine Chapters* deal with such subjects as field measurement, the addition, subtraction, multiplication, and division of fractions, the extraction of square roots, the solutions to linear equations with multiple unknowns (by the rule of double false position), the calculation of the volumes of pyramids, cones, and the like.

The problems are invariably expressed in concrete terms. The text deals with the construction of city-walls, trenches, moats, and canals, with the fair distribution of taxes across different counties, the conversion of different quantities of grain of different types, and much else besides. But to represent the work as just focused on practicalities would be a travesty. A problem about the number of workmen needed to dig a trench of particular dimensions gives the answer as $7\frac{427}{3064}$ labourers (chs. 5.5, 161.3). The interest is quite clearly in the exact solution to the equation rather than in the practicalities of the situation. Moreover the discussion of the circle-circumference ratio (what we call π) provides a further illustration of the point. For practical purposes a value of 3 or $3\frac{1}{7}$ is perfectly adequate, and such values were indeed often used. Ordinary users of mathematics clearly had no interest in the theoretical problem posed by the computation of π. But the commentary tradition on the *Nine Chapters* engages in the calculation of the area of inscribed regular polygons with 192 sides and even 3,072-sided ones are contemplated (the larger the number of sides, the closer the approximation to the circle itself, of course): by the time of Zhao Youqin, in the thirteenth century, we are up to 16,384-sided ones—a virtuoso performance indeed (Volkov 1997).

Liu Hui's comments on the chapter discussing the volume of a pyramid illustrate the sophistication of his geometrical reasoning (cf. Wagner 1979). Although he modestly makes no claims for any exceptional ability of his own, he does comment on the decline of mathematical knowledge in his day, just as Archimedes complained in the Preface to his *Quadrature of the Parabola* that, on the death of Conon, he had no one with whom to correspond on advanced mathematical questions. Both writers tacitly recognize that many of the problems they tackle were beyond the competence, and the interests, of most of their contemporaries.

The figure whose volume Liu Hui sets himself to determine (167.1–168.4) is a pyramid with rectangular base and one lateral edge perpendicular to the base, called a *yangma*. To arrive at the formula setting out its volume (namely one-third length times breadth times height) he has to determine the proportions between it and two other figures, the *qiandu* (right prism with right triangular base) and the *bienao* (a pyramid with right triangular base and one lateral edge perpendicular to the base). A *yangma* and a *bienao* together go to make up a *qiandu*, and its volume is simple: it is half its length times breadth times depth. That leaves Liu Hui with the problem of finding the ratio between the *yangma* and the *bienao*. He proceeds by first decomposing a *yangma* into a combination of smaller figures, a box, two smaller *qiandu*, and two smaller *yangma*. A *bienao* similarly can

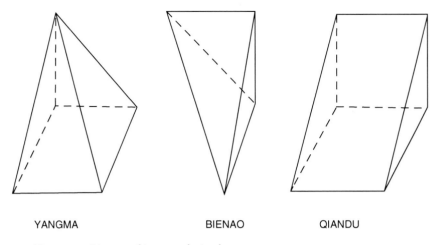

YANGMA   BIENAO   QIANDU

Figure 2.2. *Yangma, bienao* and *qiandu.*

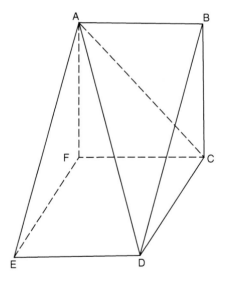

Figure 2.3. *Yangma* (ACDEF) plus *bienao* (ABCD) equals *qiandu* (ABCDEF).

be decomposed into two smaller *qiandu* and two smaller *bienao*. But once so decomposed it can be seen that the box plus two smaller *qiandu* in the original *yangma* are twice the two smaller *qiandu* in the original *bienao*. The parts thus determined stand in a relation of 2:1. The remaining problem is, of course, to determine the ratios

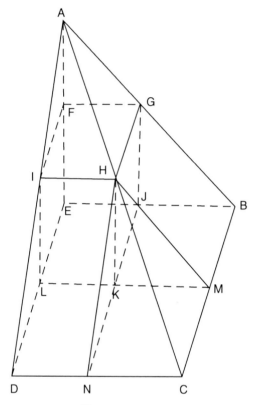

Figure 2.4. Decomposition of large *yangma* (ABCDE) (cf. Wagner 1979).This is decomposed into the box (HIFGJKLE), plus two smaller *qiandu* (HGBMKJ) and (IHKNDL) and two smaller *yangma* (AGHIF) and (HMCNK).

of the smaller *yangma* and the smaller *bienao*: but an exactly similar procedure can be applied to them. At each stage more of the original figure has been determined, always yielding a 2:1 ratio for the *yangma* to the *bienao*. If the process is continued, the series converges on the formula one *yangma* equals two *bienao*, and so a *yangma* is two-thirds of a *qiandu*, which yields the requisite formula for the volume of the *yangma*, namely one-third length times breadth times height.

    Two points of particular interest in this stretch of argument are first that Liu Hui explicitly remarks on the uselessness of one of the figures he uses in his decomposition. The *bienao*, he says, is an object that 'has

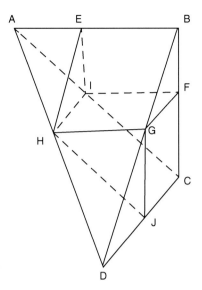

Figure 2.5. Decomposition of large *bienao* (ABCD). This is decomposed into two *qiandu* (EBFGHI) and (FCJGHI) and two smaller *bienao* (AEIH) and (HGJD).

no practical use'. Yet without it the volume of the *yangma* cannot be calculated. At this point we have yet another clear indication that, where specialist mathematicians were concerned, the interest in the exact geometrical result takes precedence over questions of practical utility.

Secondly, we may observe both a similarity and a difference between the procedure adopted by Liu Hui and some Greek methods. In such cases (as in Euclid's determination of the pyramid at *Elements* 12.3–5) the Greeks used an indirect proof, showing that the volume to be determined cannot be either greater or less than the result, and so must equal it. Liu Hui by contrast uses a direct proof, the technique of decomposition which I have described, yielding increasingly accurate approximations to the volume, a procedure similar to that used in the Chinese determination of the circle by inscribing regular polygons, mentioned above. Such a technique bears an obvious resemblance to the Greek method of exhaustion, though I remarked that in that method the area or volume to be determined was precisely not exhausted. Liu Hui sees that his process of decomposition can be continued indefinitely, and he remarks on the progressively smaller remainders that this yields. We are dealing evidently with what we would call a converging series, but although Liu Hui has no explicit concept for the limit of such, he ends his investigation with the rhetorical question 'how can there be any remainder?'

There is no suggestion, however, in any of the texts we have been considering, of giving mathematics an axiomatic base. The notion of axiom is absent from Chinese mathematics until the arrival of the Jesuits in the sixteenth century. Rather, the chief aims of Chinese mathematicians were to explore the unity of mathematics and to extend its range. Liu Hui, especially, comments that it is the *same* procedures that provide the solutions to problems in different subject-areas. What he looks for, and finds, in such procedures as those he calls 'homogenizing', qi_2, and 'equalizing', *tong*, are what he calls the guiding principles, *gangji*, of mathematics (*suan*). In his account of how, from childhood, he studied the *Nine Chapters* (91.6 ff.) he speaks of the different branches of the study, but insists that they all have the same trunk, *ben*. They have a single source or principle, *duan*. The realizations and their categories, *lei*, are elaborated mutually. Over and over again the aim is to find and show the connections between the different parts of *suan shu$_2$*, extending procedures across different categories, making the whole 'simple but precise, open to communication but not obscure'. Describing how he identified the technique of double difference, he says (92.2) he looked for the essential points or characteristics, *zhi qu*, to be able to extend it to other problems.

While Liu Hui is more explicit in all of this than the *Nine Chapters*, the other great Han classic, the *Zhoubi*, represents the goal in very similar terms. We are not dealing with some isolated, maybe idiosyncratic, point of view, but with one that represents an important, maybe even the dominant, tradition—at least among those in the forefront of Chinese mathematical speculation. 'It is the ability to distinguish categories in order to unite categories' which is the key according to the *Zhoubi* (25.5). Again, among the methods that comprise the *dao*, the way, it is 'those which are concisely worded but of broad application which are the most illuminating of the categories of understanding. If one asks about one category and applies [this knowledge] to a myriad affairs, one is said to know the Way' (24.12 ff.).

I may now attempt to sum up what our rapid and selective survey suggests. The study of just two ancient mathematical traditions already brings to light not just certain generic similarities, but also some suggestive contrasts as to how mathematics and its branches were construed. Among the former are investigations of the practical issues posed by calculation and problem-solving whether in arithmetic or geometry, as well as the appreciation of the generic links between mathematics in general on the one hand, and harmonics and certain aspects of the study of the heavens, on the other. In both civilizations we find a variety of writers who represent mathematics as the basis of the understanding of the otherwise imponderable. It was not just practising mathematicians who did so, in either case, but when they did, there are signs of their constituting themselves as something of an intellectual elite. Moreover unlike what is the case in medicine or in law, let alone in religion, where acceptance by the inner circles of existing practitioners could be influenced by considerations of birth or perceived respectability, belonging to a mathematical elite depended far more exclusively on ability alone.

Once the foundations of the subject had been laid, innovation naturally became increasingly demanding. Archimedes was not to be superseded in the West until the seventeenth century. In China, sporadic improvements on Liu Hui were made by later commentators on the *Nine Chapters* such as Zu Chongzhi and Zu Gengzhi in the fifth century and Li Chunfeng in the seventh. But it was not until the thirteenth century that major sustained advances occurred. Yet whatever may be the reasons for such intermittent progress, they did not include constraints that the elites themselves imposed in an effort to preserve their own position, as happened in other disciplines both in China and in the West.

But among the strategic differences, two stand out. While specialists argued among themselves in both civilizations, the manner in which they did so exhibits certain differences. We found many of the Greeks (not all) engaged in basic methodological and epistemological disagreements, where what was at stake was the ability to deliver certainty—to be able to do better than the merely persuasive or conjectural arguments that many downgraded as inadequate. The Chinese by contrast were far more concerned to explore the connections and the unity between different studies, including between those we consider to be mathematics and others we class as physics or cosmology. Their aim was not to establish the subject on a self-evident axiomatic basis, but to expand it by extrapolation and analogy.

Each of those two aims, secondly, has its strengths and its weaknesses. The advantages of axiomatization are that it makes explicit what assumptions are needed to get to which results. But the chief problem was that of identifying self-evident axioms that are not trivial. The advantage of the Chinese focus on guiding principles and connections was to encourage extrapolation and analogy, but the corresponding weakness was that everything depended on perceiving the analogies, since no attempt is made to give them axiomatic foundations. It is apparent that there is no one route that the development of mathematics had to take, or should have taken. We find good evidence in these two ancient civilizations for a variety of views of its unity and its diversity, its usefulness for practical purposes and for understanding. The value of asking the question 'what is mathematics?' is that it reveals so clearly, already where just two ancient mathematical traditions are concerned, the fruitful heterogeneity in the answers that were given.

Whatever notions we might entertain, a priori, about the similarity or diversity of what may be recognized as—broadly—mathematical practices in societies without writing, many would assume that once mathematics became the topic of formal reflection, that would lead to a convergence on a single uniform and standardized set of aims and methods. The historical data we have reviewed show that that is not the case. We have found quite marked differences in the views on what those aims and methods should be both as between Greece and China, and indeed between different Greek traditions. In both ancient societies skills in the manipulation of numbers and figures were highly prized, and in that sense those who displayed them were recognized as an elite. But the ways in which those who were admired for their skills chose to develop the subject, and the criteria they invoked to evaluate their own and others' performances, differed.

In this field of intellectual inquiry, the elites formed by the most skilful practitioners developed impressive programmes of research and certainly did not block all innovation even though some of them exhibit certain signs of exclusiveness. But it seems clear where one important Greek tradition is concerned, that the model of axiomatic-demonstration that served as an ideal inhibited the presentation of mathematical investigations that did not conform to that model, and in that sense deflected attention from the issue of heuristics. In both ancient societies mathematics was valued not just for its own sake, but also as a model of skilful reasoning in general. But the conception of what that comprised differed as between those who put the emphasis on certainty and those who privileged discovery, and again between those who saw mathematics as revealing invisible intelligible realities and those who saw it as a means of bringing to light the similarities and connections between things. Obviously in both cases the role of mathematics reflects certain fundamental intellectual values adopted by the society in question or by groups within it, and itself contributes to confirming those preferences. One part of the explanation for the divergences we find in the ways that mathematics developed lies, for sure, in the divergences in the goals and ideals set for reasoning and reasoners in general. Although that subject raises problems beyond the scope of my studies here, I shall have more to say, in subsequent chapters, on one relevant issue, namely the topic I have already broached of competing claims among rival elites for the hegemonic status of their discipline.[12]

---

[12] I have proposed tentative arguments on these issues in Lloyd 1990: ch. 3 and Lloyd 2002: ch. 3.

3

History

IT might be assumed that every human group has an interest in its past and therefore a concern with its history. But the conception of the past, and the nature of that interest differ, and so whether the concern is what we can call a historical one becomes problematic. The notion that time forms a continuum leading from the past, through the present, to the future, is, as the anthropologists have shown, far from universal. For some cultures the time of heroes or of gods is qualitatively different from the time of today (Vidal-Naquet 1986: ch. 2, cf. Vernant 1983: ch. 3), as also often is sacred time from profane time within the experience of people who live now (Leach 1961). Sometimes, as in some ancient Greek writers, time is not an abstract entity, but takes on the characteristics of the events that happen within it, as when Homer speaks of the *nostimon ēmar*, the 'day of return', or the *doulion ēmar*, the 'day of enslavement'.

We think of time as linear, though many peoples are reported to hold, or at least are interpreted as holding, some idea of cyclical time.[1] In one version of this, time repeats itself precisely (Eliade 1954), an idea that tends to negate any conception of history as a sequence of unique events (Thapar 1996: 5 f.).[2] Does the past start with the creation of the world or at some point closer to the present? Others have held that time will end, whether in a merely physical cataclysm or in a moral one with a reckoning of scores in a Last Judgement when God's will will be seen to be done and the destiny of his chosen people fulfilled. Besides, our own notion of linear time is hard to square with the cosmological or physical idea of time as the fourth dimension in the space–time manifold.

---

[1] Momigliano 1966 especially pointed out how oversimplified it is to identify cyclical time as 'the' Greek notion on the subject: cf. Gernet 1981.
[2] Thapar further pointed out that the notion of cyclical time is combined with that of linear time in Indian thought.

Such divergences and disagreements naturally affect what history may mean for a particular group, and whether indeed the group thinks of the past historically. Historiography, in some societies, developed by breaking free from mythology, not in the sense that it made myths redundant, but rather that it offered itself as an alternative to an account of the past in purely mythical terms, which left questions of how one got from time then to the present quite unanswered. Attempts to bring order into memory provide a powerful motive for recording events as we say chronologically, but in many societies in many contexts what is remembered is treasured as a repository of wisdom without any sense of the need—or even the possibility—either to verify the memory or to date the events claimed as remembered. Besides, which events are the important ones, and how they are to be interpreted, involve more or less conscious selection and judgement. How far a society, or a group within it, creates a history to confirm the image of itself that it wants to have accepted is a recurrent issue.

I shall be concentrating here on the particularly rich evidence concerning Greek, Roman, and Chinese thought and practice in this area, but first it will be as well to set the agenda in abstract, theoretical terms. I shall be outlining the philosophical problems in a minute, but among the sociological questions that need to be addressed in any general comparative survey of historiography are the following. Who were the historians? Were they officials, hired by rulers or the state, and if so, did they have access to official archives, and what did those archives comprise? Or were they private individuals? In any case what were the sources of their evidence, and how did they select and check it? How did they evaluate oral testimony in comparison with whatever written records were available? How did they cope with the unreliability of living witnesses in reporting their own experiences, let alone when they recounted what was supposed to have happened long ago? What difference did it make how they themselves recorded events, that is the genre and the medium they selected to do so, whether on monumental inscriptions, in oral or written poetry, or in other writings, and were whatever books that were written bought and sold openly, or only to be found in exceptional libraries, in the palaces of rulers, for instance, or in state archives? The ancient histories that are extant have all come down to us as texts, and this has the effect of 'freezing' a version of the past at a particular juncture. In addition there may be more or less determined efforts to appropriate the past and to control its interpretation. From our point of view, as consumers of history, we have, of course, to make the best use we can of whatever information is available, conscious, as we must be, of its limitations, not just in the sense of the enormous lacunae in the evidence, but also in the processing it has undergone.

Then were the historians given, or did they set for themselves, particular aims or agenda, and did they all agree about what those were or were there rival views, among the historians themselves, about their craft? We can distinguish, in principle, no less than eleven different, overlapping, non-exclusive aims, and we shall see how far the actual histories that have come down to us fit these patterns: (1) entertainment, (2) memorializing or commemorating, (3) glorification or celebration and their converses, vilification and denigration, (4) legitimizing a current regime or a newly established one, or (5) justifying past actions and policies, (6) explaining why things happened as they did, (7) offering instruction on the basis of past experience, (8) providing records for administrative use, lists of anything from the prices of commodities to the names and dates of magistrates or rulers, (9) warning, admonishing, or remonstrating with, monarchs, statesmen, or other responsible agents or groups, on moral or just on prudential grounds, (10) criticizing others' interpretations of the past, including, especially, those on offer from other historians, and (11) 'just' recording the past, i.e. telling the truth about it, saying how it was, 'wie es eigentlich gewesen', as von Ranke put it. So much for a possible checklist of aims, each of which will have a variety of subspecies depending on whether the focus of the historians' attention is political and constitutional affairs, military history, economic or social history, or whatever—not that the choice between those options is ever entirely innocent, since, as I shall be considering later, it may, and usually does, correspond to a particular political or at least educational agenda.

Then a set of questions that immediately follows on from the last paragraph is: how far were the historians aware that their aims, assigned or chosen, might prejudice, or at least would inevitably influence, their accounts? What did their own writing owe to existing literature, whether to poetry, for instance, or to rhetoric, or how far did they set out deliberately to distinguish it from other genres, or from the work of other historians indeed, and if so, on what grounds? Did they self-consciously define their own perspective or identify with one or other of the groups whose activities they were describing? In relation to any of the above aims, did they see themselves as holders of a society's, a nation's, conscience, or as the defenders of the past, or its critics, or just its observers? Did they think of their work as essentially directed towards contemporary issues, or was the study of the past undertaken in some sense for its own sake?

Any historiographical writing is faced with at least three fundamental philosophical problems.[3] (1) No description can be entirely neutral, entirely value-free. This commonplace of the philosophy of science affects all historical accounts as well. Of course we can and should distinguish between greater theory-ladenness and less. Some descriptions are closer to straight observation statements. But every description presupposes a conceptual framework that carries a theoretical load. A writer can be aware of the problem and make an effort to steer clear of the more obviously emotive terms or tendentious concepts. But even the claimed objectivity of, for example, statistical tables, is only a relative one: for how have the data been collected, how and why selected? To be sure, statistical analysis and the quantitative assessment of probabilities are not the concern of any ancient civilization: but we are often presented with bare lists, of rulers for example, that purport to be correct and complete. Yet the actual such lists that have come down to us, in writings or inscriptions, from different civilizations at differing periods are of very varying degrees of accuracy. Meanwhile the two basic points on the issue of objectivity are first that any writer is bound to have some viewpoint, some theoretical presuppositions: and secondly that every writer will choose some questions, and not others, to focus on. Even when objectivity is made an explicit goal, it is always circumscribed by prior decisions as to what it is important to be objective about.

(2) History as instruction, *historia magistra vitae* in the expression revived recently by Koselleck (1985), is also fundamentally ambivalent.[4] Instruction, we must ask, for whom, for whose benefit, by whom,

---

[3] What one may call the philosophy of history in the ancient world has been brilliantly discussed by, among others, Momigliano 1966, Finley 1975, and most recently Hartog 2003, 2005. A variety of different points of view, for example those of Nicolai and Darbo-Peschanski, is represented in Marincola's collection, 2007.

[4] The tag *historia magistra vitae* originates with Cicero (*De Oratore* 2.9.36) as part of a series of expressions he used to underline the importance of the usefulness of history. It came to be used, in the 16th and 17th centuries especially, of one view of historiography that opposed it to history as description or as rhetoric (see Grafton 2007)—not that those who used the tag then agreed on what, exactly, history was supposed to teach.

from whose perspective? Thucydides, who certainly meant his history to be instructive, makes certain presuppositions, notably that human nature is basically the same. But is that so always and everywhere? Thucydides is the diagnostician of the ills of the city-state, stasis being a prime example. But how far are they specific to a particular political regime, that is just a problem for Greek-style city-states? In a monarchy, let alone a tyranny, disagreement among political factions may not be the chief problem. It is true that greed, selfishness, and hubris have some claim to be universal, and some would say give justification enough for Thucydides' belief in the basic uniformity of human nature and the idea that history repeats itself. Maybe so. But everyone's ideas about what it is to avoid political disaster will reflect their political ideals, for sure, and of course they are far from uniform.

That is the first problem for *historia magistra*—that the instruction will only be valid for everyone, universally, insofar as there is agreement about human nature, and about how the state should be run and how inter-state relations should be managed for the best. But whose 'best' is that? Everyone's equally? But what is there to guarantee that that ideal is agreed to, and if agreed to, will guide policy and action?

Instruction, I asked, by whom? Thucydides' authority depends on his coming across as impartial, but of course he is not totally so. He has his distinctive viewpoint, on how the leadership of Pericles contrasted with that of Cleon, for instance. Of course, swept along by the force of his rhetoric, or at least by the apparent reasonableness of his value judgements, we tend to agree with him, do we not? We only rarely have good alternative sources that may lead us to question the views he was promulgating. He has certainly been enormously successful in persuading us of a certain view of Athenian demagogues— challenged only once in a while by someone as independent-minded as Finley (1962).

So any historians who set out to instruct are faced with something of a dilemma. The more they make their own values and perspective explicit, the more suspicious their readers may become (unless they happen to share those values). But *not* to have *any* preferences is, in any case (my first point), impossible, and insofar as any historian succeeds in presenting himself as quite neutral about events, the lessons the readers themselves draw from the account will be left *up to them*. They will scan the description of events for ideas about what policies succeed, which lead to disaster. But there is an obvious risk of making the general's mistake of entering the next war brilliantly equipped for the last one, but quite at a loss in the face of the new enemy. You learn from the past about the past: and that is not necessarily a good guide to the future, however fascinating it may be to ponder the reasons why the past turned out in the way it did. To be sure, history provides a rich, almost inexhaustible, source of examples, precedents, and potential analogies. But that does not get round the problem of determining which are the ones that are relevant to the case in hand. Indeed the very variety of exemplars may confuse as much as illuminate. Selection is inevitable and there is no algorithm for success.

In other words, history as historiography cannot be a reliable *magistra vitae* since we cannot rely on history as the past repeating itself. We have no option but to use our own judgement on each occasion as to whether or how far or in what respects it will.

(3) The third fundamental problem follows from my remarks about perspective and leads into even trickier issues. A historian's account of events will not be just in terms of individuals, but of groups. When wars or struggles for power are involved—and when are they not?—the rival factions will have to be identified. They may be, for example, the people, the few, the Athenians, the Lacedaemonians, the Greeks, the barbarians, the Romans, or the state of Qin, or the black-haired people, or the Xiong Nu. We sometimes assume such terms to be self-explanatory, but none is exactly neutral. True, some are more questionable than others. There is not much doubt about who, in principle, held citizen rights at Athens. But who exactly the *kaloi kagathoi* were (the 'honourable gentlemen' or 'people of the better sort') or how coherent a body 'the *dēmos*' or 'the many' (*hoi polloi*) were, are far more problematic questions.

Given that one of the aims of the historian may be celebration, the question of who exactly is being celebrated is important. Is it the whole of the population, or those in charge, or just the prince himself? Herodotus opens with the statement that he will record the great and remarkable deeds of Greeks and barbarians, and in practice he lives up to that even-handed principle, at least up to a point, even though his own preferences emerge from time to time. But so often the historian covertly or explicitly takes on the task of the glorification of the victorious, finessing the problem of who the victory really belonged to. It was the destiny of the Romans to rule (as if that were inevitable)—but 'Rome' was certainly transformed in the process of conquering most of the world it knew. Similarly in more modern times, we are to learn about the glory of 'France' or how 'Germany' deserves to be called the home of a super-race or how 'Britain' did not so much conquer, as civilize, the world. But each of those topoi presupposes a concept of the nation as a whole and a very nationalistic one at that, however the nation is constructed, whether politically, ethnically, or culturally. Detienne's recent bitter attacks on French historiography (including many of his erstwhile colleagues and collaborators) may have been overdone (Detienne 2008), but the evidence he amassed for the nationalistic tendencies in French historians was impressive—and a similar criticism can, without a doubt, be levelled at the historiographical traditions of Britain and the United States. The reputations of nations or of groups within them have all too often proved a distracting preoccupation. Writing history from the point of view of the defeated or the oppressed is a rare phenomenon and all the more precious when it occurs as something of an antidote to the customary hegemonic perspective. Yet the identity of the vanquished can be just as problematic as that of the victors.

The fundamental difficulty here is that the groups that the historian sees as the main agents in events are all constructs. The races, the nations involved are especially so—even when they correspond to the actors' own ideas of themselves (cf. Brague 2002). The same point applies also to the subgroups in question, though again the historians' labels may tally with actors' categories. Individuals are, to be sure, more easily identifiable, but they can be as much subject to stereotyping as the groups to which they are thought to belong.

One easy post-modern reaction to the impossibility of totally value-free history is to settle for it as fiction, an idea associated especially with Hayden White (1973, 1978, 1992). But that, in my view, will not do either.[5] The notion of truth we need is one that invokes the appropriate criteria for verification for the context in question. This is not to suppose that a definitive account is possible. But if historians cannot be entirely objective, they can be more or less scrupulous in setting out the evidence. They can after all be caught out getting it wrong: the burning of the Reichstag in February 1933 was not the

---

[5] Ginzburg 1992, 1999, Burke 2001, Ricoeur 2004 stand out as particularly clear-headed recent contributions to the debate on new trends in historiography.

result of a coordinated communist plot.[6] Getting an account wrong inadvertently is one thing: falsifying it deliberately—as in the denial of the Holocaust—is quite another. If no description can be complete, some omissions are more harmless than others. The historian's account cannot be submitted to an *experimental* test, as when a scientist's results are checked by another scientist to see whether they are replicable. But that is not to say that there is no difference between the selection of the evidence to present, and its fabrication.

That is at the level of what is represented as having occurred: of course the problems become increasingly difficult when suggestions are offered to explain *why* what happened happened, why things turned out as they did, why the Qin dynasty collapsed after a mere fifteen years, for instance, or why the Athenians lost the Peloponnesian War, or why Caesar crossed the Rubicon, let alone the reasons for the 'decline' of the Roman empire—though what 'decline' that was is far from transparent. Diagnoses of what that decline consisted of, and why it occurred, have an unnerving way of being adjusted to the theory that is being promoted precisely to explain it. Similarly and more generally, the choice of historical explanantia often follows, rather than precedes, the explanations on offer.

The way I have presented the fundamental philosophical problems, historiography might be thought to face an impossible task, and it is hardly surprising that in practice we find different types of compromises being made by different individuals and in different traditions, whether consciously or otherwise. Much will depend, to be sure, on which of the eleven aims I identified is given priority, or the balance between them. Insofar as entertainment becomes the sole aim, that tends to disqualify the writing as history, that is according to the more usual view, though it will still count as 'storytelling', *histoire* in the sense that is run together, in French, for instance, with 'history'. Accounts of past events are included in Shakespeare's historical plays, but they do not set out to be what we generally recognize to be history: they are not our preferred sources for understanding the past, even though Aeschylus' *Persae*, for example, has been mined by both ancients and moderns for the information it contains on the events it dramatizes, and, for sure, mere entertainment was not the

---

[6] That negative conclusion is clear, though historians still debate who precisely *was* responsible for the fire.

sole aim of historical plays either in antiquity or in Shakespeare's day. Again some writers make no pretence at objectivity but just set out to glorify. Official historians may be obliged to go in for unabashed celebration, of the victorious forces, of the all-conquering ruler, or alternatively the marvellously beneficent and wise one, though as is clear from China especially, some official historians may be fiercely independent-minded. There is a very strong tradition of remonstration, in China, the subject of much explicit comment. I have mentioned this before (Ch. 1) and shall be returning to it again.

But when the historians take their stand by the truth, the questions that then arise include how they went about deciding what that was, how they collected and evaluated the evidence available to them, how far they acknowledged its limitations, and indeed their own fallibility, how far they adopted different points of view to achieve a balance between them.

We cannot expect uniformity even within a single culture and indeed we do not find it. In both Greece and China it took some time for historiography, or something pretty close to it, to be recognized as a genre, while in ancient Mesopotamia and in Egypt that process was even more hesitant.[7] Let me rehearse first the well-known Greek data, then some of the ample evidence for China.

Initially the Greek term *historia* could refer to any research or its end product, so it spanned a wide range of what we would consider different disciplines (cf. e.g. Darbo-Peschanski 2007). What we would call geography and ethnography would be perfectly good examples, as would science and its many branches, the study of animals, or plants, or minerals, or meteorology—and of nature as a whole, *peri phuseōs historia*. Nevertheless *historikos* (without qualification) is used already by Aristotle in the *Poetics* 1451b1 when he contrasts the work that person does with poetry. Much to the chagrin of modern historians Aristotle famously considers poetry more philosophical and serious than history, since the former deals with the universal, the latter just with the particular. That tends to ignore my philosophical point that any account of what Alcibiades did or what was done to him (Aristotle's example) has to make use of general and indeed evaluative

---

[7] Feldherr and Hardy (forthcoming) provide an up-to-date overview of the state of scholarship on the development of historiography in ancient Sumeria, in Egypt, and in Mesopotamia.

concepts—as when he is said to have 'betrayed' the Athenians for instance. Aristotle's example of a *historikos* is Herodotus, though Herodotus' *historiē*, we should say, goes well beyond the historical recording of events, in particular in the Egyptian and the Scythian *logoi* which are, nevertheless, perfectly good examples of *historiē* in the general Greek sense. That general sense was never superseded, so that Greek historiography was always associated with a wide genus of inquiries.

Even before Herodotus Greek writing about human experience often presents itself as rivalling and doing better than other accounts. Much of it strikes us as composed under the aegis of the competitive. Hecataeus ridiculed the 'many tales' of the Greeks (in general) as 'absurd'. His own accounts, by contrast, so he claimed, are *true* (*alēthēs*, Fr. 1). But that did not cut any ice with Herodotus, who pretty clearly has Hecataeus in mind when he dismisses the speculative accounts of world geography as 'laughable' (4.36, cf. 42). Right at the very start of his presentation (*apodexis*) of his own *historiē* (1.1) Herodotus gives us what others, the *logioi* of the Persians, had had to say about the reasons the Greeks and Barbarians waged war with one another, though a few chapters later he contrasts that with what the Phoenicians say (1.5) which leads immediately in turn into what he Herodotus (he uses the first person pronoun, *egō*) does and does not *know*. He suspends judgement on those barbarian accounts, but says he knows (*oida*) about the first person who committed injustice against the Greeks—who turns out to be Croesus.

We then embark on the narrative, with its extraordinary mixture of Herodotus reporting eyewitnesses, recording different versions and different explanations of events, sometimes adjudicating between different views, sometimes withholding judgement.[8] We are dealing with an author who has a heightened sense of the possibilities of alternative accounts and of the need to evaluate his sources (cf. Fowler 1996). True, how far he simply constructed, that is invented, his accounts of Egypt and Scythia to suit his strategic purposes—to provide foils for Athens and Greece, in fact, as Hartog (1988) brilliantly argued—is controversial: there are some who insist that

---

[8] Herodotus 2.44 is one typical text in which he explicitly refers to his own travels and autopsy undertaken, he says, in order to establish the clear facts.

Herodotus' account of Scythia, for instance, is confirmed by independent archaeological evidence. But that he *ended up* with useful foils is
clear.

But Thucydides criticizes Herodotus in turn, without naming him.
At 1.20, he corrects an idea that is found in Herodotus (6.57) to the
effect that the Spartan kings had a double vote in the Gerousia. More
fundamentally he distances himself from anyone whose accounts (he
suggests) are 'more suited to entertain the listener than to the truth'
(1.21).[9] Their stories are beyond verification or scrutiny, having 'won
their way to the mythical' (*mythōdes*) where, in a collocation associated with unverifiability, that term clearly takes on pejorative
undertones, although elsewhere *mythos* does not always imply
'mythical' in the sense of fiction, but is a general term for story or
account.[10] Thucydides thus implicitly claims to be more scrupulous
than his predecessor in evaluating his evidence,[11] and there is an
obvious sense in which this is easier when the account deals with
recent or contemporary events, rather than with those that took place
in the distant past. Yet how you get to the truth of even contemporary
events via eyewitnesses is far more complicated than those who have
not tried it imagine. But it is not just that his methods are different:
his aim is to provide a possession for always—he means a repository
of wise advice, in the famous phrase of 1.22. This is thanks to the
assumption that human affairs obey constant principles and that
history may in that sense be expected to repeat itself. He reaches
out to future readers. His tactic to defeat his rivals is to claim that his
work is no mere competition piece (*agōnisma*), but will prove useful
for generations to come.

Subsequent Greek and Roman history is enormously varied, in
subject-matter, in the targeted audience, and in the approach that
different writers adopt. There are biographies of individuals, local

---

[9] In the terms of the aims I set out above, p. 60, it is clear that Thucydides criticizes
some of his predecessors for focusing on the first one, entertainment, while he himself lays
claims to telling the truth about the past (number 11) and offering instruction on its basis
(number 7).

[10] The ambivalence of both terms in the *mythos logos* dichotomy has been well
analysed by Calame 1996, 1999.

[11] The importance of Thucydides' claim for the truthfulness of his history has been
powerfully argued by Williams 2002. But as we shall see, Sima Qian too shares the
ambition of producing a reliable account of events from which future generations can
learn.

histories, histories of famous families, of institutions, of intellectual inquiries such as philosophy or mathematics or medicine. Many historians took on more or less official assignments, not just to record but also to celebrate and glorify.[12] Some Greek historians faced particular problems in coming to terms with Roman hegemony. In the second century BCE Polybius claimed originality for his work first because of the supreme importance of the events it dealt with—how it was that, in a matter of less than fifty-three years, so he says, Rome came to conquer practically the whole known world—and secondly on the grounds that it was the first truly universal history.[13] In the next couple of centuries a sequence of Roman historians, Sallust, Livy, Tacitus, take up the theme of the triumph of Rome, interspersing their narratives with moralizing, if often ambivalent, comments on the signs of its incipient decline, as republican institutions gave way to imperial ones, and virtue yielded to self-indulgence and vice. In the first century CE, the Jew Josephus, writing in Greek, had to accommodate Greek to traditional Jewish historiography and make room for the chosen people (Vidal-Naquet 1977, 2005). Several Christian writers in turn set themselves the task of squaring pagan history with a world-history punctuated with the singularity of the advent of Christ.

The history of Graeco-Roman historiography is throughout strongly marked by a characteristic we find also in Graeco-Roman philosophy, namely its overt competitiveness. Their own accounts, the historians claim, tell the true story, based on reliable sources: others' narratives are incomplete or biased, or merely the fictional constructs of their authors. In the process the terms *historiē* and *historia* are appropriated for the kind of research-based account the more positivist historians favour. By contrast, *mythos* often gets to be downgraded as flawed, and yet their own narratives generally contain considerable

---

[12] One of the first of these was Alexander's historian, Callisthenes, who, like many Chinese official historians, came to a sticky end after he had fallen out with his patron. He was executed after he had been implicated in a plot against Alexander's life. As we shall be noting for Chinese historians, holding an official post may give an individual a privileged position, but does not necessarily imply that the historian will identify with the policies of his or her employers.

[13] Polybius 1.1–4. He was to some extent anticipated in this ambition by Ephorus (4th century), as he recognizes, although he says that Ephorus dealt only with the Greek world (5.33). Polybius criticized the other contender, Timaeus, not just for the limitations of the scope of his work, but more especially for his failure to conduct first-hand research and for his lack of experience in military affairs (12.25–7).

doses of rhetoric quite apart from reflecting their personal political opinions.

It took far longer, of course, for the study of history to become professionalized, since that depended on its winning a place in university curricula, where in the West it was accepted as a subject for serious postgraduate study long after law, medicine, or theology.[14] Moreover the way that history came to be accepted as a key element in humanist undergraduate study in different European countries not only reflected a nationalist agenda, but also generally tallied with a distinct educational programme, geared to what students were thought to need to have mastered to take their places, in due course, among the governing cadres. Naturally enough those who taught them considered themselves something of an—academic—elite, though their claim to that position did not go uncontested by the representatives of other disciplines.

What about China? Generalization is as difficult here, as it is in the Greek case, and on certain issues, such as, particularly, the compilation of composite texts, scholarship is currently in a state of flux. A text such as the *Spring and Autumn Annals, Chunqiu,* used once to be attributed straightforwardly and in its entirety to Confucius, and other classics were traditionally represented as going all the way back to such legendary figures as the Yellow Emperor. Now these works are seen as put together from strata of very different periods and provenances, where the text we read is principally the result of editorial work done in the Han dynasty if not later, in some cases very much later. As archaeological work progresses and versions of more and more texts are discovered in tombs that can be given definite dates, that gives us direct access to *a* version of a canonical writing. But it immediately poses the question of the relation between that

---

[14] The overt competitiveness I remarked on in Graeco-Roman historiography continues to mark later European work, with the added feature of the frequent rivalry between different nationalistic traditions. Within just the English-speaking historiographical tradition, indeed, the acrimony of the exchanges that followed the publication of Carr's *What is History?* in 1961, with interventions by Berlin, Elton, Butterfield, and Trevor-Roper among others, may be cited as an example where there was not just an intellectual point at issue, namely the extent to which the historian was bound to be influenced by his or her own beliefs and preoccupations. The dispute spilt over into a debate within the elite over control of the curriculum in the universities, with prominent members of the profession arguing over how and what undergraduates should be taught at Cambridge and elsewhere. Evans in Carr 2001 outlines the controversies.

version and the later edited work that has been transmitted through the commentary tradition. The notion of a *text* itself has, many think, to be revised: we should think rather of different schools or traditions of the transmission of writings that had no single archetype, where there is no such Urtext which it is the prime duty of modern scholars to try to recover. The problems of interpretation remain severe even when we can supplement literary evidence with epigraphic and archaeological, in order to get some bearing both on the provenance of the text and on the events it purports to describe.

Nevertheless, some basic points are reasonably secure. First it is clear that, as in Greece, what we may call historiography developed from earlier genres—court chronicles, almanacs, annals[15]—even though there is no ancient Chinese category that corresponds exactly to the Greek *mythos* in the sense of fiction, a type of writing with which proper, truthful, 'history' could be contrasted. The first Chinese universal history that offers a narrative account of the major dynasties in a well-defined chronological framework is the *Shiji* compiled by Sima Tan and his son Sima Qian around 90 BCE.[16] But the *Spring and Autumn Annals* offers a precedent for a—minimal—record of events in chronological order, and among the commentaries on that text, the *Zuozhuan* provides a model for an account of the past that offers judgements on the reasons for success or failure. The *Zuozhuan* evidently drew on a mixture of oral and written sources, that we now find difficult, or rather impossible, to disentangle, with obvious consequences for its usefulness, to us, as a historical source. This and other commentaries on the *Spring and Autumn Annals* generally owe more to a concern for literary or rhetorical style, to a delight in the elaboration of anecdotes and to the exploration of the opportunities for moralizing that that presents, than to any single-minded devotion to establishing a reliable account of the facts. Thus although the *Shiji* owes something to some earlier discussions of past events, its claims to originality are high. Even while later historians, such as Ban Gu,

---

[15] For the idea that Chinese historiography derives from, or at least owes much to, divinatory practices that go back to the use of Shang oracle bones, on which predictions were made, but also outcomes recorded, to form something approaching an archive, see Vandermeersch 2007.

[16] Sima Qian certainly distances himself from some of the more extravagant stories about early times, particularly in relation to the founding of legendary dynasties, but he does not deploy a category that is the equivalent of 'myth' in order to do so (cf. Lloyd 2002: ch. 1).

the author of the *Hanshu*, criticized Sima Qian for his style, ideology, and alleged inaccuracies, in ways that resemble the rivalry we find in Greece, the *Shiji* continued to act as the chief model that all subsequent Chinese historiography used.

Secondly, the universal histories that start with the *Shiji* and continue with the long sequence of dynastic histories, from the *Hanshu* onwards, are not *just* history in our sense. Over and above the account of events, the biographies of individuals and so on, they include treatises on such subjects as the calendar, astronomy, even the waterways, and 'geography'.[17] This is not just because of some interest in those subjects for their own sakes, but in order to provide the most important information that rulers, ministers, or anyone aspiring to office, would need to carry on the business of government. The treatises are not there for literary enjoyment, but to instruct— and not just about the past.[18]

Thirdly, most of the authors involved held official positions themselves, which impinged on, even on occasion dictated, the nature of their work as historians. We can trace the gradual rise, in China, of the conception of the office of historian as such. Both Sima Tan and Sima Qian held the post of *tai shi*, but their duties were as much to do with astronomy as with historiography. According to the *History of the Later Han, Hou Hanshu* (25: 3572.1 ff.), the responsibilities of the *tai shi ling*, included (1) being in charge of the calendar, (2) choosing auspicious dates for state functions, and (3) recording propitious or adverse omens as they occurred. So it was more from personal ambition that they composed the *Shiji*, rather than because they were ordered to do so, as Ban Gu was later instructed to compose the history of the Han.

The disadvantage of an official role was clearly that the historian could not afford openly to incur the displeasure of the powers that be. At the same time, official historians could tap sources of information that were not available to private individuals. Sima Qian himself

---

[17] How far the Chinese categories of *di li*, ('earth patterns' or better 'terrestrial organization') and *zhou jun* ('provinces and commanderies') tally with 'geography' is, however, problematic. See Dorofeeva-Lichtmann 1995, 2001.

[18] The *Shiji* and its successors thus perform a remarkably complex set of functions. At different points the goals of their work comprise, in different combinations and proportions, the entire gamut of possible aims I identified above, p. 60, with the possible exception of the first, entertainment, and the last, the exclusive version of the von Ranke claim.

points out that he had access to official archives. He frequently complains that much had been lost, destroyed, or misunderstood (*Shiji* 130: 3288, 3296, 3319): yet the material records available to him were still considerable and made his position, in his attempts to investigate the past, far more favourable than that of—say—a Herodotus. The accumulation of available archival material may even have been one factor stimulating the extraordinary growth of Chinese historical writing after the Han, though by Tang times the individual authorship of such works had become more or less submerged in what, by then, had been turned into state-sponsored group projects for the production of very considerable corpora of official histories.

Their official posts, however, fourthly, did not prevent these historians from expressing independent critical opinions. From early on in Chinese culture there is, as I said, a strong tradition of reprimanding or remonstrating with rulers. To criticize the king, later the emperor, directly, was recognized to be highly dangerous, and in fact many advisers, including several notable historians, such as Ban Gu, paid for their independent-mindedness with their lives. When Sima Qian fell out with Han Wu Di, he avoided having to commit suicide only by accepting the humiliating punishment of castration, a choice he made, so he tells us, specifically in order to continue his father's work.

However, the Chinese developed sophisticated techniques of oblique criticism of those in power. Commenting adversely on past policies and behaviour was an effective way of indirectly registering disapproval of present ones. Sima Qian, in an interview with an important minister reported in the *Shiji* 130: 3299 (cf. *Hanshu* 62), has of course to agree that, unlike so often in the past, 'all under heaven' is nowadays ruled by an enlightened monarch, Han Wu Di, but he justified his history in part by saying it was still important to spread abroad the record of the emperor's great deeds. But that was not all that he was doing. In the body of the *Shiji* itself (18: 878.4 ff., cf. 6: 278.9 ff.) he suggests that learning from the past can provide 'a key to success and failure in one's own age'. There is no trumpeted claim that the work is a 'possession for always': but he reaches out beyond his immediate audience to future readers who will learn from his account of events. To that end, it seems, he deposited one copy of his text in an archive he calls the Famous Mountain, and another in the capital 'to await the sages and scholars of later ages', as he tells us himself (*Shiji* 130: 3319–20).

But as Chinese historiography developed and came to be recognized as a well-defined, official genre in its own right, the price that had to be paid for this was clear. The independent-mindedness that Sima Tan and Sima Qian had shown was increasingly difficult to maintain in the face of the demands of an official agenda, and the roles of glorifying and legitimating tended to win out over those of instructing, warning, and admonishing.

If neat conclusions as to the nature of ancient historiography are out of the question, given its polyvalent character, let me now nevertheless attempt to draw some of the threads of this discussion together. I started by emphasizing the fundamental problems that face any ambition to record the past neutrally. But there have, of course, been more, and less, resolute attempts to do so, with more or less well-focused attention to that goal as opposed to others. What we may still wish to call historiography is evidently not so much a single well-defined genre as a family of loosely related ones, varying according to the roles and functions of the authors or compilers, the aims they set themselves or were set by others, and the actual uses to which their accounts were put.

Several hypotheses that might at first sight seem to be attractive as a basis to account for the differences between different ancient traditions do not stand up well under scrutiny. So far as antiquity goes, no straightforward correlation can be established between the nature of the political regime, or even the particular political views of the historians themselves, and the mode of historiography favoured. Autocratic regimes no doubt seek greater control than do more liberal ones over the work of those who record their own deeds and performance. But the consistently monarchical political set-up in ancient China was not without its severely independent-minded commentators. Besides, autocrats themselves may look for more than flattery: they may indeed want to find out about the past and charge historians to report on this with some respect for verifiable facts. Conversely, those who lived in democracies certainly did not necessarily tailor their accounts to please the particular leaders who happened to be in power, but neither did they always abstain from over-optimistic glorification of the workings of democracy.

Every historian's oeuvre is bound to a greater or lesser extent to reflect their personal views, their sense of the merits or demerits of the age they take as their subject, their hopes and disappointments.

But the heterogeneity that is such a feature of the material we have been considering stems mainly from the very variety of the options historiography may set itself. The choice between them will not necessarily be determined by external factors, by patrons, or potential audiences, but will also reflect the historians' own self-image, their sense of their responsibility, their pride in their work, their ambitions, not least to outdo their rivals, either by doing *their* kind of history better than they, or by advocating and practising a brand new kind of historiography. As in several other of the disciplines my studies here are devoted to, in historiography too competitiveness is often an important stimulus to innovation. Yet against that, historiography has often found itself constrained to remain within the framework set by a traditional agenda, especially when that corresponds to the requirements of officialdom.

The two most powerful motive forces that recur (where both ancient Greece and China in particular are concerned) are first the desire to commemorate, or frankly to celebrate, and second the wish to draw lessons from the past to apply to the present and the future. But first there is, on occasions at least, some tension between these two, insofar as the first, in its glorificatory mode, is clearly one-sided, while the second, to be convincing, has to attempt even-handedness. Secondly, where a balance is sought between them, there is the problem of achieving this, indeed the—philosophical—impossibility of employing a totally value-free conceptual framework in which to cast a description of events. The basic difficulty with the Koselleck programme is, as I noted, that what we take from the past depends crucially on a judgement of what is relevant—where we may be as likely to be misled by the analogies of history as illuminated by them. Ignoring past events is foolish, but assuming that they are a guide to the future may also be a source of mistaken judgements. Very few historians seem to have been capable of recognizing the deep-seated ambivalence of their whole enterprise. That may be understandable in ancient times when great efforts were needed to establish historiography as an independent genre. But even with many modern practitioners of the craft, the questions of what the discipline should comprise, its aims, and methods, remain at points unresolved, and the threat of a descent into subjectivity, if not pure fiction or naked ideology, still looms.

4

Medicine

OF all the subject-areas that I have chosen to examine in these studies, medicine might seem to be the least problematic, at least from two points of view. On the one hand, humans everywhere have always suffered from diseases, much as their opinions about the nature of those diseases differ. On the other, over a considerable range of problems, to do with the causes of diseases and how to treat them, some claims that can be made for objective understanding are well founded. Most people would agree that there is more in common between human experience of disease across the world than there is in our religious or artistic experience, for instance.

But both those remarks call for qualification. It is true that Western biomedicine can give robust answers to a number of questions to do with diagnosis and therapy. But even Western biomedicine has its limitations—and not just where mental disorders are concerned. The early successes of biomedicine, in identifying the causes of malaria and bringing it under control, for example, made it look as if its complete triumph was imminent and inevitable. But in 2009 there are still plenty of conditions, both physical and more especially psychological, that are poorly understood, and even more where no effective treatment is available. In these circumstances it is more readily understandable that alternative traditions of medicine have not died out and even continue to flourish. In India and China especially, for instance, other styles of medicine are not just practised, but are taught in institutions that survive in close proximity to Western hospitals and universities. Where the sick have a choice, they do not all necessarily opt for Western biomedicine either as their first, or even as their last, resort. Indeed it is not just Western medicine that has spread across the world: the same is true also of Asian medical theories and practices.[1] One of the aims of this chapter is to explore what there is in common between modern biomedicine and other learned medical traditions, at least in respect of the mechanisms by which elite status is constructed and maintained.

On a narrow view of the goal, health may be defined just as a matter of a normally functioning body, one whose processes and structures do not deviate from what statistical analyses will show to be within the normal range. But very few would accept that that is all there is to well-being. On a wider definition of health, one endorsed in a modern medical dictionary indeed,[2] that involves 'the attainment and mainte-nance of the highest state of mental and bodily vigour of which any given individual is capable'—and that may clearly be adversely affect-ed even in the absence of a determinate diagnosable condition. Some may even go further and think of health as freedom from uncleanness or impurity of any sort, not just from pathological disease. Again some may say that true well-being is conditional upon social integra-tion—being at one with the society in which you live—in which case, again, how the body functions will not be the prime consideration. On the other hand, how the society itself functions may be of great importance. On that view, an individual or a group cannot feel at ease living in a society that they judge to be unjust or inequitable.

The discussion of medicine thus has a tendency to lead into a discussion of everything else, values and morality included. But if we concentrate more narrowly, as I shall here, on the notions of disease and illness and their treatment, there is still an amazing range of problems to come to terms with. One fundamental and recurrent question is who can claim to know the answers to the nature of an affliction, its cause or causes, and what to do to alleviate it. The spectrum of possibilities ranges from societies where there are no experts in the domain, to those where there are clearly demarcated professionals and access to their number is very tightly controlled. When that happens, the role of such elites can prove to be quite ambivalent, on the one hand furthering research and promoting theoretical analysis, but on the other blocking innovation that does not tally with the core assumptions of the elite in question.

---

[1] This has been documented for Chinese medicine by Kleinman et al. (1975) and for other Asian medicines as well in Hsu and Høg (2002) for example. Cf. also Leslie 1976.
[2] I cite Black's *Medical Dictionary* in its 41st edn. (Marcovitch 2005: 317).

In the first type of situation (frequently documented in the ethnographic literature[3]) it is up to the patients themselves to decide that they are unwell. They may well have their own ideas about why that is and what they are suffering from—the equivalents of a diagnosis—and friends, relatives, and other members of their communities may well chip in with their views on the subject. But in the final analysis the patients decide that they are sick and equally determine when they have recovered. The first will generally involve withdrawal from the ordinary activities of the community, the second reintegration in social life. Meanwhile the help they receive, their treatment, will include not just personal moral support and sympathy, but also community activities similarly expressing solidarity with them. If it is generally believed that there are malign spirits or hostile shamans at work, then rituals will be undertaken to counter their effects.

Before I turn to the opposite end of the spectrum, to societies with well-established learned traditions of medicine, I should say a little about the very extensive middle ground. In most societies particular individuals or groups gain a reputation for their medical knowledge in general or in particular matters. This may be because they have had more experience, or more perceived success, than others in deciding what people have been suffering from and more importantly in alleviating their complaints. Those who help in childbirth may well be a marked group whose expertise is not necessarily limited to what we call midwifery. Others may have particular knowledge of herbal and mineral remedies, yet others may have special skill in dealing with sprains, bruises, fractures, and dislocations.

In many ethnographic reports the term 'shaman' is used, admittedly often rather loosely, of individual men or women reputed to have special powers for good or evil, including in matters of diseases and their cures.[4] In most cases those powers will include the ability to

---

[3] One classic study is that by Gilbert Lewis of the Gnau of Papua New Guinea, Lewis 1975. Recent studies in medical anthropology have brought to light the amazing variety of ideas entertained in different societies on health and illness, both physical and mental. See e.g. Kleinman and Good 1985, Lindenbaum and Lock 1993, Good 1994, and Nichter and Lock 2002.

[4] The literature on shamanism is immense, ranging from Eliade's classic study (1964), to popular general overviews (such as Vitebsky 1995 and Drury 1996), including various attempts at psychological and neurophysiological explanations of the phenomenon (Devereux 1961a, 1961b, Silverman 1967), analyses of the political ramifications of shamanism (Thomas and Humphrey 1994) as well as many detailed ethnographic studies of particular societies (such as Humphrey and Onon 1996 on the Daur Mongols).

communicate with gods or spirits in trances and other out-of-body experiences. Such communication may form part of a society's regular experience, involving rituals in which the society as a whole joins in, and that need to be carried out at set times to ensure that the gods and the spirit world are well disposed towards the group. But apart from providing leadership on such occasions, shamans may be called in in crisis situations, when someone is seriously sick for instance, when the shaman's responsibility will be not just to say what should be done, but to do it.

How individuals become shamans varies a great deal, but often special powers are noticed in quite young people who are then encouraged to seek the advice and tutoring of experienced shamans, who may hand on some or all of their own, often highly esoteric, personal knowledge. But in the ethnographic literature apprenticeship is rarely described as a formal matter. The neophyte's training is more likely to involve participation in ritual activities and acquiring certain practical skills than in verbal instruction, while book learning is of course out of the question in societies without writing. Meanwhile the shaman's reputation depends crucially on how others evaluate their powers, and those are sometimes rated more highly by outsiders than by members of their own group.[5] In many societies, as Descola 1996 has documented for the Achuar, for instance, it is assumed that whenever misfortune strikes, some person is responsible, and that someone is usually a shaman believed to be acting either directly or indirectly through the spirits he or she controls. The frequency of misfortune then contributes to bolster the belief in the powers of shamans in general and of particular ones in particular situations.

It is certainly not the case, however, that shamanic societies accept individual shamans uncritically or gullibly.[6] There are plenty of records of scepticism or doubt being expressed about whether a particular person does indeed possess the powers claimed for them. But to doubt an individual's reputation is very different from rejecting the

---

[5] This was noted by Shirokogoroff (1935) in his study of the Tungus.

[6] See Shirokogoroff (1935: 332 ff., 389 ff.). The story of the Kwakiutl Quesalid (reported by Boas 1930: 1–41 and popularized by Lévi-Strauss 1968: 175 ff.) is a poignant illustration of how initial scepticism can be turned into belief. Quesalid was at first extremely critical of the ways of the local shamans, whom he considered frauds. To expose them he used other techniques he learnt from shamans from neighbouring groups and discovered that they were thought to be effective. The sick reported remarkable recoveries, and Quesalid found himself, willy-nilly, a shaman.

whole idea that such exceptional powers exist. The latter denial faces insurmountable obstacles when no alternative framework of understanding exists.

True, not all misfortunes, not all diseases, may be attributable to malign agencies, whether human or superhuman. Some, as Lewis 1975: 197 noted for the Gnau, 'just come'. Mundane mishaps, spraining an ankle, stubbing a toe, the common cold, may be treated just as that, as mishaps. It may be recognized that it was because a doorpost was eaten away by termites that it collapsed. Thus far the causal chain is entirely 'naturalistic'. But the question that may then arise is why the termites attacked *that* doorpost in *your* house, the 'why me?' question popularized by Evans-Pritchard, and that may lead to imputations of malevolent intentions to agents, human or demonic.

In the face of grave misfortune, including the onset of a serious disease, the tendency may be to look for a responsible agent, and that tendency is more readily understandable in that it follows the model of how behaviour in fellow human beings is normally to be explained, namely by identifying motives and intentions. Once such a pattern of belief has become firmly established, it is, strictly speaking, impossible to refute, for even if an alternative 'naturalistic' account can be produced, that does not *rule out* the possibility of intervention by some agency in initiating that naturalistic process.[7]

Every society needs to be able to draw on considerable knowledge of foodstuffs and that will extend also to drugs and poisons. Such knowledge is handed on from one person to another, and from one generation to another. In basically illiterate societies, that is vulnerable to the vagaries of oral transmission. The situation is very different in societies with written records, not that they are immune to corruption, selective bias, and misinterpretation. However, in such societies the institutionalization of medicine is not just possible, but in a way even inevitable.

So at the opposite end of the spectrum from those societies where there are no medical experts at all and everyone has an equal say in what went wrong and why, there are those societies (like our own) where knowledge in this domain lies in the hands of a well-defined group of professionals. They may or may not be marked out by the

---

[7] This was a notable factor in the persistence of witchcraft beliefs in 16th- and 17th-cent. England (Thomas 1971).

possession of qualifications that have some standing in law, and they may or may not have been recruited by way of formal instruction ending in tests or examinations. There may be and often is more than one literate and articulate group of such claimants to expertise, in competition with one another and disagreeing not just about practices and theories but about the very concepts of health and disease themselves. But entry to any elite group will certainly depend on acceptance by most of its existing members who thereby exercise a more or less strict control on recruitment and indeed on subsequent performance and behaviour.

If we review three of the major ancient societies that produced learned medical traditions, namely China, Greece, and India, what they shared, in terms of theories and practices, and where they diverged, are alike remarkable. At a very general level, some sense that disease is a matter of some disorder or imbalance is widespread. That imbalance may be one within the body—between its component substances or normal processes—or again between the soul or mind and the body, or yet again between the person as a whole and the environment. That last case illustrates how in all three ancient civilizations well-being may be thought of as a matter of being in tune with the cosmos as a whole. Health was often connected with values and morality. Immoral behaviour was alternatively interpreted as a sign, or as a cause, of ill health, and was often described as itself a sickness.[8]

But important divergences also existed on how the component elements to be attuned were conceived, and in each case these naturally reflect more general cosmological or physical concepts and theories. Greek and Indian medicine both attached considerable importance to humours, though entertaining different ideas as to which humours were the key ones and on their role in the body, whether as normal constituent elements or as pathogens or as the end products of diseases. It may be that similarities in this case owe something to diffusion and to actual contact between these two societies at different periods in their histories, though dating Indian developments is especially difficult, given the multiple strands that went to form the two major classical texts, the *Caraka Saṃhitā* and *Suśruta Saṃhitā*.[9]

---

[8] I have documented this for ancient Greece in Lloyd 2003.
[9] See e.g. Zimmermann 1987, Zysk 1991, 2007.

But the Chinese, for their part, concentrated more on processes than on constituent substances: they entertained distinctive medical notions that in turn reflect their views on normal and abnormal interactions within the body.[10] Health was often construed in terms of the free circulation of qi_1 (breath/energy) around the body, where certain diseases were put down either to the blockage of that circulation or to the irruption of heteropathic, that is pathogenic, qi_1, *xie qi*. Some specifically Chinese therapeutic procedures, such as acupuncture and moxibustion, were eventually related to such concepts, though it would be foolish to suggest we are in a position confidently to identify why those procedures were originally developed in China.[11] But then we are equally in the dark about why venesection, for instance, was favoured to the extent that it was in ancient Greece.[12] Such divergences in preferred treatments give the lie to any naive assumption that, once medicine achieved the status of a learned practice, the same therapies would tend to be used throughout the world. That was simply not the case and I shall need to return to the issues that that presents.

While we can identify certain leading ideas that recur in different forms in each of those three societies, in no case was there a single rigid orthodoxy in medical theory and practice even within the learned elite—and that is before we take into account marginal or peripheral traditions with which elite medicine continued to be in competition in all three cases. The Greeks especially disagreed fundamentally on the nature of disease, on their causes and cures, and not just on basic pathological questions but also on the underlying epistemology and methodology that should guide good medical practice.

---

[10] See Sivin 1987, and cf. Unschuld 1985, 1986.

[11] Harper 1998 discusses the evidence for the transformations in the modes and use of moxibustion and acupuncture that derives from the Mawangdui medical texts. Cf. Kuriyama 1999.

[12] Brain (1986) tentatively suggested that one possible factor that may have contributed to the persistence of the practice of venesection in ancient Greece and indeed down to modern times in certain parts of Europe was that the anaemia that resulted may have provided some protection against malaria. Whatever basis that hypothesis may have, the popularity of the treatment depended on a combination of factors, including the conservatism of doctors who were taught a practice that they believed to be sanctioned by tradition. Patients, for their part, came to expect a therapy that appeared to correspond to deep-seated ideas of the need to evacuate superfluities from the body—and that despite the dangers that some ancient doctors drew attention to. Thus the Hippocratic treatise *Aphorisms* (5.31) warns that venesecting pregnant women may lead to miscarriage.

The learned elite was particularly articulate on such issues, but insofar as we can reconstruct the views of other practitioners, the herbalists, for example, or those who practised temple medicine, they were not short of their own ideas on just *why* their remedies could be claimed to be successful. In the shrines, after all, the cures were said to be brought about by the god in person, and many plant remedies were also believed to be efficacious because they were under the aegis of Asclepius or other healing gods, after whom they were often named. But this pluralism is not confined to the Greeks. The ancient Chinese and Indians too proposed divergent opinions on plenty of medical questions without necessarily setting up sustained overt polemics with the views with which they disagreed.

However, all three societies eventually came to possess writings that acquired canonical status, from which the subject was usually taught, and this is obviously a key point in the construction of an elite, for entry to such depended first and foremost on mastery of the canon. In China, the earliest compilations of the *Huangdi neijing* date from the turn of the millennium.[13] In Greece the so-called Hippocratic Corpus was first assembled in the late fourth century BCE, though much of its later European influence reflected Galen's reinterpretation, in the second century CE, of what he decided were the best elements in it, the ones that corresponded to his own theories and practices. In India I have already mentioned the Ayurvedic classics, the *Caraka Saṃhitā* and *Suśruta Saṃhitā*, that also represent scholarly compilations of work stretching over several centuries. Each of those canons appears to modern philological scholarship to contain highly divergent material, divergences that lead modern specialists to attempt to identify different strata emanating from different schools and periods. But to those for whom these writings contained the essence of medical expertise, those discrepancies were not signs of possible inconsistency, so much as sources of useful variation.

In China and Greece especially, notable efforts were made not just to systematize the key concepts, but also to accumulate medical experience. In both those societies considerable pains were taken to record the case histories of individual patients.[14] Inevitably the terms

---

[13] See Sivin 1987, Keegan 1988.

[14] For Han dynasty Chinese case histories, see Hsu 2002, and for the later development of the genre, Cullen 2001, Furth, Zeitlin and Hsiung 2007: pt. 2. There is a sharp contrast

used in such accounts are theory-laden and tied to the conventions of the tradition in which they were drawn up. But one object of such records was to describe the courses of individual complaints in all their complexity, so that other doctors could learn from the authors' own experiences, although a second aim was to vindicate the doctors' own claims to medical expertise. In Greece in particular the case histories seem to pay particular attention to combinations of symptoms that might indicate a fatal outcome. Certainly some Greek doctors were explicitly advised not to take on such cases (as in the Hippocratic treatise *On the Art*, ch. 3).

A second major area of inquiry in Greece especially used dissection to investigate the bodies of humans and animals. The study of anatomy is so obviously a part of modern Western biomedical training that we might take such research to stand in need of no particular justification. Yet in fact it originated in Greece in connection with a distinctive, more than purely medical, programme.[15] The first Greek to carry out animal (though not human) dissection systematically was Aristotle, and he explains the reasons for this very clearly, namely to exhibit the forms and final causes of the structures in the body, to show the beauty and craftsmanship of nature, indeed. In the absence of such teleological motivations, such human dissections as the Chinese carried out were often directed rather to another practical aim, namely to establish the causes of death where foul play was suspected.[16]

Moreover in Greece, while human dissection at Alexandria in the late fourth and early third centuries BCE led to some notable anatomical discoveries, such as that of the nervous system, both dissection and vivisection, whether of animals or of humans, remained as controversial

---

between the role of case histories in ancient medicine, where one of the functions they serve is as an archive of experience, and that of modern case reports that often concentrate on the exceptional, and that are sometimes considered a threat to, or at least a distraction from, so-called evidence-based medicine. This seeks to draw up rules to aid the modern biomedical physician in diagnosis and in the evaluation of performance in the face of the truly massive quantities of data and of the secondary literature dealing with its interpretation that are now available. That modern information overload is undeniable: but quite how to deal with it remains controversial: see Sackett et al. 1997, and cf. De Camargo 2002. On the general methodological issues of inference from case histories, and on their role in the development of modern psychiatry, Forrester 1996 is fundamental.

[15] I have outlined the Greek debates on the pros and cons of animal and human dissection and vivisection in Lloyd 1987: 160–7.

[16] On dissection in China, see Kuriyama 1999.

as teleology itself. Many doctors rejected the technique as contributing nothing to medical practice and indeed that was largely true, even though we find Galen insisting that in surgical interventions knowledge of the internal structures of the body, the nerves, arteries, and veins, for instance, was essential to avoid unnecessary damage to the patient. Meanwhile the idea that nature exhibits providential design was flatly denied by the Epicureans among others. As is again clear from Galen, human dissection had died out long before his day, even though he was himself a staunch advocate of the practice of both the dissection and the vivisection of animals.

In both the examples I have taken, case histories and dissection, it was members of the literate elite who pioneered the techniques, stimulating much new research, but also using the new methods to display their own learning. Galen records the public dissections at which competing experts showed off their anatomical knowledge and attempted to expose the ignorance of their rivals. On one occasion this involved the dissection of an elephant, where predictions were made on such matters as the structure of its heart, and on this, as in several other encounters, the supporters of rival experts, and other bystanders, placed bets on who would be proved right. Both the prestige that went with victory, and the humiliation of public defeat, were considerable.

One of the key features that all three learned medical traditions share is thus the elaboration of certain doctrines and procedures. The actual doctrines that were advanced diverge, as I have noted, in remarkable ways, but from the point of view of fostering an image of their learning, what was important was the elaboration itself. Pulse diagnosis, humoral theory, the rationale of acupuncture therapy and of venesection, all came to be the subjects of intense theoretical development, illustrating what, in Lloyd 2002: ch. 6, I called the 'momentum effect', whereby once a theory or practice had come to be accepted and to be believed to prove its worth, very considerable efforts were devoted to its elaboration and justification. Looking at this phenomenon from a cross-cultural perspective, one might con- clude that the very success of certain procedures, or at least their fashionableness, were factors that eventually served rather to inhibit the exploration of alternatives. The situation has certain analogies with that I described in relation to Greek mathematics, where the axiomatic-deductive style of demonstration, once invented, came to be, in certain quarters at least, a preoccupation bordering on an obsession.

The learned medical elites, thus constituted, showed remarkable staying power. One might have thought that inadequacies in the matter of actually delivering cures would have undermined them. But then the question of whether some treatment had been effective was often a highly subjective matter. Even when the patient died, the doctor might claim that he or she had done everything possible to prevent that. Conversely, sometimes patient and practitioner colluded in registering success. Even when, as happened often enough in both Greece and China, the practitioners themselves recognized that they had failed, in prognosis or in treatment, they could put that down to their own misapplication of the principles, rather than to the principles themselves. Moreover the recognition of failure could be used as evidence of their own scrupulous honesty, thereby creating a greater degree of confidence in their patients than if they had claimed infallibility.[17] In some Greek texts when mistakes are recorded, the writer notes that he does so to help others avoid repeating them: congenital humpback, the fifth-century BCE writer of the treatise *On Joints*, ch. 47 notes, cannot be cured by ordinary methods of reduction. Every attempt he made, and he made several, was a failure. Recognizing one's errors could be represented as an important first step in improving practice.

Powerful learned medical traditions were generally jealous of their reputations and discouraged dissent: those who were accepted among the elite were not normally expected to challenge the core teaching of the tradition that had enrolled them, although to be sure that sometimes happened.[18] Yet in all three ancient societies I have been considering,

[17] I have argued elsewhere (Lloyd 1987: ch. 3) that some Hippocratic writers may have recorded their mistakes in part to contrast their—honest—medical reports with the extravagant claims made on behalf of temple medicine, where the inscriptions at the shrines of Asclepius at Epidaurus and elsewhere record 100% success.

[18] In Greece, especially, intense rivalry existed between different *learned* traditions, as well as between them and marginal groups, such as the root-cutters or drug-sellers. Already in the Hippocratic period, ambitious individuals exploited the room for manoeuvre that offered in order to build up their own personal reputations. In Hellenistic times different schools or sects flourished, named after particular doctors (such as the Herophileans or the Erasistrateans) or according to a particular methodology ('Empiricists' or 'Methodists'). Secession from one group to join another, or even to set one up for oneself, was common: the Methodists, for instance, were inaugurated by a dissident Herophilean, Philinus of Cos. The best succinct account of Hellenistic medicine is that in von Staden 1989: ch. 1, and cf. Nutton 2004, chs. 9 and 10.

important elements of pluralism subsisted. As I have noted, learned practitioners were faced by other individuals and groups whom they often criticized as naive and ignorant, but who nevertheless continued to attract a clientele, sometimes a substantial one. Traditions of religious healing continued to be very popular in Greece down to the end of pagan antiquity, and while door-to-door salesmen of charms and incantations were generally easy to dismiss as charlatans, that was not the case with the cult of Asclepius.[19] That was practised in imposing shrines and numbered highly educated and successful public figures among its adherents. They included the orator Aelius Aristides in the second century CE. Even when belief in the pagan gods and heroes as healers lapsed, in Europe, they were replaced by Christian saints, and Christ himself, in that role. That implied not the denial of the possibility of divine intervention in curing (and indeed in causing) diseases, but rather the appropriation of that belief and its restriction to the one true faith.

Knowledge of plant and mineral remedies was never limited to the circles of elite medical practitioners. While they might seek to control that aspect of treatment with learned classifications of plants and complex explanations of why they worked as cures, there were plenty of ordinary people in all three ancient societies, as in those reported in the ethnographic literature, who relied on purely empirical knowledge to underpin their traditional, or personal, treatments. It is striking that in early modern Western medicine, one of the chief challenges to the dominant—Galenic—doctrines came from Culpeper whose claim for a hearing came from his personal, as he saw it more detailed and empirically proven, knowledge of plant remedies. While he broke with tradition by writing in the vernacular, he made his own claims for learned, esoteric knowledge in his use of astrology and reference to the connections between herbs and planets. Already in late Greek antiquity itself, there was an ongoing tension between, on the one hand, the more theoretical Galenic schemata that brought plant and mineral treatments within the orbit of natural philosophical theories based on the four elements and the humours, and on the other, the focus of interest that is found in Dioscorides where plants were classified in part rather by their perceived or imagined therapeutic effects (Scarborough and Nutton 1982, Riddle 1985, Touwaide 1997).

---

[19] I discussed this in Lloyd 2003: chs. 3 and 8.

Similarly in China, while in the sixteenth century Li Shizhen saw himself as preserving knowledge, as much as innovating in this field, the corpus of material he was able to collect and arrange concerning plant remedies opened up a considerable range of new possibilities.[20] As with Dioscorides, his account drew on local traditions many of which had previously been neglected or ignored. In ancient and early modern times, elite doctors could learn much from folk medicine if they kept an open mind and did not automatically assume they knew better than their less learned rivals. Indeed that still remains true, to an extent, today, to judge from the ongoing research undertaken into the still insufficiently understood active properties of herbal remedies from around the world.

Even though modern biomedicine has, as I said at the outset, extraordinary successes to its credit, the general pattern that we have found in ancient medicine, of a tension between elite insiders and more or less peripheral groups can still be found. Indeed some of the non-medical personnel with whom modern medicine is de facto in competition see themselves as having a very different set of responsibilities from those of medical care. I mentioned the problems posed by psychiatric cases, where Foucault showed, in a series of brilliant studies (1967, 1973, 1977), the dramatic changes that took place in the early modern period both in the understanding and in the treatment of those labelled 'demented', 'deranged', 'irrational', or 'insane'. Where today too the psychologist will be concerned to establish the degree of severity of the mental illness of any given case referred to them,[21] the same individuals may be treated by other agencies not as patients in need of treatment, but as criminals to be brought to justice.[22]

---

[20] This is discussed by Métailié 2001.

[21] As Luhrmann 2000 pointed out, the degree of severity of the case is often the primary initial concern of psychiatric staff when a patient presents for treatment. Moreover they are often under pressure from the threat of possible litigation initiated either by the patients or their families, if it could be represented that they had underestimated the gravity of their patients' conditions. The patients, for their part, learn that if they talk of taking their own lives, that is going to get them greater attention and more immediate treatment, including possible hospitalization.

[22] The issue of the effects of an explicit recognition and labelling of a new category of a physical, mental, or social disorder on the incidence of those diagnosed as exhibiting it has been opened up by Hacking 1991, 1992b, 1995, citing such examples as child abuse and multiple personality disorder.

The subsequent handling of the case will vary fundamentally, depending on which agencies claim, or are given, responsibility for dealing with it, for all that the initial treatment of the individual may, and usually does, involve physical restraint. But while sometimes the various different agencies may agree on which of the two, therapy or punishment, is called for, there are many instances where the nature of the case is disputed and radically different interpretations of the symptoms are put forward by different groups intent on establishing that they have the relevant expertise to deal with the case. Where the psychiatrists take charge, the physical treatments available—drugs and ECT, for instance—may be successful in calming the patient but do little to bring about a cure. Moreover why they have the effect they do is often poorly understood, as also are the causes of the disorder in the first place. In ancient societies the means of restraint available were, of course, appreciably less sophisticated and often frankly brutal.[23] But some ancient doctors appreciated that what helped their patients most was to talk them through their condition. 'Healing by the word' thus shares some features with modern psychoanalysis,[24] even though the theories that underpin the latter are distinctive, while the perceived effects of the former depended on the charisma of the healer as much as on the self-understanding that patients achieved in their exchanges with their carers.

It may seem far-fetched to compare any variety of ancient medicine with modern biomedicine with its unprecedented basis in physics, chemistry, anatomy, physiology, let alone molecular biology. But we should recognize that every learned medical tradition produces its own, often elaborate, rhetoric of self-justification, with modes of argument developed to put down rivals, to refute objections, and in general to provide the elites in question with a carefully constructed rationale. We should not underestimate the confidence that the great masters of traditional Chinese, Indian, and Greek medicine felt in the powers, or at least the potential, of the traditions to which they were

---

[23] This is not just a judgement we might make: it is a view expressed, for example, by the fourth-century CE Greek Methodist doctor Caelius Aurelianus when he complains that many of the customary treatments for what was diagnosed as madness were violent. The patients were chained up, kept in the dark, and flogged. But Caelius himself accepts that some patients will have to be tied up, although he insists that care should be taken not to injure them. Cf. Lloyd 1987: 25–6.

[24] Greek 'healing by the word' is the subject of a classic study by Laín Entralgo (1970).

heirs. In psychological terms their patients must often have been reassured by the authority with which their doctors pronounced on what had to be done to alleviate their conditions.

True, medicine is not just a matter of psychology: it can sometimes be judged by its results in ways that are not mirrored in some of the other learned disciplines that I have discussed, such as philosophy or historiography (and cf. Chapter 5 below on art). But it shared many of the same features that we have found elsewhere in our study of the ways in which learning gets to be constituted and learned practitioners get to make authority claims. If in medicine certain modes of appeal, to recognizably efficacious results, are distinctive,[25] the history of the subject amply illustrates how justifications in terms internal to the learned tradition itself, that is to say in terms that depend on prior acceptance of the general validity of that tradition, also played their part. The very elaboration of Galenic, traditional Chinese, and Ayurvedic medicine, organized around imposing corpora of texts, provided resources for such justifications that seemed to give them a pretty secure basis, certainly ones that the ever-present but marginalized outsiders found it hard to challenge.

Modern biomedicine now has its publicly and legally recognized credentials and yet it continues to face competition from alternative practitioners. In the ancient world, doctors—of whatever kind—had to work harder to persuade their patients that they had the knowledge and skill to cure them. But what many ancient and some modern doctors alike appreciated is that getting their patients to believe in their ability to help is not just a crucial first step in convincing them to accept treatment, but may be part of the therapeutic process itself. The dilemma there that persists in modern biomedicine is that the more esoteric the ideas, explanations, and justifications the doctor has to draw on, the more mystificatory or at least less accessible they will appear to be to many of their patients, who may well feel helpless in the face of the problem of evaluating the options open to them or even unaware that they have any options.[26]

---

[25] Yet how results are to be evaluated often remains, as I noted, the subject of controversy, both between doctors and their patients, and within either group.

[26] Thus Bates 2000: 517 even argued that in our present world, 'effectiveness and patient-friendliness may, at certain points, be mutually exclusive'.

So if we return to our original question and ask what medicine is, it seems necessary to distinguish between producers and consumers. One group of producers has the authority of modern biology to draw on, but other practitioners too express or have expressed their confidence that their approach is the right one, that they have a true understanding of health and disease and the true welfare of their patients at heart. Even so in certain quarters of twenty-first-century industrialized societies, the authority with which those other groups speak does not begin to equal that of modern biomedicine.

But if we turn to the consumers' perspective, we have to register first that some societies do not recognize medical experts as such at all, secondly that in others the room for alternatives is limited, and third that where there is a choice, not everyone opts for what biomedicine would represent as the best therapy, in general or in particular circumstances. Consumers are then faced with difficult decisions, and have to make more or less well-informed judgements about which kind of doctor to consult. They will do so on the basis not just of their reactions to the prevailing fashions or assumptions, but also of their own, or their acquaintances' reported experiences. They may be perfectly happy not just to try one style of therapy for one disease or illness and another for another, but also to switch from one style to another in relation to a single complaint. For some, the primary consideration may be whether a mode of treatment fits in with their expectations of what is appropriate: they may pay more attention to felicity, in other words, in the anthropologists' jargon,[27] than to efficacy, though that distinction breaks down when the very felicity of the procedures is judged to *make* them efficacious. In such a case it is enough if the therapy is held to be as it should be, to meet the patients' own beliefs concerning what is appropriate in the circumstances. The fulfilling of that criterion then becomes the only mode of efficacy that is demanded.

Biomedical practitioners, with a battery of tests to call on, may pronounce a patient all clear: alternative practitioners, on the basis of their different criteria, may do the same. But the patients themselves have their opinions and feelings, which medical experts may label ignorant, misguided, deluded, even neurotic, but which from the

---

[27] For this distinction, see e.g. Tambiah 1968, 1973. I shall return to this in the next chapter.

patients'—consumers'—perspective are what counts. Biomedicine is no doubt set to make even greater advances in the techniques at its command. But the possibilities of mismatch between what biomedicine pronounces to be the case and what individual patients feel, are unlikely ever to be completely removed. If so, alternative styles of medicine, with their more or less articulate elites to promote them, are likely to continue to bear witness to the complexities of our understanding of what it is to be truly well, and it would surely be foolhardy to suppose that biomedicine has nothing to learn from its rivals.

5

Art

WHEN views about what counts as art, let alone as good art, have been and continue to be so disputed, within the Western world to go no further afield, what hope is there, one might ask, of arriving at a coherent cross-cultural account of what we in the West call the aesthetic experience? The widely divergent theories to be found in Goodman (1976), Geertz (1983), Bourdieu (1984), Eagleton (1990), Gell (1998), and Pinney and Thomas (2001)—to name just some of the leading recent commentators—indicate the lack of any consensus on how to tackle the problems. While some have focused on the political, economic, and ideological dimensions of the issues, others have attempted to bring art within the orbit of a general theory of symbolic systems. But all have emphasized, in their different ways, the difficulties in the cross-cultural application of the Western category of the aesthetic (cf. Ingold 1996).

My own tactics in this chapter will be to start from a context where mundane, quantitative, evaluations are made on a day-to-day basis, namely in the commercial sale of art. I shall then consider briefly some of the profound changes that have taken place, in Europe and elsewhere, in the production and appreciation of art, before proceeding finally, by way of an imaginary confrontation between Western and non-Western perspectives, to examine on what basis, if any, cross-cultural comparisons may be attempted. The elites we are dealing with, in this case, are constituted first by the artists—the painters, sculptors, architects—themselves, and secondly by connoisseurs who create fashions and influence taste. Meanwhile the pressure to innovate, in both cases, arises from the competitiveness within both types of elite, though innovativeness may, to be sure, be circumscribed when traditional styles and traditional aesthetic judgements are in the ascendant.

In industrialized societies, and not just in the West, art is a highly prized, and highly priced, commodity. Works by famous painters and sculptors, of the past and of the present, European, Indian, Chinese, Japanese, African, Mesoamerican, Inuit, are bought and sold for enormous prices at salerooms across the globe, New York, London, Tokyo, Shanghai, Mumbai. Works that the painters themselves gave to restaurant-owners to pay for a meal come to fetch prices that would cover the costs of millions of hours' labour of the workforces of those in Third World countries who are lucky enough to be employed.

Meanwhile outside the commercial market, no self-respecting major city is without its museum exhibiting as wide a selection of the world's art as it can afford, for the delight and edification of its visitors. The museum shop will stock replicas and illustrations of the major works as well as a selection of the considerable numbers of books written to help their readers to understand and appreciate the objects they see. These inform them about the schools into which the works should be divided, the names of the styles they cultivate, and the details of the artists' lives when these are known. Anyone can thus become something of a connoisseur, though not one to rival the self-styled real experts whose opinions are the major factors that help to determine the prices of the works that are bought and sold, the rises and falls in the fashionableness of particular modern artists as well as of long-dead ones.

Connoisseurship is a profitable business. Of course it carries its responsibilities and hazards. Called upon to authenticate the work of a great master, where hundreds of thousands, even millions, of dollars may hang on the verdict, the connoisseur has to resist the temptation to be unduly influenced by those considerations. Their reputations as connoisseurs will depend on carrying their colleagues, or enough of them, with them, so it is in their interests to 'get it right'. But those who 'discover' a new or neglected period, movement, or school, and who manage to persuade their peers, and a handful of rich patrons, that the works in question are hitherto unrecognized masterpieces, stand to make fortunes. One Western example was Bernard Berenson who 'discovered' early Italian, especially Florentine and Sienese, painting in the opening decades of the twentieth century, and who made a considerable fortune by authenticating these and other works of art, as well as from the commissions he charged for selling them to rich American and European collectors. But the phenomenon is not just a modern, nor just a Western one. As Craig Clunas (1991, 1997) showed, in China in the sixteenth and seventeenth centuries, certain collectors and writers, notably individuals such as Gao Lian and Wen Zhenheng, and members of the extended Wang family, successfully promoted the merits of particular Chinese calligraphers, painters, and ceramicists, in whose works they had, as it happens, themselves invested heavily. They thereby scored a double victory: the prices of those works went up, as did also their own prestige as arbiters of taste.

Wherever there is a market for art, questions as to the relative quality of different works will be subject to controversy and the answers liable to manipulation by forceful persuaders. Are there indeed any objective standards in the matter? While what a particular work will fetch at an upcoming auction can sometimes be estimated fairly accurately, prices are subject to wide fluctuation over time. The auctioneers, and to some extent the connoisseurs on whom they rely, are in business not to let prices fall. But within the ranks of the latter, different views rival one another and that tends to undermine any stable consensus in the short, let alone the medium, term.

But if good art is controversial, art itself also is. Major changes in the perception of what counts as art can be brought about by the painters and sculptors themselves and by art critics and philosophers writing about them. The nineteenth-century Impressionist revolt against the styles of art taught in the schools, and promulgated by the French Academy, is one of the best known examples of that. But there have been many others. One earlier movement, that of the Romantics, insisted on a quite different mix of technique and genius from that of more traditional, classical, art, whether in painting, in music, or in literature. But it was all very well to say, as Plato had said long before, that true artistic inspiration shares something with madness (though a madness that Plato insisted should be under the auspices of the divine): the problem was always to identify true inspiration. Earlier still the painters and sculptors of the Renaissance overturned conventions as to how the human body was to be depicted, and the history of ancient Greek and Roman art is one of more or less constant change, as new techniques were developed and new styles of representation came into favour—often in the teeth of the opposition of conservatives. Plato, for one, considered that innovation in music undermined morality and threatened the good order of the state. 'A change to a new type of music', Socrates is made to say in the *Republic*

424c, 'is something to beware of, as a hazard of all our fortunes. For the modes of music are never disturbed without unsettling the most fundamental political laws-and-conventions (*nomoi*)' (cf. Barker 1984, chs. 7 and 10).[1]

Again self-conscious innovation is not just a Western phenomenon, even though a certain preoccupation with the concept of mimesis certainly is. From the fifth century CE onwards a sequence of Chinese writers theorized about what makes paintings effective, what gives them force, efficaciousness, shi_3 (Jullien 1995: chs. 4 and 5). Influential Tang dynasty studies, by writers such as Zhang Yanyuan (ninth century), discussed the appropriate styles of paintings for different kinds of subjects and had profound effects on subsequent work. At a superficial level, those changes may be relatively easily understood as analogous to changes in taste that we have been used to in the West, as fashions alter and practitioners and aesthetic experts influence others' views. But if we consider the Chinese category of *tu* (conventionally translated 'diagrams') a further point concerning conceptual boundaries emerges. *Tu* is in any case closely related to *hua* ('painting'). But the items labelled *tu* in our Chinese sources range from cosmograms, representing the cosmic forces of creation, symbolic or magical charts, used, for example, to guide the initiated to enlightenment, all the way to technical illustrations of the construction of artefacts such as silk-reeling machines.

Thus the Chinese category spans the decorative/aesthetic on the one hand and the educational/pedagogic on the other. A series of wide-ranging studies recently edited by Bray, Dorofeeva-Lichtmann, and Métailié (2007) has further brought to light the shifts that occurred, from the Warring States period down to modern times, first in where the emphasis lay as between those two functions, and secondly in the relative importance attached to *tu* and to the written texts that generally accompanied them, with *tu* eventually losing out to texts, at any rate in the eyes of the Ming literati. This provides a salutary reminder of the imperfect match in the conceptual maps relevant to

---

[1] Evaluating the divergent ancient Greek attitudes towards innovation in such areas as painting, sculpture, and architecture is complicated by the fact that in general the 'fine arts' (as we should call them) were not systematically distinguished from all the other crafts, skills, and technical processes that the term *technai* could cover. But music was considered a fundamental item in the education of any citizen.

'art' in China and in Europe and of the shifting understanding of the Chinese categories, as well as the European ones, in question.

But if change has always been endemic to artistic production and appreciation, from the start of the twentieth century new movements have succeeded one another in Europe with particular rapidity, post-Impressionism, expressionism, cubism, Fauvism, vorticism, Dadaism, surrealism, post-surrealism, hyper-realism, movements that were often inaugurated with explicit manifestos setting out why they represented the only, or the supremely, worthwhile art. In the process other styles have sometimes been dismissed not just as not good art, but as having no claims to being art in the first place. While in many societies over long periods traditional styles are held up as the model to be followed, there have been many exceptions. Sometimes, though not always, these coincide with other more general challenges to accepted values. However, in general the conservativeness of what is taught in the academies or art schools or by accepted masters may well provide some indication of the stability of those social values themselves.

Some visual artists nowadays refuse to produce works that fit easily into the usual categories of items that can be bought and sold or even deposited in galleries and museums. Some have sculpted snow or sand knowing their work to be subject to imminent destruction, emphasizing thereby its transient nature (though there is usually a photographic record to which interested parties can be referred).[2] Such ephemerality differs from that which we associate with a theatrical or a musical performance, insofar as in those cases a script or a score exists that can serve as the basis of further performances, even though they will never recapture exactly the individual interpretations of a character in a play or a musical cadenza. The further problems that arise in those cases relate, of course, to the question of the nature of the identity that can be ascribed to works of art in different media.

Among critics and commentators, some have taken up even more radical positions than those of the actual practitioners of the avant-garde. Some have insisted that beautiful natural objects—*objets trouvés*—should be classified as art. Their shapes and colours may

---

[2] Contrast the use of sand in Japanese gardens where the patterns, if disturbed, are carefully recreated or restored. Sand 'paintings' in primitive art have been discussed, for example, by Goody (1995: 211).

be just as aesthetically pleasing as sculptures made by humans and accordingly deserve a place in our museums alongside the works of Donatello, Rodin, or Henry Moore. An even more extreme view was expressed by a group now long since forgotten, who called themselves, after the slogan they adopted, the N.E.Thing Goes company. On their view *anything* can be considered art: it only had to be labelled as such, that is it only had to be thought by someone to be art for it to be classified as such. The group produced actual labels, indeed, which its members attached to objects, from Chartres cathedral to broken cups and saucers. Yet to make the category all-inclusive was to rob it of any discriminatory power. If everything is art, nothing is.

At this stage in the argument, a cynical appraisal of the state of the question would have it that, while the art market knows exactly what it is doing, namely maximizing the value of the works it sells as art, that must be set against a background of conceptual anarchy and chaos. The old assumptions about art have been effectively demolished as arbitrary only to be replaced by a complete sense of aporia or confusion.[3]

But to answer the fundamental question of whether, or how far, the category of 'art' is applicable cross-culturally, we have to broaden our horizons and consider the issues from the perspective of societies that are not preoccupied with the rises and falls of prices at Christie's or by the needs of museums. There is no doubt that *we* in the West value and enjoy *their* art,[4] and we generally suppose that we can judge the quality of different works, ranging from masterpieces to run-of-the-mill productions. More or less exotic carvings or textiles are brought back from remote parts to London or New York and admired in our museums and sold for high prices in our galleries. But is that not just a typical example of the way the West appropriates other peoples'

---

[3] Cf. Eagleton's critical remarks (1990: 372–9) on the impasse of post-modernism.

[4] The bafflement we are more likely to register at the music performed in other societies points to the differences that exist in the criteria brought to bear in that domain (see Blacking 1987 for a discussion of cross-cultural comparison in ethnomusicology). Similarly in literature the appreciation of poetic or prose works in a given language is generally well beyond anyone who does not command a considerable mastery of that language. Judgements as to whether two works in different languages do or do not belong to the same 'genre' are notoriously difficult, and attempts to explain why particular genres or styles were cultivated in particular societies at particular historical conjunctures often seem to misfire. I have in mind the superficiality with which such questions as why the Greeks developed epic and tragedy, or why the novel took such different forms in China and in Greece, are generally discussed.

cultural products and in the process distorts and misinterprets them? To answer that, we have to recover as much as we can of the views of the producers and users of those objects—to get away from our, observers', categories back to their, actors', ones, in other words—making the best use we can of cases where the ethnographic reports have been careful not to superimpose Western interpretations.[5]

Lévi-Strauss, who famously illustrated an influential study of the problem with a photograph of a carved Tlingit club that he had on his desk as he wrote *La Pensée sauvage,* did as much as anyone to insist on the need to recontextualize the objects that the West tended to label 'art' all too swiftly. Part of that recontextualization is straightforward. That club had a use: it served its original owner as a weapon to kill the fish he had caught. So the first way in which it could be evaluated was in terms of its *functionality,* in other words how it worked as a weapon. Yet to serve that purpose, it did not need to be carved elaborately or indeed decorated at all. The second set of considerations in play is the *skill* with which the carving was executed, and the third the *symbolic appropriateness* of the carving in question—not that these three criteria are necessarily sharply distinguished from one another. To do its job well, it was right that it should represent, indeed should *be,* a monstrous sea animal. This one depicted a predatory creature, but others depict the prey on which the implement is used. To understand the symbolism one evidently has to know a great deal about the cosmology, and the values, of the society in question.

To appreciate this it is useful to invoke the notion of *felicity* that has been used in connection with the interpretation of magic and ritual.[6] Let me take a second example, the elaborate carvings on the prow-boards of ocean-going canoes on the Melanesian island of Kitawa studied by Scoditti (1990) as well as by Gell (1999) and Campbell (2001). Are the carvings believed to increase the seaworthiness of the canoes—their efficacy in that sense? That may not be the right way of posing the question—certainly it is not the only way of approaching the issue. Rather it is the case that the carvings are integral to what

---

[5] Geertz (1983: ch. 5) in particular was one who emphasized the importance of the deepest immersion in the values and world-view of the society producing the art, if we are to avoid a merely sentimental and deluded 'appreciation' of it. Cf. also Gell 1998.

[6] As noted in Ch. 4, Tambiah's studies, 1968 and 1973, provide classic statements of the contrast between 'felicity' and 'efficacy'.

makes a canoe a *proper* canoe, and that involves a whole range of considerations besides how it performs at sea. The canoes themselves are used in the *kula*, the circle of exchange between different islands that occupies a central place in Kitawan society. To succeed in the *kula* is a man's highest ambition. So great attention is paid to every aspect of the construction of the canoes that will be used for these journeys. The fine carvings not only give the patron and the users a sense of pride and achievement: they are designed to secure a psychological advantage over partners and rivals, to dazzle and indeed upset them by displaying what Gell (1999: 166) called a 'physical token of magical prowess'.

A banal example from our own society will help to illustrate the basic idea of 'felicity'. Whether or not we are Christians ourselves, we would not think a wedding ceremony in church had been correctly performed if certain symbolic acts are not carried out properly—putting the ring on the fourth finger of the bride's left hand, for instance, or showering the couple with confetti. It may be that no one now holds that such a gesture actually contributes to increasing the couple's fertility, however much that may have been part of its origin. But what is at stake for Christians and non-Christians alike is not so much the efficacy of the complex set of rituals in church in that sense, as rather their appropriateness, the way they meet people's expectations of what is right and proper in the circumstances, their felicity in other words.

In the case of the Kitawan canoes, the further point is that the carvings are direct testimony to the skill and prestige of the carver and so of the group to which he belongs. Becoming a carver is a matter of a long apprenticeship, during which any member of the society may attempt to judge the apprentice's progress, but it takes the master carver himself to say when the apprentice can really do the job properly. The designs carved on the prow-boards consist of a mass of intricately organized graphic signs, and while, according to Scoditti, anyone in the community can appreciate something of their aesthetic quality, the full significance of the symbols is an item of special, in a way esoteric, knowledge that only the expert can judge.

On the one hand, then, if Scoditti is right, aesthetic experience can be shared, up to a point, by everyone in the society: but on the other, the evaluation of the true quality of the workmanship is in the hands

Prow-board from kitawan canoe. *Source*: Scoditti 1990.

of the carvers themselves.[7] This does not rule out innovation, for each carver will create his own distinctive style, but it is only members of his own peer group that are in a position to say how good that is. They constitute, in fact, an artistic elite, though not a social one. They depend on rich patrons to commission their work—but the patron's own prestige grows when he secures the services of a master carver, in a way that bears obvious analogies to the situation in, for example, European baroque art, where patrons and artists supported one another, the ones financially, the others in terms of renown (cf. Haskell 1963). There is a constant interaction between the artists and their prospective clients, not that the latter can dictate how the artists should go about their work. Meanwhile this elite is not an exclusive one, designed to keep outsiders away. The carvers, including Scoditti's

[7] There are parallels, but also contrasts, between the situation on Kitawa and that described among the New Guinea Abelam by Forge 1967: 82–4. In that society aesthetic judgement concerning such matters as form and proportion is said to be the concern of the artists themselves alone, while the rest of the community is interested, rather, in the effectiveness of the designs as a component in rituals that are designed to ensure the society's future prosperity—in their functionality in that sense. So the parallelism is that in both cases the ultimate arbiters of aesthetic qualities are the artists themselves: but the contrast is that according to Forge, such qualities are not a matter of *general* interest among the Abelam.

own teacher, are keen to hand on their skills to their chosen pupils. But the skills are such that very few actually succeed.

As a third example let me take a more complex case where far more than a merely utilitarian functionality is in play. Body-painting in many Amazonian societies has been well documented and much admired, but what has sometimes been neglected is the nexus of beliefs, about clothing and disguise, with which such practices are often associated, as Viveiros de Castro (1998) especially has demonstrated.[8] What appears as a jaguar may be a shaman in disguise who has adopted the 'clothing' of a jaguar temporarily. Conversely jaguars may be believed on occasion to adopt human disguises. Appearances may be deceptive, but they are nonetheless important for that, since the new disguise, the new clothes, may go with a new role for the individual concerned, whether the individual is an animal, an ordinary human, or a shaman. Against the background of these ideas, body decoration is no mere decoration, but the acquisition of a distinct personality, whether temporary or more permanent.[9] But the pleasing character of the decoration—we may surely say its appreciation as an object of beauty[10]—contributes to that transformation. Again there is nothing particularly surprising about this combination of roles, as a means of effecting that transformation and as attractive decoration, for does not the pleasing representation of a saint in a Christian church add to the satisfaction the faithful may feel in communing with, and praying to, the holy person so portrayed?

[8] Compare the somewhat different use of body-painting on Mount Hagen in New Guinea, studied by Strathern and Strathern (1971). There in different social situations, such as funerals, warfare, ceremonial exchanges, complex meanings concerning social positions and intentions may be conveyed by decoration that varies on the three axes of (1) degree of elaboration, (2) colour, and (3) texture (cf. Layton 1991: 116). Some of the separate elements have fairly clearly demarcated significances, whether singly or in combination, though some, such as the colours black, red, and white, exhibit a marked ambivalence (Strathern and Strathern 1971: 162ff.). However, the individual may and to some extent must make choices to use the code to convey the personal messages he or she may wish to get across, whether discreetly or overtly. These are occasions for display and are used to make statements about an individual's or a group's role or status. In a later study, Strathern (1979) emphasized the continuity between inner and outer selves and accordingly developed a further contrast between Hagen body-painting and mere cosmetic decoration.

[9] That may similarly be effected by the use of masks, attested across the world even more widely than body-painting: see e.g. Napier 1992.

[10] This is not to say that the body-painters' ideas of beauty are the same as 'ours', just that they can and do discriminate between examples that are more and those that are less satisfying, using aesthetic judgements among other criteria. Descola (1996) describes the enjoyment that the Achuar derive from painting their faces for different occasions. This can be a social activity, and fun, but that does not diminish its ritual importance and seriousness.

For my fourth example let me consider the comparisons and contrasts that exist when outsiders are confronted with even more richly contextualized situations. Take the experience of someone visiting a Maori meeting house, a building of great importance to the tribe, often magnificently adorned with what to the non-Maori will appear strange and exotic carvings and textiles.[11] We may compare that with a non-Christian visiting a great medieval cathedral or a non-Muslim going to a mosque.

The significance of the Maori meeting house, like that of the mosque, is underlined, for example, by the fact that shoes must be removed before entering, just as it used to be the case that women were not allowed into Christian churches if their heads were not covered or if they wore short sleeves—a prohibition that still survives in some places. The building itself is often a simple rectangle built of wood and with a high ceiling and carved wooden posts and beams. The non-Maori will have no difficulty recognizing half-human, half-animal figures, carved on pillars and posts stretching from floor to ceiling, tiered like north-west American totem poles. But of course the non-Maori will be (initially) totally ignorant of the names and significance of each of these highly individualistic figures. For the Maori, by contrast, the range of possible understandings is far wider. The figures will be associated with a rich set of stories recounting their exploits, revealing their complex personalities, powers, and spheres of influence.

Then there are the panels of textiles and further carvings that occupy the space along the walls between the pillars. The non-Maori will certainly be impressed by the technical skills displayed in both the carving and the weaving, but to all intents and purposes will see the latter just as abstract designs.[12] Yet for the Maori these woven panels, known as *tukutuku*, are reminders of stories, relating to the origins of the tribe and of the world in general, to the deeds of heroes and legendary figures down to the present generation. The apparently abstract, but very distinctive, patterns often serve as aides-memoires concerning such exploits. One design, known as *roimata toroa* (the tears of the albatross) relates to the story of how a great chief, named Ruakapanga, loaned two mighty

---

[11] I am most grateful to Dr Amiria Salmond for advice on Maori art and on the problems of cross-cultural evaluation of art in general. On Maori meeting houses as an index of agency, cf. Gell 1998: 251–8.

[12] Compare Boas 1955: ch. 4 on the cosmological symbolism in some apparently abstract designs of textiles and basketry that can be found in many societies across the world, and cf. ch. 6, in that study, on those of north-west coast American Indians in particular.

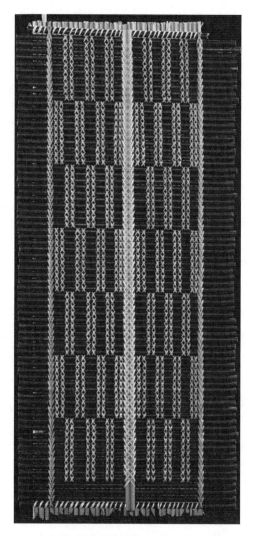

Tukutuku panel made for Te Hau ki Turanga, 1935–6: roimata toroa (the tears of the albatross). Museum of New Zealand Te Papa Tongarewa (registration numbers ME015746/112).

birds to help Pourangahau to fly to Aotearoa (New Zealand) to be the first man to cultivate it by planting kumara. But while Ruakapanga insisted that care should be lavished on the birds, this order was forgotten—with disastrous results—the infestation of the kumara with pests.

Another pattern, called *poutama* (stairway to heaven) recalls how Tawhaki climbed to heaven to bring back the baskets of knowledge:

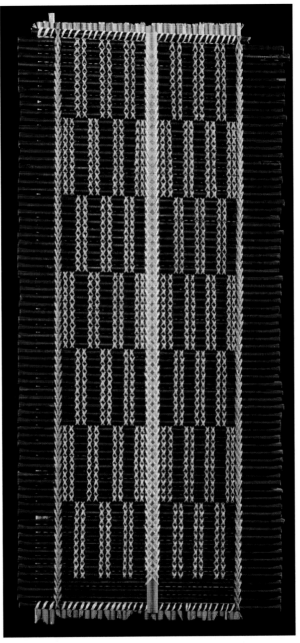

Tukutuku panels made for Te Hau ki Turanga, 1935–6: roimata toroa (the tears of the albatross). Museum of New Zealand Te Papa Tongarewa (registration numbers ME015746/112).

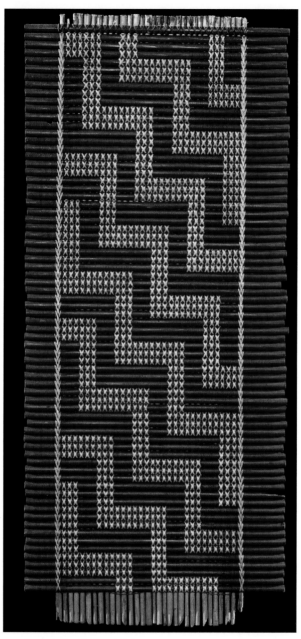

Tukutuku panels made for Te Hau ki Turanga, 1935–6: poutama (stairway to heaven). Museum of New Zealand Te Papa Tongarewa (registration numbers ME015746/115).

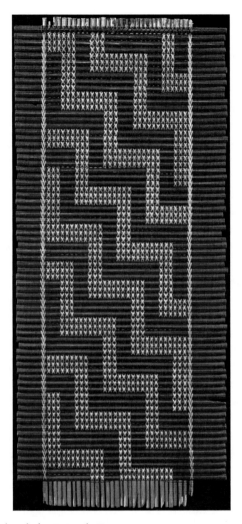

Tukutuku panel made for Te Hau ki Turanga, 1935–6: poutama (stairway to heaven). Museum of New Zealand Te Papa Tongarewa (registration numbers ME015746/115).

but the design also denotes the progress and advance that ensure the future success of the tribe and its members. Tawhaki, moreover, is not simply a mythological figure: he has living descendants who can trace their genealogy back to him through scores, even hundreds, of generations. None of these layers of meaning is directly portrayed, in the sense of given a representational depiction, in the textiles, which, to the uninformed eye, look as if they were just abstract designs.

But if we turn back to Europe, many modern visitors to a medieval cathedral will be similarly baffled, though here too there are some representational figures where anyone can appreciate part at least of what is represented. That is, they may recognize the faces and figures of men and women (though they may be saints or God himself) in the stained glass windows. Yet their identities will not always be given by their being named, and besides, the names will mean nothing to the outsider. However, as in the Maori case, they will also be faced with symbols, the cross, the chi-rho, whose meaning they will not understand, any more than they will the significance of the iconic figures, the lamb, the fish, the dove. Stations of the cross that will enable the faithful to repeat Christ's last journey, in the church itself, may not even be recognized as representing a journey.

What the two pairs of experiences I have imagined have in common is that up to a point, but only up to a point, anyone, insider or outsider, can enjoy the decorations and ornaments of such buildings and appreciate something of the craftsmanship that went into their construction. But what for the outsider may be merely a source of a visual pleasure, for the insider is an experience rich in edification and instruction, a commemoration of values and beliefs the community holds dear.

But it is not just what the insider understands that is different from the understanding of the outsider: what the insider *sees* differs too, and the outsider may never be in a position to respond to the total experience of the building in the way that is accessible to someone brought up in the society—not that there is a single definitive appreciation of any building or any work of art, painting, sculpture, textile, music, dance, to be had by anyone. We are used to acknowledging that we have to *learn* to appreciate art and that training the eye, and the ear, may be a highly complex business and one that may involve practical interactions with the environment (Ingold 2000). But those processes nevertheless *begin* with the basic pleasurable experience that comes even to the comparatively untrained eye and ear.[13] The

---

[13] That is not to say that any 'eye' or 'ear' is totally innocent. On the contrary, both are deeply implicated in the active interpretation of sensory inputs, as Gregory (1970) long ago showed conclusively for the eye. The point is an important one for the philosophy of science (see below, Ch. 8) but for now it is enough simply to note that from childhood we all begin to learn, from those who are responsible for bringing us up, how to respond to our experiences, particularly—as Aristotle already remarked—in the matter of pleasures and pains.

initial response to such a pleasure can occur in any context in the presence of any beautiful object, and this may give us a bridgehead for cross-cultural comparison. Again let me emphasize that this does not depend on *what* is considered beautiful, or how that concept is cashed out: the point of similarity is that some objects or experiences will be picked out as more pleasurable than others (cf. Tooby and Cosmides 2001).

But two problems now need to be confronted. First, the trained eye may be so accustomed to fine objects of a particular type and executed in a particular style that those that do not conform to those patterns are rejected as positively ugly and yield no pleasure at all. Secondly, the origin of the pleasurable experience is what is perceived as beautiful and that category is not only complex and tied to a whole constellation of other ideas and values, but is also evidently far wider than that of art.

But to the first question it should be conceded that no claim can conceivably be made for a uniformity, across all peoples at all times, in what, in the visual domain, they respond to with pleasure, even though some have speculated that there may be a universal, biological, or psychological origin of art (Aiken 1998, cf. Mithen 1996, Solso 2004). The cross-cultural claim I would defend relates merely to the point that we all respond with pleasure to *some* objects to *some* degree. However, just as our eye and ear need training to arrive at a positive appreciation of certain experiences, so, it has to be said, they may also need to be *un*trained, to overcome certain types of negative response that have become habitual through ignorance or prejudice.

That takes us to the second question, and again a defensive reply is in order. First, no claim can be sustained that there are universal criteria governing what is perceived as 'beautiful' any more than there are for what is 'pleasant'. Secondly, we should concede that the objects that give pleasure are generally far wider than those recognized to be the products of human craftsmanship.[14] However, in the experience of art there is, as I mentioned before, the added dimension of the interaction between the artists and their audiences.

---

[14] This is not to presuppose that distinctions between what is natural and what made by humans are always salient or drawn according to the same criteria in different societies, as many studies that have questioned the cross-cultural applicability of the dichotomy between nature and culture have shown (cf. Viveiros de Castro 1998, Descola 2005).

It is foolish of patrons to try to dictate how their painters should paint, though such attempts have often been made. Nevertheless, more positively the patrons' appreciation can contribute to confirming the potentialities of the style within which the artists work. Innovation, in that context, in other words, will depend not just on the genius of the artists, but on how their works are appreciated, that is it will be encouraged by the positive response they receive. To that extent it is a communal matter.

Our categories are evidently not the equivalent of those that other actors use. But that should not lead us to conclude that it is always mistaken to talk of other people's experiences as aesthetic ones, whether or not they, the actors themselves, have a vocabulary of terms that can be brought into some kind of correspondence with those that we generally use ourselves. Some certainly do. One example among the many that may be cited comes from Hughes-Freeland's discussion of Javanese dance (1997). While she points out that there is no Javanese term for 'art' as such, distinctions are drawn between the 'coarse' (*kasar*) and the 'refined' (*alus*) in the evaluation of courtly performances. What falls into each category may be difficult for an outsider to predict, but the important point for my argument is that a distinction is clearly made between them. 'Primitive art', as I noted before, has indeed been systematically hijacked by Westerners and others. The objects displayed in the sections of museums devoted to Africa or South America or Polynesia have been stripped of their original context, even when they have not actually been stolen. They certainly often owe their label as 'art' to the impositions of outsiders' categories. But that just leaves all the work of interpreting their significance—in all its complexity—in their original context still to be done.[15]

The defence that modern connoisseurs might make is that any object can be evaluated from a variety of perspectives and that includes perspectives not imagined by the original makers and owners.

---

[15] Some ritual objects that the uninformed may think to be fine examples of 'primitive art' may be considered by those who make and use them to be perfect exemplars of the ugly. Thus Horton 1965: 12 remarked, in connection with some Kalabari sculptures, that there is evidence to suggest that some of them evoke 'not merely apathy, but actual revulsion'. 'Thus one can refer to a man's ugliness by comparing his face with a spirit sculpture', though when the comparison is with a badly carved piece—with the 'sculpture of a god carved by one who does not know how to carve'—there is an additional factor in play, namely that the sculpture fails to conform to local conventions or expectations.

That may be the case, though there are always risks in overriding the actors' own categories. A second less aggressive approach would be to suggest, as I have done, that while the appreciation of the fine and beautiful is often deeply enmeshed with that of the symbolically felicitous, the religiously uplifting, the ritually appropriate, the functionally well adapted, the ideologically embedded, or even the politically correct, that is not to say that the first component cannot be identified independently of the others: the aesthetic experience is not reducible to one or other of those other elements nor even to a combination of them. When we encounter different manifestations of human creativity in different places and times, we have to suspend whatever preconceptions we may have about 'art' and be prepared to broaden our understanding of what aesthetic experience may include. But if we do so, we have many things to learn about the range of human aspiration and sensitivity.

So at the end of this discussion we may take stock of some of the particular difficulties that confront the cross-cultural application of the notion of art. Evidently the criteria invoked to judge what is beautiful—whether in nature or in objects made by humans, and whether or not a sharp distinction is drawn between those two—vary widely. They do so as between different individuals in different communities and even between different members of the same community—where some stake out a special niche for themselves as connoisseurs or leaders of taste, or indeed if they are craftsmen themselves, as the producers of objects that should be prized.

My argument has been that such commonalities as we can discern are to be found at a deeper level. *Some* recognition of *some* distinction between the attractive and the ugly, the refined and the coarse, the admirable and the dull, is common, if not universal. That point remains however much we differ in what we admire and in how we might go about explaining our preferences if indeed we think they need some justification.

But one lesson that can be drawn from the observation that the eye needs to be trained to see the beautiful is that there is no reason to limit ourselves to what we are used to, in our Western perception of art. We can acquire an appreciation of others' views on the subject, learn from others' perceptions of the fine, although, as with learning another language, such an appreciation may always remain imperfect—and it certainly requires harder work than is usually imagined, since it depends on acquiring new skills, new understanding, even a new vision of the world.

Art thus exemplifies the problems of elite versus common views in a particularly striking way. As with other questions to do with values, the issue of how far they are open to challenge, and if so, by whom, and in what conditions, may be hotly disputed, whenever, that is, tradition is not held up to be, in some sense, sacrosanct. The limits within which both the artists themselves and those who evaluate their work can innovate are set by the need to carry their peer group and beyond them the wider public.

As for where most Western reflections on art will start, namely with the history of art as it is taught in our art schools and universities, we need to be aware that there are many other considerations in play in bids to swing opinion towards favouring some aesthetic experiences over others. We come back to the commercialization and commodification of art with which I began. The final irony is that while there is an obvious mismatch between the market forces at work and those aspects of the art of other societies and periods from which I claimed we can learn to see things afresh, those who produce 'primitive art' for the tourist trade and the wider market do so in a way that turns its back on the original value-laden and contextually rich circumstances in which it had initially been created.[16]

---

[16] There are perceptive remarks in Hughes-Freeland 1997 on the deliberate modifications that Javanese dance undergoes when directed at foreign, especially Western audiences. On the issues of the commodification of art and of musical performance in general, see e.g. Greenwood 1978, Shepherd 2002, Kaul 2007, and Taylor 2008.

6

Law

WE do not expect laws to be the same everywhere. The question of
the extent to which it can be claimed that there are or should be
objective universal moral principles is, of course, another matter
entirely on which I have developed some arguments in an earlier
study (Lloyd 2004: ch. 11). But in respect of cultural diversity, law is
more like art than it is like mathematics, though we saw reason to
doubt too easy an assumption of uniformity where the latter is
concerned. We encounter a bewildering variety both in notions of
law and in ways of administering it. Not every human society has a
formal legal system, but those that do generally see it as fundamental to the proper ordering of human relations and a mark of a
superior civilization. Other groups that lack such a system are no
better than beasts. Yet any such view is open to two immediate
objections. First, societies that have no written laws, nor officially
recognized legal officers—judges, magistrates—may nevertheless be
perfectly able to deliver justice. Secondly, is the codification of the
laws always an unmixed blessing? Confucius thought not, on
the grounds that people would be distracted from internalizing the
principles of good conduct and from practising virtue. If the laws
cover every issue of importance to do with right and wrong, there is
less incentive to think about such matters and to regulate one's
behaviour according to the highest standards.[1]

Among the recurrent fundamental questions on our agenda in this
chapter are first the relationship between law and morality, where the
second term is, as noted, certainly as problematic as the first. Moral
issues are not necessarily all subject to legal provisions. In our society

---

[1] See *Zuozhuan*, Zhao 29, Graham 1989: 276. A similar view is expressed also in the
Daodejing 57, associated with the legendary Laozi.

lying in court is, but not lying in many other contexts.[2] Conversely, law codes often lay down rules for behaviour outside the domain of what we consider morality, prescriptions and proscriptions relating to diet and dress, for instance. However, when they do so, breaking those rules will generally be considered not just a misdemeanour, but a crime, maybe even an act of sacrilege. The concept of the unclean, which I mentioned in Chapter 4 and to which I shall return in Chapter 7, may span religion, morality, and medicine, breaking down the barriers between those three and treating all three as a seamless whole. We shall have occasion, here too, to distinguish a more inclusive notion of morality from a less inclusive one.

Secondly, there is the issue of how the law is interpreted and applied. Legal codes lay down general rules, but those who administer them have to decide particular cases. Even when there are plenty of recorded precedents to refer to, there is always scope for debating which laws, which precedents, are applicable to the case in hand. Within what limits do judges have discretion? When they are thought to overstep the mark, or are suspected of bias or corruption, how can they be challenged and what sanctions are they subject to? Who guards the guardians in other words?

That takes us, thirdly, to the origin and status of the laws. Are they recognized to be made by humans, or are they—or some of them at least—thought to come from God, incorporated in a holy text, or revealed to priests, prophets, sages (cf. Brague 2007)? Does the divine intervene in other ways, as when trial by ordeal is held to unmask the guilty, or when perjury is believed to lead to divine retribution?

That in turn is connected to a fourth issue, namely the possibility of change and innovation in this domain. Are the laws, in whole or in part, thought to be immutable, because, for instance, they encapsulate God's commands? Or can they be changed, and if so, by whom? Who are the experts in such matters, if there are experts, and in virtue of what qualities do they achieve that status?

---

[2] Attitudes towards lying may differ appreciably in different societies. Herodotus, 1.136–8, remarks that the Persians considered lying utterly disgraceful. But for many Greeks in many situations there was nothing particularly reprehensible about lying. Indeed those who did so and got away with it were admired for their *mētis*, their cunning intelligence, as Odysseus especially was. He even attempted, unsuccessfully of course, to hoodwink Athena when he meets but does not recognize her, when he finally lands on Ithaca, *Od.* 13.253–86.

Fifthly, is there a separation of powers, between the legal and the political authorities? Is the law used to curb the activities of those who rule, or do the latter simply manipulate and control the laws to do whatever they like and indeed give it the cloak of legality?

Finally, how do attitudes towards the law, and its status, change when the rules in question relate not to intra-state affairs but to inter-state ones, where they cannot be enforced by officers acting for a single sovereign state. The main focus of my discussion will be the laws of individual societies, but I shall end with some brief remarks on the ongoing problems presented by the field of inter-national law.

There are rich materials on these issues that we can consider from ancient China and Greece, but let me begin with some brief remarks about three other societies that will serve to bring out some of the variety in the ways in which justice is dispensed (cf. Diamond 1971). The first is a society, the Barotse, that has no written codes, indeed no writing at all; the second, ancient Babylonia, produced one of the most detailed codes extant from antiquity, that of Hammurabi; and the third, Islamic societies provide an example where the basic law code, the Sharīᶜa, is divinely sanctioned.

I mentioned before, in connection with reasoning ability (Chapter 1) the evidence that Gluckman (1967, 1972) collected concerning the self-conscious pride the Lozi show in their connoisseurship of skills in argument that orators may display, where the chief context in which they do so is, precisely, in courts of law. The Lozi do not have written rules governing the procedures of those courts which are, rather, a matter of tradition and custom. They say that while outsiders, Wes-terners for instance, may excel in other domains of human activity, they, the Lozi, are experts on legal issues, including, for instance, evaluating those who speak on either side of a case brought to trial or who are responsible for arriving at a determination of guilt or inno-cence. As I noted before, their language possesses a rich vocabulary of terms to describe the virtues and vices shown in oratory. These are virtues in speaking, not in morality itself, of course. But when it is a judge who displays them, the quality of the justice he dispenses is improved, just as it is marred when he does not stick to the point, let alone when he is inconsistent. While particular skills in speaking are a gift that belongs to exceptional individuals, any member of the community may be capable of appreciating them. You do not have to belong to an elite cadre to do so.[3]

The Code of Hammurabi dates from between 1792 and 1750 BCE when the king of that name reigned in Babylonia. We know of even earlier codes, that exist in a fragmentary state (Pritchard 1969: 159ff.), but none appears to have equalled that of Hammurabi in comprehensiveness. It lays down procedures and specifies penalties for both civil and criminal cases (as we should call them). It covers, for instance, the relationships between slaves (of various kinds) and free persons, and sets out differential tariffs for crimes against those of different social status (Richardson 2000: 105). But a comparison between Hammurabi and other documentation that we have concerning particular cases that were brought to trial brings to light certain discrepancies between Hammurabi and actual practice. This suggests that, despite appearances, the code was not a compendium of actual legal decrees and ordinances, so much as a *model* for such. Students of the law, future magistrates for example, would learn how to tackle complex cases, how to square apparently conflicting principles and determine which applied to the case in hand, how to adjust penalties to the circumstances of the plaintiff and the defendant, and so on. The slippage between Hammurabi and what we otherwise know of how the law was administered indicates that that code, at least, was in certain respects an idealization. If that is correct, that means that more of the responsibility for delivering justice would fall on the shoulders of the magistrates in charge. Moreover, insofar as the code had an educational function, it was not aimed at just anyone, but designed to train an elite.

At the same time Hammurabi emphasizes the divine authority that underpins his code. The gods Anu and Enlil ordained him to demonstrate justice within the land: indeed it was when the god Marduk 'commissioned' him 'to guide the people aright, to direct the land,' that he 'established law and justice in the language of the land' (Pritchard 1969: 164–5, cf. Richardson 2000: 29 and 41). Babylonian rulers were not god-kings, like Egyptian pharaohs. But they can claim they speak with the support and approval of the gods, and nowhere is this more important than in the administration of justice.

---

[3] Contrast the situation I described for Kitawa skills in carving in Ch. 5, where the carvers themselves alone have full understanding of the merits of the work.

Islamic societies are among the many, past and present, that have a system of law, the Sharī'a, that is divinely sanctioned.[4] It derives, in the first instance, from the immutable teaching of the Ḳur'ān, which in principle deals with every aspect of daily life, not just religious, but financial, sexual, social, down to rules for diet and dress and for carrying out such responsibilities as the *ḥajj*, the pilgrimage to Mecca. But when the Ḳur'ān does not, in fact, itself pronounce directly on a subject, it has to be supplemented by *ḥadīth*, the sayings of Muhammad, and they in turn by what was agreed unanimously by his companions (*ṣaḥāba*). While the Ḳur'ān and *ḥadīth* together constitute the core code, they are distinguished from the *fiḳh*, the 'understanding of details', interpretive law, that includes the inferences of scholars down the generations. They are, and are recognized to be, subject to variation and change.

This means that those who, at a local level, are responsible for administering justice, the judges or *ḳāḍī* (or *qadi*), have a fair amount of discretion. For them, interestingly, written depositions count for less than oral testimony, and in assessing the latter the key factor is the uprightness of the witnesses.[5] The *ḳāḍī* make use of a corps of accredited witnesses, appointed according to settled procedures of evaluation and certification (Schacht 1964: 82, Geertz 1983: 191) and they may include women experts in matters of childbirth and sexual irregularities. But it is not just that the reliability of testimony depends upon the reputation of the person testifying: the judgement in any given case is likely to reflect the social standing of the disputants.

The immutability of the Ḳur'ān is a formidable bedrock principle. But in practice there is a good deal of room for manoeuvre and for change, though not usually proclaimed as such. There are and have always been plenty of disagreements between different Muslim sects, and different commentators within them, on such matters as the

---

[4] See e.g. Schacht 1964, Rosen 1989. Judaism is another example where, as in Islam, distinctions are recognized, within Halakha (divine law) between what is laid down in the Torah, and what in the Mishnah and the Babylonian Talmud, and again in the writings of those who have interpreted those texts. While the first possesses divine immutability, it is acknowledged that there have always been changes in the interpretations proposed by generations of rabbis.

[5] Schacht 1964: 125 ff., 200. This is not just a feature of Islam: Grafton 2007: 97 notes the same phenomenon in early modern European historiography, and a similar point goes back to Graeco-Roman antiquity: see Humphreys 1985.

modes of reasoning that can be permitted when applying the Ḳur'ān and *ḥadīth* to particular cases.[6] But if, in certain circumstances, innovation occurs, that is in the name of supplementing the holy texts and oral teaching, not to modify them, and such new interpretations are in the hands of a learned elite, no subject on which lay individuals can pronounce. Meanwhile Sharīᶜa vividly illustrates how the category of the legal may expand to cover not just human relations, but the whole of human life. Allah, it is said, is well aware of everything you do. The distinction between legality and morality that we draw is thus eroded. Every human act, being known to God, has to be consonant with the law that he ordained.

I turn next to China, where I have already noted Confucius' view that the introduction of written laws is regrettable, since it distracts people's attention from internalizing, and practising, virtue. The key concept in this domain, in Confucius' view, is *li₁*. This is often translated 'rites' or 'ritual', but it covers not just ceremonial, but also the proper conduct of all human relations, starting with those with your own family.[7] The real test of the *junzi*, 'gentleman', is how he behaves in relation to all those he comes in contact with, his prince, other superiors, but also inferiors, then his behaviour as a host, as a guest, among friends, to strangers, and of course especially to his own relatives.

Good social relations, on this view, depended on a recognition of the differences in social roles, and on a hierarchy of values. In a famous passage in the *Lunyu* 13.18, when a choice is put between family and strict observance of the law, Confucius is represented as coming down on the side of the family. The Duke of She boasts of a paragon of virtue in his state, a son who bore witness against his father who had stolen a sheep. But to this Confucius counters that where he lives, they have a very different idea of uprightness, namely that it consists rather in fathers covering up for their sons and sons for their fathers.

---

[6] One issue is the acceptability, or otherwise, of reasoning by analogy from issues covered by the Ḳur'ān and *ḥadīth* to other cases, and another is the weight and value of consensus. How to deal with non-believers is another question on which different Muslim authorities have taken different views, though most have recognized a distinction between the 'people of the book' (including Jews and Christians) and others.

[7] However, the Confucian texts use a different word for 'right', or 'righteousness', namely *yi₂*.

Yet Confucius' views were opposed both by the Mohists and by those, dubbed the Legalists, or School of Law, who saw *fa*, a term that covers law, order, and standard, rather than *li₁*, as the key to good order. The Mohists, as I have explained before, are badly represented in our sources, but one of their reported principles was that of a 'concern for all' (*jian ai*), an idea that evidently contradicted Confucius' idea that the role or the status of the people you are dealing with should affect the way you behaved towards them. The Mohists still upheld the law, and had some difficulty in squaring their belief that you should not kill people with their acceptance of the death penalty for certain criminals. There are convoluted discussions, in our sources, to show that 'killing robbers is not killing people'. But on the fundamental point of disagreement with Confucius they were clear that the whole world is your proper sphere of action, and that your concern should be with everyone equally, not with some more than others.

As for the School of Law, one of the most articulate representatives, Han Fei, attacked both Confucius and Mozi—and their followers. Their disagreements spread confusion. 'If you approve the frugality of Mozi, then you must condemn the extravagance of Confucius. If you approve the piety of Confucius, you must condemn Mozi for his impiety (or perversity, *li₂*)' (*Hanfeizi* 50: 1085). It is absurd to think that virtue can secure good order. They may have praised the ancient kings, *Hanfeizi* 49: 1051 ('Against the Five Vermin') puts it, but they did so for the wrong reasons. 'Benevolence may make one shed tears and be reluctant to apply penalties; but law makes it clear that such penalties must be applied. The ancient kings allowed law to be supreme and did not give in to their tearful longings. Hence it is obvious that benevolence cannot be used to achieve order in the state' (trans. Watson 2003: 103). We shall come back shortly to the point that while the 'ancient kings' could be invoked as models to follow, quite what they should be taken to stand for was a subject of some controversy.

Evidence for actual legal codes in China goes back to the sixth century BCE. I have noted before the role of Chinese 'philosophers' as counsellors to kings, and several important figures, such as Hui Shi in the fourth century, are reported to have drawn up such codes or to have advised rulers on them. One major point of controversy, as we have seen, is on whether law or virtue was the key to good order. Many of the penalties that the codes prescribed, beatings, brandings, amputation, castration, were harsh, and in severe cases it was not just the guilty individual who would be punished, but his entire family, his relatives 'to the third degree', that is, on the usual interpretation, the members of all three clans, the father's, the mother's, and the wife's. Incoming rulers often made a bid for a reputation for humaneness, by mitigating some of those penalties, but periods of relative leniency were generally punctuated by longer ones of great severity.

But any modification to the laws inevitably raised the question of their legitimacy—where there was no Chinese equivalent to the idea that they are divinely sanctioned and can be read off from a sacred text that incorporates the word of God. But if the laws are correct, should they not be permanent? On what basis and within what limits could change be tolerated? The sage kings of antiquity were accepted on all sides as paradigms of virtue and wisdom, but what they stood for was disputed.

Both the *Shangjunshu* (the *Book of Lord Shang*, otherwise known as the *Shangzi*) and the *Lüshi chunqiu* develop sophisticated arguments on the issue. The *Shangjunshu*[8] first reports a point of view according to which the laws should not be changed. 'I have heard', says a person named Du Zhi, that unless there is a hundredfold improvement, one does not alter a *fa* (law, standard), just as one does not replace a tool unless the results are ten times better. 'I have heard that if you take antiquity as standard, there will be no mistake, if you conform to convention (li_1) there will be no deviation.'

But to that Lord Shang replies: 'Former generations did not all have the same doctrines: which antiquity shall we take as standard? The Emperors and Kings did not repeat each other; to which convention shall we conform? Fu Xi and Shennong taught and did not use punishments. The Yellow Emperor, Yao, and Shun punished but spared the families of the condemned. Coming down to Kings Wen and Wu, each established standards fitted to the times, instituted conventions as affairs prompted them. Since conventions and standards were fixed according to the times, restrictions and commands were appropriate to the circumstances.' So there is no one way of bringing order to one's generation.

Similarly the *Lüshi chunqiu* contains a chapter (15.8, cf. Knoblock and Riegel 2000: 367–71) called 'scrutinizing the present' (*cha jin*)

---

[8] *Shangjunshu* ch. 1: 1.26–2.2, trans. Graham 1989: 270, modified.

which opens up the problems, and as prime minister in the state of Qin, Lü Buwei would have had more than a merely abstract interest in them. The *fa* (laws/standards) laid down by former kings were important for their times, but times have changed. Besides, the books that contained their principles have been altered in the transmission, and bits have been added and others omitted. So there are problems of authenticating what they taught. This is not a rejection of ancient wisdom, but a warning that one should not follow the 'fixed' standards mechanically. Rather one must work out what the former kings, on the principles they adopted, would have prescribed for the changed circumstances of the present day. To rule the state without laws leads to *luan* (disorder, chaos, anarchy), but to guard the laws without modifying them leads to rebellion or revolt, *bei*.[9] Those who do not dare to debate the laws are the multitude, but those who die preserving them as they are are those who hold offices charged with managing them—a perceptive comment on where the interests of officialdom lie. Both those groups are contrasted with those who respond to the times to modify the laws: they are the worthy rulers.

These and other writers insist that laws have to be adapted to the prevailing situation. This is the view expressed, for instance, by Du Zhou in the *Shiji* 122: 3153. But if that savoured of possible arbitrariness, or at least subjectivity, there were other passages that proclaimed that objectivity and impartiality are essential to the implementation of the law. The *Guanzi* (21.3: 157.29–31, Graham 1989: 275–6) is one text among many that uses the popular analogy with the scales. 'The scales are the means of finding the number for a weight. That in spite of everything people do not try to influence them is not because at heart they don't want profit; the counterpoise is unable for their sakes to increase or decrease its number, the beam is unable for their sakes to estimate as lighter or heavier. Men don't try to influence the scales because they know it would be useless. So when there is a clear-sighted ruler on the throne officials have no opportunity to bend the law, magistrates have no opportunity to practice partiality.'

This was fine in principle, but with the increasing elaboration of the law, over time, there were considerable problems. The documents that

---

[9] Interestingly enough, Lü Buwei goes on to suggest an analogy with medicine, precisely to make the point that treatments should change to cope with the transformations in diseases.

are extant relating to the actual administration of justice in the Han dynasty (Hulsewé 1955, 1986) certainly show an extraordinary attention to detail, as the magistrates concerned attempted to decide how a particular case in hand related to the general principles they were supposed to apply. In that connection we have collections of records of individual cases that parallel in many respects the Chinese clinical case histories we reviewed in Chapter 4. Both medical and legal cases have in common first that they provide a database for future reference.

Secondly, they could be cited, if need be, as evidence of the care with which the doctor or the judge carried out their responsibilities—and minor magistrates were evidently often keen to demonstrate their conscientiousness to their superiors. In the legal cases the outcome is a verdict and a penalty duly imposed. Although the parties in the dispute have some opportunity to make their own statements concerning it, there is nothing like the sustained debate between defendants and plaintiffs that are familiar from Greek law courts (see below). Rather, the expectation is that the guilty party will confess to their crime and accept the appropriate punishment that the law ordains.

This emerges from a story recorded in the chapter that the *Shiji* devotes to 'harsh officials' despite its obvious fanciful details. In this (*Shiji* 122: 3137) a boy is punished by his father for allowing a rat to steal some meat. To redeem himself, the boy catches the rat and brings it to trial—indicting the animal, beating it until it confessed, writing out a record of its version of what happened, comparing that with the evidence, and drawing up a proposal for punishment. After that he takes the rat and the meat into the courtyard, where he holds a trial, presents the charges, and executes the rat. The father was astonished that the boy had carried out the whole procedure like an experienced law officer. The anecdote is, to be sure, exaggerated, but it substantiates the point that an arrest was generally expected to be followed by a confession, sometimes extracted under torture. Elsewhere (*Shiji* 122: 3153) Sima Qian notes that the very possibility of being charged often led the accused to take to flight. Sima Qian himself, of course, writes from first-hand experience of imprisonment, after he had fallen out with Han Wu Di, although he chose the ignominious punishment of castration and rejected the nobler course of suicide, precisely in order to continue his father's history.

The magistrates formed a well-trained professional cadre whose meticulousness in the matter of recording their activities is evident from our sources. But the elaboration of the laws and the proliferation of precedents were, by Han times, causing a fair amount of confusion. In the *Hanshu* (23: 1101) we read that in relation to the death penalty alone, there were 409 articles covering 1,882 cases, and that there were no fewer than 13,472 cases of judicial precedents for crimes deserving death (Hulsewé 1955: 338). By that stage there were justifiable complaints that corrupt officials could exploit the very complexity of the provisions to their own advantage.

We thus find intense debates, throughout the Warring States period and on into the Qin and Han dynasties, on at least four fundamental questions concerning the law, namely on how important written codes are for good government, on whether the only realistic way to ensure order was to prescribe the severest punishments for misdeeds, on whether all are equal before the law, and on whether the laws should be preserved intact over the ages or adapted to the circumstances of each generation. Yet on one other question there was far more general agreement, namely that it was the duty of the ruler—after the unification, the emperor—to ensure that the macrocosm and microcosm should be in harmony with one another. To that end we find in texts such as the *Lüshi chunqiu* and the *Huainanzi* sets of 'monthly ordinances' (*yue ling*), of the rules of behaviour that the prince should observe, month by month through the year, to ensure cosmic harmony. Moreover those ordinances also specify the dire consequences if he does *not* do so, the natural and social disasters that will ensue (not that those two categories are thus distinguished).

This does not imply a belief in some transcendent being, a providential God or Craftsman, who is in control of the universe. Rather, the idea is that the entire universe, the heavens, the political dispensation, and the individual human body are inherently linked: all manifest the same patterns of the interactions of the five phases[10] and of *yin* and *yang*. So the way the ruler conducts himself has cosmic repercussions. He cannot allow political and social disorder (*luan*) on pain of provoking cosmic calamities.

---

[10] On the concept of the five phases, see above, Ch. 1. While some of its primary spheres of application are in what we would describe as the physical or cosmological domains, political dynasties were thought to follow one another in the same styles of sequence as that described in the Mutual Conquest order.

Of course there were plenty of actual rulers who ignored all such warnings. But just as there were positive paradigms provided by the sage kings, Yao, Shun, and Yu, so the tyrants Jie and Zhou, the last rulers of the Xia and Shang dynasties respectively, could be invoked as negative examples of the way in which princes could lose their Mandate from Heaven. Meanwhile it was, as I have observed before, the duty of advisers to reprimand rulers who did not have the welfare of their people—of 'all under heaven', *tian xia*—at heart, even though the risk those advisers ran was to incur the rulers' displeasure and the price they then had to pay could be anything from mere loss of office to mutilation and death. The references to macrocosm–microcosm interactions may have been idealistic rhetoric, but it drew on deep-seated beliefs that many leading thinkers made it their business to articulate.[11]

As in China, so too in ancient Greece, there are radical disputes on fundamental questions to do with law and morality, shifts in the meanings of key terms, puzzlement over the respective contributions of good laws and good magistrates in securing justice, and conflicts between more, and less, egalitarian arrangements for dispensing it. But less emphasis is placed, in Greece, on the notion that the ruler has cosmic responsibilities and less on the duty of advisers to reprimand them when they fall short in that respect. Identifying *who* to reprimand, in the Greek case, was often difficult, when policies were decided by the people in assembly, not by princes. Conversely the idea that questions of guilt and innocence should be determined by voting, that is by counting heads, was distinctively Greek and indeed without parallel in any ancient society. That was, of course, the democratic way of arriving at political decisions, but politics is never far from the law in ancient Greece.

Our earliest literary evidence comes from Homer, where a famous scene depicted on the Shield of Achilles (*Iliad* 18.497 ff.) represents elders dispensing justice. They sit round in a sacred circle and judge the issue relating to some question concerning the recompense for a

---

[11] As Loewe (2006: ch. 1) and Lewis (1999: 354) especially have emphasized, a considerable body of texts from the late Warring States period onward is devoted to considering ways in which to try to curb the arbitrary exercise of power by autocratic rulers.

murder that has come before them. Two talents of gold have been set
down in the middle to be awarded to the judge who gives the 'straight-
est judgement' (*dikē*) in his speech, though it is not explained who
contributed this valuable prize, nor how it was decided who should get
it. Nor is the case itself clearly described. On one interpretation, one
side says that it has paid compensation for the murdered man in full,
but the other claims that it has received nothing. But on another
reading of the Greek, the first party seeks to absolve itself by making
full payment (in the future) while the second refuses to accept any
compensation. Not only is the Greek text indeterminate, but we
should bear in mind that this is a description, in words, of a scene
that is supposed to be portrayed on the Shield. However, what are
described are clearly some more or less formal arrangements used to
resolve a case that otherwise threatened to degenerate into feuding
and revenge.

The term used for 'judgement' in that text is *dikē*, the standard later
Greek word both for justice and penalty. But elsewhere in Homer that
term is used without any overtones of justice, simply to describe what
is usually the case. In the *Odyssey* at 14.59 the slave Eumaeus excuses
himself for giving his guest, the unrecognized Odysseus, a small gift,
saying it is the *dikē* (custom) of slaves such as himself to do so, since
they are in fear of those who rule them. At *Odyssey* 11.218, when
Odysseus tries to embrace his mother in the underworld and finds she
is an insubstantial shade, she says that that is the *dikē*, the way things
are, when mortals die.

Themis is a second term with a similar range of meaning. When at
Iliad 9.132 ff., Agamemnon, promising to hand back Briseis to Achilles, swears that he has not been to bed with her, as is *themis* among
humans, that indicates simply what is usual, rather than what is
lawful, let alone moral. But Eumaeus uses that term, in the same
speech from which I have just quoted, to say it is not *themis* to
dishonour strangers, and there it means what is right and proper,
for all strangers and poor people are under the protection of Zeus (*Od.*
14.56–8). Again at *Odyssey* 9.112 ff. in the account of the non-human
society of the Cyclopes, we are told that they lack *themistes*, that is
the rules and regulations and customs that govern proper human
interaction.

Zeus elsewhere too is sometimes cast in the role of protector of
human justice. At *Iliad* 16.384 ff. he is said to send a furious rainstorm

as a punishment on men who 'violently give crooked judgements [or ordinances, *themistes* again] in the assembly and who drive out justice [*dikē*] paying no attention to the wrath of the gods'. Yet as later authors were quick to point out, in Homer the people and behaviour that were approved by one god might well be anathema to another, and Zeus himself is famously hoodwinked when seduced on Mount Ida by Hera in *Iliad* 14.292ff.

But in Hesiod the principle that Zeus rewards the good and punishes the wicked is made more explicit. At *Works and Days* 225f. the good are said to be 'those who give straight judgements to strangers and to natives and who do not stray from what is just'. The just city enjoys peace and prosperity while the unjust suffers plague and famine. For the misdeeds of a single man, indeed, Zeus may punish a whole city (*Works and Days* 240). The message is that the cosmic dispensation is in good order. But meanwhile among the humans with whom Hesiod and his brother have to deal there are 'bribe-devouring kings', rather different from the elders on the Shield of Achilles. Hesiod is certainly not afraid to criticize them. But the bitterness with which he does so, and the stridency of his invocation of the eventual retribution of Zeus, suggest that he is more hopeful than optimistic that those in power will listen to him and mend their ways.

The contrast with the ideas we find in the poems of Solon in the early sixth century BCE is striking. He was responsible for constitutional reforms at Athens when he was called in to help resolve the political and economic crises from which it was suffering. Law codes covering a wide range of topics begin to be attested, in Greece, from the century before Solon, though some of the figures involved, Lycurgus at Sparta, Zaleucus at Locri Epizephyrii, belong to legend rather than to history. We know of fragmentary laws from Dreros that date from around 600 BCE, but the first detailed epigraphic evidence for a fairly comprehensive code comes from Gortyn.[12] This dates from the mid-fifth century, though some of its provisions are thought to go back at least to the previous century (Willetts 1967). Like Hammurabi, it distinguishes penalties both by the status of the

---

[12] However, just how systematic the Gortyn code can be said to be, and indeed how far it is correct to see even Solon's legal provisions as aiming at comprehensiveness, continue to be the topic of scholarly debate: see Davies 1996, Osborne 1997, Hölkeskamp 2005.

individual committing the offence, and by that of the person against whom it was committed.

Solon's provisions were at once political and legal. Although eligibility to hold office was restricted to the higher property classes, every citizen had the right to participate in the assembly and in the law courts (*dikastēria*). The key move, as Aristotle recognized (*Athenian Constitution* 9.1), was that, given the right to vote there, the people (*dēmos*) controlled the constitution. Aristotle underlines the difficulty Solon had in persuading people of his impartiality, a topic he repeatedly addresses in his extant poems. Like Hesiod, he invokes Zeus as sanction, comparing the swiftness and certainty of the vengeance he takes on the unrighteous with the sudden scattering of the clouds by the wind in spring (poem 13: 17 ff.). But Solon puts far more emphasis than Hesiod had done on human responsibility for human affairs. It is from its great men that ruin comes to a city (poem 9). The Athenians should not blame the gods for their troubles: they are responsible for them themselves (poem 11). As for his own efforts to secure justice, the earth itself will, in time, bear witness on his behalf, for when he abolished loans secured upon the person and cancelled debts, he removed the boundary-stones that marked estates that had been mortgaged (poem 36), though he is careful to insist that he 'wrote ordinances for commoner and nobleman alike, making justice straight for each one'. The language of Zeus' sanction continues. But Solon is fully aware that the fate of his constitution rested with the sovereign people of Athens.

Solon was appointed to sort out the problems of a single city-state. But Greek awareness of the differences in the laws and customs that different states, both Greek and non-Greek, adopted comes, in the fifth century, to be expressed in a whole variety of writers, historians, tragedians, medical writers, and philosophers. Homer's geography was largely imaginary, though Egypt already figures as an important country. But as knowledge of both Egypt and Persia increased, the Greeks began to realize the antiquity, the power, and the magnificence of some of the civilizations by which they were surrounded. They were 'barbarians' for sure—just as the ancient Chinese dismissed their non-Chinese neighbours as inferior peoples. But while the Chinese might easily despise the Xiong Nu, it was far more difficult for the Greeks to ignore the impressiveness of the pyramids or the achievements of the empire controlled by the Great King of Persia.

But if the *nomoi* (the term covers laws, customs, and conventions) of different peoples differ, where did that leave those that any Greek state set up? The issue could hardly be ignored, given the frequency with which political and legal institutions were debated in theory, and constitutions and laws in fact modified. Several different types of reaction or response appear in fifth- and fourth-century writings on the topic. The realists, or cynics, argued that the laws had no natural, objective, basis. They were instituted in a forlorn attempt by the weak to curb the strong (as Callicles puts it in Plato's *Gorgias*) or were promulgated by the strong merely to give a veneer of legitimacy to their appropriation of power (Thrasymachus in the *Republic*). Xerxes' invasion of Greece was not just (*dikaios*) according to the *nomos* the Greeks maintained, but according to nature—indeed according to the law (*nomos* again, *Gorgias* 483e) of nature, what he did was just, for as the Athenians put it in the Melian dialogue (Thucydides 5.105) it is 'a necessity of nature always to rule whatever one can'. On that view the one principle that could claim objectivity is that might is right—a principle all too obviously applicable to the relations between states, as well as to those of rival groups within them.

An even more extreme position is found in Antiphon's *On Truth*. There it is conceded that one should not break the laws and customs of one's own state if there is any danger of being found out. But otherwise one should follow 'nature'. The laws are artificial agreements. To break them, if you are not found out, does you no harm: but going against what is natural (and that would mean not acting to maximize your own interests) *does* harm you whether or not you are discovered.

Against these attacks on the basis on which the law could be held to secure justice, two main types of argument were mounted. There are, some claimed, exceptions to the relativity of *nomoi*. In Sophocles' *Antigone* (453 ff.) Antigone says that the obligation to bury her dead brother is an unwritten but sure law/custom (*nomima*) set up by the gods, that no mortal can gainsay. Elsewhere Herodotus has Xerxes, no less, say that the law that heralds should not be killed holds for all humans (7.136). Pericles in Thucydides says that the Athenians obey not just the laws that have been set up to protect the oppressed, but also those that are unwritten but acknowledged to bring shame on those who break them (2.37.3).

A debate between Hippias and Socrates in Xenophon's *Memorabilia* (4.4.18ff.) serves to illustrate both how common the idea of unwritten laws was and how difficult it was to specify what they covered. The two of them agree that worshipping the gods and honouring one's parents count as such, and Socrates includes incest and is unmoved by Hippias' observation that that is not universally upheld. He is not swayed either by the analogous argument in the case of repaying benefits, for that too is a rule that is often broken. However, the claim that transgression of divine laws never goes unpunished is precisely the point at which (as in Hesiod) theodicy degenerates into what the realist will call mere wishful thinking.

The second line of argument defending justice comes from Plato, that committing injustice positively harms the soul (the precise opposite of Antiphon's claim when he said that it was being unselfish that harmed you). Injustice is like a disease damaging the soul and disrupting the balance within it. No one wants to be diseased: so if you appreciate that that is what injustice does to you, you would avoid all wrongdoing. The paradoxical conclusion is that no one does wrong willingly, but only out of ignorance of the dire consequences to their psychic well-being. Virtue, as in the other Socratic paradox, turns out to be knowledge.

The whole argument turns on what happens to our souls: it does not depend on our relations with other people, nor on the harm that wrongdoing does them. Nor is our reputation relevant—for it is recognized that the truly just person is sometimes thought to be unjust and vice versa. The thought-experiment with Gyges' ring in the *Republic* (359cff.) is designed precisely to bracket any consideration of how others rate you. Given a ring that ensures your invisibility, how would you behave? If you really understood that injustice damages your soul, you would never commit wrongdoing even if you were never to be found out.

In Plato this set of ideas is underpinned first by his metaphysics—the transcendent Forms guarantee the objectivity of Justice itself, the Good itself, and the rest—and then by his cosmology, his belief that the universe is under the control of a benevolent, craftsmanlike force. The cosmos as a whole manifests order, regularity, and indeed beauty, a theme developed especially in the *Timaeus*, with astronomical among other arguments. On this account human legislators should model themselves on the pattern set by the divine creator of the universe himself. Just as the divine Craftsman introduces order into the world, so it is the duty of human lawgivers to imitate the pattern of a just cosmos in just social and political institutions. Whereas in the

Republic he had put his faith in the philosopher-kings as guarantors of justice, by the time he came to write his last work, the *Laws*, those human paragons of virtue are seen to be too idealistic and the focus shifts on the role of the laws themselves. The fiction of the founding of the new state of Magnesia enables Plato to start from scratch and to evade the problems of transforming existing political and legal arrangements. Many detailed provisions in the new laws will be subject to modification during the first ten years, but thereafter, once perfected, they will be declared to be immutable (*Laws* 772b–c). However, whatever aura of unchallengeability Plato hopes they will acquire, there is a clear sense that he realizes that merely human laws, however admirable, are always subject to human second thoughts.

Plato's psychological argument for justice is certainly original: his cosmological one belongs to a long line of Greek philosophical speculations in which the idea of the orderly cosmos is conveyed with a variety of political and technological images, not that earlier philosophers agreed on quite how that order was to be represented. Some of the Presocratics (Xenophanes, Anaxagoras, Diogenes of Apollonia) saw the universe as under the control of a single, king-like, power: but others (Anaximander, Empedocles) pictured the relations between cosmic forces as a balance of equal powers, while Heraclitus even used the images of War and Strife to convey the idea of constant interaction between opposites.

But not only did the philosophers not agree among themselves: they did not cut much ice with those who were in positions of actual political power and responsibility. Plato embarked on an expedition, indeed several, to try to persuade Dionysius II, the ruler of Syracuse, to take up something like the role of a philosopher-king—only with an eventual disastrous outcome. Plato was thrown into prison and had to be rescued by Archytas, a figure who certainly looked far more like an actual philosopher-king since he combined great originality in both mathematics and philosophy with a successful career as a statesman, being elected repeatedly as general in his home state of Tarentum. But from Plato's point of view Archytas could not do as a model. His state was a democracy and so liable to all the shortcomings that Plato associated with any such regime: besides, being elected was not the way you became Plato's style of philosopher-king.

The great disadvantage, in Plato's eyes, of the actual institutions of Athens was that the assemblies and law courts were in the control of ordinary citizens who had no training, no particular expertise whether political or legal. To others, of course, that was precisely the great strength of democracy. In practice, however, although the citizens of Athens were in no sense professionals, they acquired very considerable experience in political and legal decision-taking (far more than the vast majority of the citizens of modern Western-style democracies). The business of the assembly was prepared by the council, which had representatives from each of the tribes, who served in turn as *prytaneis*—a kind of executive body that was responsible for the day-to-day handling of affairs of state. But since no one was allowed to serve for more than a total of two years on the council, there was no question of an oligarchic or other faction gaining permanent control there. The assembly, constituted by the full citizen body, was where the real political power lay (Hansen 1983). It took decisions that ranged, in the fifth century, from whether to go to war or not, and even on the strategy and tactics of waging it, to the constitution itself. Moreover the officials who were appointed or chosen by lot to take responsibility for certain affairs were subject to two other forms of control. First there was the *dokimasia* in which their eligibility to hold office was examined. Then when they had finished their term, there was the *euthyna*, or scrutiny of how they had conducted themselves, and especially of their financial accounts.

Eventually in Athens the elaborate provision for the legal system included separate courts, under different magistrates, for different types of case. The council and assembly tried some cases themselves. The Areopagus had responsibility for certain types of religious cases and for homicide, though both its importance and its precise role changed over time. In addition we hear of no fewer than ten other courts, though not all were operational at the same time (MacDowell 1978: 35–6, cf. also Osborne 1985). These were the Odeum, the Painted Stoa, the New Court, the Inserted Court, the Court at Lycos, the Kallion, the Triangular, the Greater, and the Middle, as well as perhaps the most important of all, the Heliaia, the court presided over by the *thesmothetai*, the lawgivers.

Even though the main courts were under the control of magistrates, they did not act in any way like modern judges. Both verdicts and sentences were decided by the 'dicasts', who combined the roles of judge and jury, deciding questions of law as well as of guilt and innocence. They often numbered several hundred, and we even hear of cases tried by the entire annual panel of 6,000 dicasts. Manning the courts took up a large amount of time of a considerable proportion of the citizen body, and from Pericles' time payment was instituted for jury service. Moreover the dicasts for any one case were chosen by lot on the day from those on the panel who volunteered. This proved a generally effective device against attempts to prejudice the outcome by bribing the jurors, not just because there were often so many of them, but also because no one could tell in advance who the jurors for any given case on any given day were going to be.

One of the most striking features of Greek democracies was the principle of equality before the law. Every citizen had access to the legal system and decisions were there taken on the principle of one man one vote.[13] However, we have to qualify this egalitarianism in several respects, most importantly, first, in that it extended only to adult males who were full citizens. Slaves, foreigners, and women had some rights, but not the whole range of those that citizens enjoyed, and in particular not the right to belong to the assembly and so participate in the political decision-taking process. Then two other anti-egalitarian features should also be mentioned. As remarked already for the Gortyn code, the seriousness of some offences varied according to the status first of the person committing it and then of the person offended. Finally we should not imagine that free speech in the assemblies meant that the opinions of all the citizens carried equal weight. It is clear that powerful individuals, wealthy or well-born ones for instance, had more than an ordinary share of influence.

One strength of the Athenian legal system was that it was, even with those important reservations that I have mentioned, egalitarian, and another was that, as noted, the fact that the jurors were chosen by lot meant that there was less chance of bribery there—and virtually no opportunity to influence their composition. Yet to judge from the number of cases of perjury we hear about, bribing witnesses (as

---

[13] Yet one possible disadvantage of the principle of a decision by majority vote was that there was less incentive to continue debate to see whether a consensus could be reached: cf. Lloyd 2005b: 128f. Moreover, as Cohen has argued (1995: 87), frequent recourse to the courts had complex consequences. The litigiousness of the Athenians could sometimes be a safety valve to prevent feuding between individuals or groups from degenerating into physical violence. But it could and often did have the effect of perpetuating such feuding—as prosecution was followed by counter-prosecution and ever-increasing numbers of supporters were drawn in, on either side, as both parties strove to wipe out an earlier legal defeat by a new victory.

opposed to jurors) was common enough. One weakness was that vexatious prosecutions (by *sykophantai*) were common. Again impartial witnesses were a rarity: in general, indeed, witnesses were not *expected* to be impartial. Those called on were generally relatives or friends or others who had some obligation to those who asked them to testify on their behalf (Herman 1987, cf. Humphreys 1985, Todd 1990). The prejudices of dicasts, and their gullibility in failing to see through the corrupt informers by whom they were surrounded, are not only satirized in comedy but denounced at length by, for example, Isocrates (15.15–38). Those who manipulated the assembly and the courts often themselves complained, in a standard rhetorical trope, that those bodies were subject to manipulation (Thucydides 3.37–8).

We should certainly not imagine that the institutions of democracy, at Athens or anywhere else, ensured clear-headed, well-reasoned, just decisions in political or legal matters, any more than did the institutions of oligarchy or of monarchy—which equally reflected the interests of those who set them up. The actual record of Athens in the fifth century is, to put it mildly, mixed. It includes miscarriages of justice not just against individuals (such as Socrates) but against whole states. What had started as a defensive alliance against the threat of Persian attack was turned, by Athens, into an empire, and those states that stepped out of line, or did not join in, were savagely coerced.

Most of the writers on whom we rely, Thucydides, Plato, Aristotle especially, were critical of democracy. Many retreated to the idealistic view that the best safeguard of justice was virtue, combining that with policies for inculcating that in the young. But prescriptions for education inevitably reflected the view their authors took on whether humans, left to their own devices, would be selfish, greedy, and unprincipled, or whether they would be capable of acting justly and fairly, provided that they had not themselves been wronged—or even if they had. The anti-democratic, authoritarian, former view, in one version or another, is the one that dominates in our sources. Aristotle pinned his hopes on the idea that rulers and the ruled would be content each to take their turn in either role. That is idealistic to the point of naivety. But when in the *Politics* 1269a19–24 he warned that changes to the law were liable to undermine the authority of the law itself, his basic conservatism is apparent (Brunschwig 1980). At the same time his ideas on the inadequacy of the law on its own to secure justice are supplemented by sophisticated reflections on equity, *epieikeia* (Brunschwig 1996). This is a principle that aims, among other things, to ensure that the complexities of the individual case are taken into account. As he puts it at *Nicomachean Ethics* 1137b26ff., equity corrects the law when it is defective owing to its universality.

The Greeks were extraordinarily energetic in exploring the pros and cons of different legal and political arrangements, not just in abstract theoretical debates but in situations where they could and did implement the policies they approved.[14] But hardly surprisingly they found no solution, in principle, let alone in practice, that guaranteed justice. Many of the institutions they adopted reflected the small-scale, face-to-face, nature of Greek city-states.[15] By the same token, however, those states were no match for the rising power of Macedonia and then of the kingdoms carved out of Alexander's conquests by his successors, most of which then fell, in turn, to the might of Rome.

In those regimes the law reverted to patterns we associate with central government, whether monarchical or (in the Roman republic at least) oligarchic. The extent to which the dispensation of justice depended on your ability to persuade your peers of the merits of the case varied accordingly. But it came increasingly to be in the hands of officials, magistrates appointed to positions of authority, more or less venial, corrupt or impartial, as luck would have it, though they operated eventually under the Roman empire, within the framework of impressively detailed legal codes. The sequence of enormously influential Roman writers on jurisprudence not only drew up comprehensive provisions covering every aspect of law, but also distinguished its various domains, as for instance between the *ius civile* (that applied to Roman citizens) and the *ius gentium* (in one sense equated with the *ius naturale* that applied to non-Romans as well). Their work formed the basis of most subsequent European elaborations in the field, as Garnsey 2007, for instance, has shown in the case of property law. However, nowhere in later times did securing justice in private affairs with fellow citizens and others depend on the kinds of opportunities,

---

[14] But while we know from Aristotle that the doctrine of natural slaves was denied by some theorists, no attempt was ever made to abolish that institution in Graeco-Roman antiquity, other than by force of arms by the slaves themselves.

[15] Aristotle thought the population of the ideal state should not be larger than could be addressed at a single assembly (*Politics* 1326b5ff.).

and hazards, that were presented by the mass dicasteries of classical Athens.

What lessons should be drawn, I may now ask in conclusion, from what has had to be, in so vast a field as the law, a particularly selective survey of just some of the data? In view of their variety, it is not just difficult, but out of the question, to pronounce on what 'law' is and has been, across the board, let alone to attempt normative judgements on what it should be.[16] What we recognize as 'law' may be the name for the arrangements, whatever they may be, whereby a society uses some mode of coercion to ensure some kind of order: but what order that is, for whose benefit it is instituted or imposed, and how the arrangements work, differ radically. Different societies, contemporary or historical, have made very different provisions and used different institutions to administer justice, right wrongs, or secure order, provisions that imply considerable divergences in the underlying notion of law. Sometimes the dispensation of justice is under the aegis of the divine, but that is far from always the case. Often, punishable offences include far more than what we would consider criminal activities, for example breaking dietary rules. Sometimes it is not just humans who can be brought to trial, but also animals and inanimate objects.[17] The questions of who decides what counts as offences, and of what kind, and who determines what should happen when they have been committed, have been answered very differently in different societies. Sometimes the whole process is made as impersonal as possible: no human judge is involved, but the issue is decided by ordeal. But often particular individuals, specialists or those with particular authority, are given responsibility for seeing that things are as they should be and indeed for saying how they should be in the first place. Even though in both ancient China and Greece we find idealists expressing the view that government should be for the benefit of society as a whole, other writers—and sometimes the very same ones—also often

[16] Cohen 1995 mounts a successful attack on what used to be prevailing functionalist and evolutionary views of the development of the law, first the idea that the law always promotes the harmonious functioning of society, and secondly that one can distinguish between less and more evolved solutions to how that should be achieved.

[17] Provision for bringing animals and even inanimate objects to trial is found in Athenian law (MacDowell 1978: 117–18) and figures also in Plato's *Laws* (873d–e). Similar ideas recur in the European Middle Ages (see Evans 1906).

recognize that in practice the law just serves the interests of the powerful, whether they be kings, or wealthy oligarchs, or democracy itself.

Thus at the limit the study of law shades into the study of human social relations in all their complexity. But how far does it seem possible to arrive at some conclusions on the three main interrelated questions that I have been concerned with throughout these studies, namely on the role of elites, the constitution of learned disciplines, and the possibilities of innovation? The dispensation of justice, I said, is not always in the hands of a corps of officials trained for the task. Often, head men or chiefs are in charge in virtue of their political position, not of their understanding of the niceties of the law. There will be no occasion for learned scrutiny of written codes, where none such exists, though of course there may be disputes over what orally transmitted custom or tradition lays down. But the more elaborate the written code, the more that will call for expertise in its interpretation.

When a professional cadre of experts is constituted, the learning that marks them out may be a matter of their command of a body of texts, and if that includes some that are considered sacred, the expertise they have to display may be as much religious as legal. Islam provides a striking instance where different levels of the law are distinguished, some with direct divine authority, others only with indirect. The proliferation of laws and precedents in ancient China may be a response to the intricacies of the cases that came before the courts. But it is obvious that the more complex the subject, the greater the sense an elite cadre may have of the distinctiveness of the knowledge and experience they command. It is then not in their own interests to simplify the provisions they have to put into practice.

The possibilities of innovation, equally clearly, correlate, at least up to a point, with the relationship between law and religion, and between law and the political regime in question. The laws that God has ordained are immutable. Only outsiders, heretics, blasphemers, would question the authority of the book that is the basis of the claim that God did indeed ordain them. In societies under the rule of kings, everything will depend on how far the ruler himself, and his ministers, are open to advice. We saw that in China there is a well-developed custom of reprimanding rulers when they are thought to have stepped out of line. Thus they may be told that their Mandate is under threat whether because their rule is too harsh, or conversely because it is not harsh enough. When the laws are seen to have been made by humans, then other humans can make a bid to change them. But, as the experience of Greece exemplifies, radical innovation in legal matters is bound to be bought at the price of instability. If the law depends on consensus, and is modified in response to changes in opinion, how durable is the new consensus? Indeed how much of a consensus remains?

Great individual lawgivers may rely on their personal authority to gain acceptance, though of course that is no guarantee of how long their work will last. When new laws or regulations are the outcome of a majority vote, there is the ever-present risk that the next assembly will countermand them. Learned elites, in this context too, are a mixed blessing, with the converse strengths and weaknesses. Their very professionalism may carry weight: but by the same token it may inhibit criticism and restrict innovation, when allowed at all, to the contributions of members of the elite cadre itself.

Meanwhile, to end on a realistic, if pessimistic, note, if the tensions between law and morality are often strained within any given nation-state, the situation as regards international relations is even more acute. Of course we now have provisions that set out to regulate commercial disputes, intellectual property rights, even territorial boundaries, and do so with greater or less effectiveness. In addition to the International Court of Justice, we now have an International Criminal Court. Yet its operations have to be acknowledged to be highly selective and the background assumptions of the judges in question are far from uniform. It is predominantly those who are considered by the United States or the European Union to have committed war crimes, crimes against humanity, genocide, who are brought to justice—if they can be caught—in processes that to ordinary people appear enormously cumbersome, protracted, and expensive. As for the enforcement of resolutions taken by the United Nations, that depends on getting agreement in the Security Council to send armed forces as 'peacekeepers'—where decisions can be thwarted by the veto of any one of the permanent members. Nothing remotely resembling a standing international law-enforcement body exists or is likely to be possible, for two main reasons. The first relates to ongoing disagreements on moral questions. While there may be a consensus that genocide is evil, what counts as such is often hotly disputed even though sometimes with highly specious arguments used by those who seek to deny that any genocide occurred. The second and maybe more important factor relates to the reluctance of most states to yield any portion of their sovereignty even when individual politicians may privately acknowledge that it is in the interests of humanity as a whole that they should do so. Genuine political leadership, in that regard, is often in short supply.

The law, we must conclude, operates more or less efficiently within the context of intra-state relations. But unwritten laws, to encapsulate shared moral principles, remain as much in the realm of utopian dreaming as they ever did in the days of ancient Greece and China.

7
Religion

By what criteria should we judge a belief or a practice to be 'religious'? If we are content to settle for an ostensive definition, we can readily agree, to start with, that Christianity, Islam, Judaism are religions. But obviously we should not limit religions just to monotheistic ones, for we have also to include polytheistic ones, modern Hinduism, for example, or ancient Greek and Roman polytheisms. And what about the more, or less, philosophically oriented theisms and pantheisms? Should some idea of a personal god or gods be a defining characteristic? If so, Buddhism becomes problematic, as does Confucianism, though both these have or have had priesthoods, which on some views is a typical institution of religion. Again if we chose to make belief in a single—usually benevolent—supreme deity constitutive of religion, dualist systems such as Zoroastrianism would be ruled out. Shinto and the Dao hold, in some sense, to the divinity of nature and accordingly have a very different sense of the numinous and the spiritual from that which is associated with anthropomorphic deities. While belief in gods in the form of humans is undoubtedly widespread, there are evidently major obstacles to accepting such a thesis as that put forward by Guthrie (1993) that the tendency to anthropomorphize is the major source of religions across the world.

Many different suggestions have been proposed as to the origins of religion and concerning the cognitive constraints under which it operates: we shall be considering some of these in due course. The relations between religion and society, religion and science, religion and morality, are all problematic. One issue that needs to be mentioned straight away concerns 'natural' religion. Some have held that religious experience is universal, often introducing a distinction between 'natural' and 'revealed' knowledge of god to that end. To be sure, that contrast has itself been construed in very different ways.

Rousseau provides one classic statement of the division, associating 'revealed' religion with the dogmatic, but he did so in a context where he was very conscious of the need to protect his own position in the turbulent and dangerous controversies, between Protestants and Catholics of different persuasions, of his day. That did not prevent *Émile* from being condemned, and indeed in places publicly burned, in the very year of its publication, 1762.

Now if there is such a thing as natural religion, that is compatible with it taking a variety of forms, reflecting a variety of modes of religious experience. But if, at the opposite extreme, there is one source of true revelation, most of what may pass as the religions of the world has to be discounted as deluded, or worse condemned as heresy. This is an important theme in Harrison 2002, who even goes so far as to claim that the concepts of 'religion' and of 'the religions' (in the plural) were invented in the Enlightenment, in particular in the seventeenth and eighteenth centuries in England.[1] But while the issue of the naturalness of religion certainly came to the fore in the controversies surrounding the Reformation, and in the wake of the development of science, the questions of the origins of beliefs in the gods, and of how they should be worshipped, were intensely debated already in pagan Graeco-Roman antiquity—and indeed, as we shall see, also in ancient China. Harrison indeed concedes that the *locus classicus* for the contrast between natural and revealed knowledge of God is in the New Testament (Romans 1: 18–23)—which undermines, rather, his thesis that religion 'did not exist in antiquity' (Harrison 2002: 14). In this area, as in our other studies, it is vital not to impose modern Western categories and to do justice to the great variety of ideas and practices to be found in different societies across the world.

Indeed the enormously rich ethnographic records provide abundant evidence concerning that variety, much of it germane to the question of the roles of elites in this field. In some societies the spirit world is accessed by special figures, 'shamans', who act as intermediaries between that world and everyday life,[2] but in many others there are no such specialists. In many, rites of passage have to be carried out as

---

[1] Cf. Masuzawa 2005 on 'world religions', where she takes that discourse to be a matter of European history and its manifestations to be 'very much an American phenomenon' connected indeed with university curricula (Masuzawa 2005: 32–3).

[2] Some of the extensive secondary literature on shamanism is mentioned in Ch. 4, n. 4.

the individual becomes increasingly incorporated into the society and introduced to its more profound and arcane concepts and practices concerning relations not just with other human beings, but also with the divine world.

In the extreme case of the Baktaman, studied by Barth (1975), there are six or seven stages in such initiations, where at each successive stage the individual is taught that what was learned at the previous one is deeply flawed, morally unsound indeed. They discover for instance that in an earlier rite they broke an important taboo, not just inadvertently, but because that was what they had been instructed to do. The whole sequence is under the control of elders, but only the most senior members of the society can have any confidence that there are no further surprises in store for them—and that merely in virtue of their age.

Again, some religions have elaborate bodies of myth underpinning their beliefs and rituals, in others there is far less by way of narrative support. How far does any story of the origins of the world and of the current order belong to the religious register—where the entities that are invoked may be gods and spirits, or world-masses, water, earth, sky construed as divine? Should we suppose that an entity has to be the object of explicit worship for the attitude towards it to be counted as religious? Or is it enough that whatever is labelled divine evokes awe?

A similar demarcation issue arises in relation to ancestor worship, a central feature of the rituals and beliefs in many societies, including, for example, in China in antiquity (see, for example, Puett 2002) and still, if to a lesser extent, today. What should be considered the distinctive characteristics that convert gestures of affectionate remembrance into elements of religious praxis? When does a collection of treasured heirlooms turn into a veritable shrine? Is this a matter of prayers and rituals on special occasions, or does it depend on some belief that the dead are intentional beings and are capable of being offended as well as of helping to ensure the prosperity of the living? But what kind of active agents are they supposed to be and what powers do they have? More generally, can gods or saints intervene directly in human lives, and how do they do that? Do they underpin humans' attempts to foretell the future, and how does that occur? Are the faithful supposed to be able to understand the workings of the Holy Spirit, for instance, or is it enough just to believe that some such manifestation of the Godhead *is* at work?

Religious belief has often been associated with an anxiety over death (Tylor 1891). But when the dead are thought still to haunt the living is this because their rites of passage to the world of the dead have not been correctly performed, or alternatively because they themselves were sinners? Is life after death granted to everyone? When reincarnation is an article of faith, it may be conceived as a mechanism whereby justice is secured. The very fact of being reborn may be a sign of imperfection, when, that is, the desired goal is to escape the cycle of rebirth, as in some Greek beliefs and in Buddhism. The nature of the reincarnation that awaits the individual may be thought to reflect the way that individual has behaved in this life, or in previous ones. Your being reborn as a higher or as a lower creature reflects the moral quality of your behaviour and so may be a vehicle of cosmic rewards and punishments, as also, of course, without any idea of transmigration, is the belief in heaven and hell.

When, as in both ancient China and Greece, religious beliefs and practices came to be the subject of critical examination, just how the gods and spirits were supposed to be able to do what was attributed to them became a subject of controversy. Greek anthropomorphism had at least the advantage of vividness: statues of gods and goddesses in human form were everywhere in the temples, and divinities were brought on stage in both tragedy and comedy, sometimes clearly recognized by all as such, but sometimes incognito (as Dionysus initially in Euripides' *Bacchae*). But criticisms of the absurdity of the very idea of gods in human form began to be mounted from the sixth century BCE on. They are repeated by one philosopher after another, including by some of the most eminent, such as Plato. Meanwhile other attacks (as by the sophist Critias) advanced the cynical line that the gods were invented by some unnamed individual for the purposes of social control, to deter people from wrongdoing by the threat of divine retribution. Yet such rationalizations appear to have made little or no impact on the actual practices of the worship of anthropomorphic deities in the Graeco-Roman world. That certainly tends to favour those who would define religion not in terms of beliefs, but rather in terms of practices (cf. Keane 2008). Beliefs may come to be challenged (how are they to be justified?), while practices continue simply because tradition dictates that they should.

Similar developments occurred in China from the third century BCE when a number of writers explicitly rejected popular beliefs in spirits, ghosts, demons, and the like. Xunzi rationalized the origin of such beliefs, saying they arose from fear or confusion and denying that rites to propitiate them did any good.[3] Wang Chong in the first century CE in turn produced a battery of arguments to expose the errors, inconsistencies, and fallacies in many common beliefs.[4] Yet as in Greece, the attacks of the intellectuals seem to have had little effect in practice. The commitment to ancestor worship certainly continued to be strong. It was a major factor contributing to the legitimacy of imperial rule (Puett 2002), and at different times the state actively supported religious institutions, temples, and priesthoods associated with Daoism, Buddhism, and even the worship of Confucius (Overmyer et al. 1995, Robinet 1997).

One central and recurrent problem relates to the tension between the personal and the communal. Various traditions of mysticism have been attested in for example ancient pagan Greek religion, in Sufism, and in Christianity, where, for all their differences, what they all shared was experiences that were, in some sense, beyond the reach of words (see James 1902). That ineffability tended to block all ordinary comprehension, but for the faithful, it did not detract from, but rather often contributed to, the persona of the mystic as the role model of the truly religious.

Since the Romantic movement, especially, many in Western societies may believe that most religious experience is intensely personal. The worshipper has an intimate relationship with the god, saint, or spirit to whom he or she prays. At the same time much religious practice is a matter of group activity. Large masses gather in St Peter's Square to hear the Pope give a Christmas or an Easter blessing. Even larger ones circle the shrine at Mecca. However, when, as in some monotheistic religions, participation is enjoined, and any failure in that regard is subject to sanctions, then the personal convictions of the participants may be far less deeply engaged than when a single devout worshipper addresses his or her guardian spirit. The engagement of participants may in some circumstances be simply a response to a perceived need for social solidarity or merely a sign of great

---

[3] *Xunzi* 21, cf. Knoblock 1988–94, iii. 108–10.
[4] Of the many sections in the *Lun Heng* where Wang Chong takes up these themes, *ziran* (18: 365 ff.), *bushi* (24: 482 ff.), *qiguai* (3: 73 ff.), and *shizhi* (26: 519 ff.) are worth mentioning especially.

enjoyment in continuing the customs handed down through the generations. Yet it is clearly difficult to make either deep personal commitment, or communal participation, or a combination of the two, into defining characteristics of religion.

Another Western phenomenon of relatively recent date is the sense that religion is threatened by science, when some article of belief is seen to conflict with what science is able to establish—at least to most people's satisfaction.[5] True, there were ancient Greek antecedents for this, when certain natural philosophical ideas were thought to undermine common religious beliefs. Some certainly got into trouble for suggesting, for instance, that the sun is a red-hot stone comparable in size to the Peloponnese (Anaxagoras), while Aristophanes pilloried Socrates for similar views, a factor that contributed, according to Plato at least, to his trial and eventual execution, though it is important to register that that was a private prosecution, not one initiated by any equivalent to an established Church. However, the believed conflict took on an altogether more serious aspect with the rise of science in the seventeenth century, when that was seen to contradict the teaching of the Bible.[6]

Faced with that problem, the first tactic often tried, and still in use today, is to deny that science had indeed established conclusively what it purported to show, whether it be heliocentricity, or the great age of the earth, or the evolution of species. But a more subtle response was to suggest that the words of some sacred text that appeared to conflict with what science maintained were to be understood in some special

[5] Needham 1925 contains a series of articles that are eloquent testimony both to what was perceived at the time to be a deep-seated conflict between religion and science, and to the variety of proposed 'solutions' to the 'problem'. Malinowski's chapter, entitled 'Magic Science and Religion', still adopts the framework of evolutionary hypotheses which had been at the core of Frazer's work as well as Tylor's. According to such views, those three— but in the order magic, then religion, then science—represented three phases in the development of culture (cf. Tambiah 1990). That idea has certainly gone out of fashion. But there still remain the problems of demarcating religion from magic and from other modes of belief and practice such as theurgy, demonology, theosophy, even rank superstition. For a more recent discussion of the problems of the relationship between science and religion, see e.g. Brooke 1991.

[6] Yet paradoxically enough, many of those in the forefront of ancient and early modern investigations of nature were deeply religious persons, seeing the regularities of nature as testimony to the work of a benevolent creator God. Some modern historians have accordingly considered scientific research to owe a good deal to a belief in God, not to have undermined any such belief, as in the case of Weber's now heavily criticized thesis of the influence of what he called the Protestant Ethic on the rise of capitalism and other modern modes of rationality (Weber (1930) 2001).

way, for example merely figuratively. Indeed the figurative understanding of aspects of religious discourse is often favoured in other contexts besides those involving some perceived conflict with science, as in many of the paradoxes that permeate religious beliefs, as I shall discuss further below. In the Christian doctrines of the Trinity, the Virgin Birth, and Transubstantiation, for instance, there has been a constant tension between, on the one hand, the need to take these articles of faith literally, and on the other, the difficulty of doing so—and the corresponding need to have recourse to the idea that discourse about God is exceptional. Some have argued that where that discourse is concerned, the law of contradiction has to be suspended, while others have rejected any such move as stripping statements about God of the minimum requirements of intelligibility.[7]

When the tactic of the figurative in turn seemed inadequate, religion had rather to retreat and define the area over which it could claim authority as a matter not of the understanding of the natural world, but of salvation or of morality, though in the latter case a further potential rivalry emerged not from the side of science but from that of philosophy, from which some might argue religion borrows most of its ontological and epistemological arguments, as well as some of its moral ones, in any event. Yet something of a victory could be snatched from the jaws of apparent defeat, when religion could insist that it was indeed a domain apart, ministering not to a need for scientific explanations, nor even to one for a basis for morality and social justice, but rather to a sense that humans had more to live for than could be catered for by merely mundane concepts of well-being, namely a secure relationship with god.

It soon becomes clear that most attempts at providing crisp necessary and sufficient conditions for a belief or a practice to count as religious run into severe obstacles. A quick comparison between different types of approach reveals extraordinary varieties and discrepancies. Geertz (1973: 90ff.) for instance offered an extended commentary on his proposed multi-part definition, namely that religion is '(1) a system of symbols which acts to (2) establish powerful, pervasive, and long-lasting moods and motivations in men by (3) formulating conceptions of a general order of existence and (4)

---

[7] Dascal 2006: 237ff. reports the controversy on just that issue between Leibniz and Honoré Fabri in the late 17th century.

clothing these conceptions with such an aura of factuality that (5) the moods and motivations seem uniquely realistic'. But Horton (1960), criticizing Durkheim's view of religion as derived from human social relations, put it that 'religion can be looked upon as an extension of the field of people's social relationships beyond the confines of purely human society', though this was an extension in which humans see themselves as 'dependent on their non-human alters' (Horton 1960: 211).[8] Yet if we go back to Tylor (1891: i.424) religion was, on a minimum definition, simply a matter of a 'belief in Spiritual Beings' (cf. Goody 1961).

Thus for some, mood or emotion is the key, for others, a sense of what transcends merely human capabilities, for yet others rather the covert ideological underpinning of human social relations, and that is before we get to Marx's famous dictum, that religion is the opium of the masses, designed to hoodwink them and divert their attention from the class struggle. A recognized priesthood, set places of worship, well-marked rituals, a sacred text may all have claims to be sufficient conditions. However, the possible circularity in such formulations is obvious in the use of the terms 'priesthood', 'worship', 'ritual', and 'sacred' themselves. Moreover to treat any of these as necessary conditions is no doubt to be unduly restrictive. On the other hand, just to appeal to some sense of spirituality is open to the opposite objection of being far too loose, as also is any appeal to some idea of powers other than, and stronger than, mere human ones. Those who recognize no god and subscribe to no organized, institutionalized, faith, may be awestruck by the power of a tsunami or an earthquake, but not think of those in religious terms at all.

But if, as many have pointed out, the difficulties of definition are formidable (cf. e.g. Saler 2000, Whitehouse 2004), we may still tentatively identify certain recurrent, if not universal, features of what are

---

[8] In a later article, however, Horton argued for closer analogies than are normally recognized between African traditional thought and Western science (Horton 1970), though few have followed his lead. Both share, indeed, a commitment to invisible entities: but the way they proceed to use them exhibits fundamental differences. Among the important contributions to the debate between 'intellectualist' and 'symbolic' interpretations of religion, sparked in large measure, by Horton, are Sperber 1975, 1985 and Skorupski 1976. That controversy was part of an even more extensive debate on understanding 'apparently irrational beliefs' (cf. also Winch 1970, MacIntyre 1970, and already Wittgenstein in his lectures on religion, notes on which were eventually published in 1966).

generally accepted as religious beliefs. Boyer (1994, 2001) has argued, with some plausibility, that one such recurrent feature is the combination of common-or-garden ideas—to do with agents, motives, more or less transparent cause–effect relations—and highly counter-intuitive ones (cf. also Pyysiäinen 2001, Pyysiäinen and Anttonen 2002, Atran 2002). It is certainly the case that many religions exploit paradox. God is omnipresent, for example. We understand well enough what it is to be in some location, and to be in one location generally rules out being in any other. But such a rule may be suspended where divinity is concerned, indeed not just divinity itself. Shamans are reported to be able to leave their bodies and travel to another world to commune with the spirits that live there, while their bodies remain where they are for all to see. In Greek antiquity there are stories of wise men such as Abaris and Aristeas who were able to transport themselves to the spirit world (Bolton 1962), and Pythagoras was said to have been seen in two different places at once.

Of course it is recognized that such events do not normally happen: indeed a claim that they have happened in some particular instance may ordinarily be greeted with some scepticism.[9] But religion specializes, one might say, in the abnormal, the miraculous, often treating it as a test of the faith of the faithful *that* they believe. As Tertullian in the early third century CE put it: 'the Son of God is dead: this is to be believed, since it is absurd. Having been buried, he rose again: this is certain because it is impossible.'[10] The sacred thus marks itself out from the profane: yet the profane still has to serve as the yardstick from which the sacred deviates. This is true as a matter of analysis, though some religions claim, to be sure, that they are all-embracing.

---

[9] I documented this in my brief discussion of shamanism in Ch. 4 at n. 6, while pointing out that it is one thing to express doubts about one particular shaman, quite another to be sceptical about shamanic experiences as a whole. Obviously the difficulties of nonconformity are greater in a society that adopts a monotheistic religion, since those who do not adhere to it will be categorized as infidels, not just as sceptics. Moreover such a religion will usually have its own methods of legitimating its priests and officiants, and sanctioning them too if they step out of line, so that the gap between how an individual performs and how the system as a whole functions is less liable to open up. The phenomenon of a hierarchy closing ranks in the face of a perceived shortfall from an ideal standard of behaviour on the part of its priests can, to be sure, be illustrated from 20th-cent. examples as well as those from earlier times.

[10] Tertullian, *On the Flesh of Christ*, ch. 5. What he wrote was 'credibile est, quia ineptum est' and 'certum est, quia impossibile est', on which a group of variant expressions of this general type came to be modelled.

God oversees everything, every aspect of human life,[11] and every detail of the physical world, a view that tends to obliterate the distinction between sacred and profane.

In that context there are interesting analogies and disanalogies with other disciplines where authority claims are made, such as medicine. The exceptional nature of the expertise in question helps to ensure the special status of those claiming to possess it. But there is something of a double bind. The more exceptional that expertise is, the more the ordinary layperson may need persuading that it is genuine. Where medicine is concerned, patients may come to accept that the strange treatments they are offered—along with strange explanations of their rationale—do indeed produce some of the results claimed. They may have to revise their ideas of health and true well-being in the process. Failures, meanwhile, as I discussed, can be put down to the misapplication of the correct methods, not to any flaws in the methods themselves. The situation as regards prayers is in certain respects similar. Their *not* being answered may be ascribed to the lack of devotion of the person making the prayer. Conversely when some outcome corresponds to their wishes (they prayed for rain, and it came) that provides support enough for the general belief in the efficacy of prayer, despite the frequency of apparent failure.

Again, how a sacred religious book comes to be treated as such bears a generic resemblance to how a medical text (for instance) achieves canonical status. The cumulative approval of an inner circle of experts will count for much in the latter case, even though it will only be in extreme instances that positive divine revelation is claimed for a medical book. Sacred religious texts are, of course, far more often held to contain the words of God or of his prophet. But once the status of sacred is acquired, disbelief about the contents of the text will certainly have to be suspended—on pain of being excluded from the ranks of the faithful. In that context, in a way, the more counter-intuitive the ideas and stories the text contains—tales of miracles, mysteries, paradoxes—the better, at least from the point of view of using the text as a test to distinguish the true believer from the heathen infidel. Creeds and vows in general perform the function of establishing commitment.

---

[11] As I pointed out in Ch. 6, the idea of an all-seeing God has profound implications for morality, even though different areas of the law have more, or less, direct divine sanction.

This is in no way to doubt the sincerity of those who believe, nor indeed the comfort they may derive from their faith.[12] But the religious case differs from the medical one especially because religion is so tied up with issues of group solidarity. Not holding to medical orthodoxy carries no social penalties for the layperson, even though, as I noted, aspiring practitioners may find themselves not accepted into the ranks of the elite. But not subscribing to the religious beliefs and practices of the community to which you belong normally comes with high costs of potential isolation. The more universal the claims made for the religion, and the more the insistence that it is the one true faith, the greater will be the problems facing dissidents. Some will struggle to reconcile themselves with the doctrines and practices they disagree with, others will try to change them, and yet others will give up, abandon the faith, even suffer martyrdom, voluntarily or perforce. Evidently religion shares with the other learned disciplines we have discussed, that relations of power are implicated. Although religions are so variegated, a recurrent feature is the special authority to dictate to others that derives from a particular relationship to the divine.

But the question of who can claim such a special status raises an important issue. In some religions, or at least in some sects of some religions, it is only the religious leaders, the priests for example, who have direct access to God. Ordinary laypeople have to use intermediaries, the priests themselves, just as those priests may use saints as their route of access to the Godhead. But in other religious regimes, no such intercession is necessary, and everyone without exception can approach God directly. That does not mean that power relationships are, in the latter case, abolished altogether, for it is still usual for there to be some people, elders for instance, who are more authoritative in religious matters than others. Inspiration may be within the capability of all, but still be very unevenly distributed. The point is rather that intermediaries serve a double function, of giving access, but also of implying its difficulty and controlling its means.

If the domain of the sacred may be structured in a variety of ways, the further question of its relationship with political power is just as

---

[12] Boyd and Richerson (2006) outline the arguments that have been advanced for the view that religious belief may contribute to a society's success (however that is judged). However, as Geertz for one pointed out (1973: 114 ff.) religion does not necessarily deliver comfort, for it may well convey a heightened sense of the horrors of ordinary existence.

complex. Weber (1947) contrasted the personal charisma of many religious leaders with other modes of authority, 'traditional' and 'legal/political'. Those are useful analytic distinctions, though in practice they are sometimes eroded. In the early days of Christianity, as Peter Brown showed (2003: ch. 7), bishops were often the most important political leaders in their communities, combining religious with secular authority. Yet as Detienne's collaborators have recently reminded us (Detienne 2003) religious sects sometimes act as some kind of countervailing force to the political institutions of government. Discussing the secret assemblies of the Poro Senoufo, for instance, Zempléni (2003) showed how they provide a framework for open, egalitarian debate that falls outside the official hierarchical political structures of the community (cf. already Little 1965, 1966).

Religious hierarchies are often structured in terms of degrees of purity, where the converse notion of the impure is marshalled to underline the inferior status of individuals or groups and the unacceptability—even the danger—of certain behaviours. As Mary Douglas (1966) argued, what is considered unclean in any society takes one directly to the centre of its notions of values and morality. Physical cleanliness is never just a matter of the physical, but overlaps with the psychological, moral, and religious applications of the concepts of purity and pollution. You must be clean before entering a holy place, and this means not just washing your hands, but, as it may be, examining your conscience, confessing your sins, asking for absolution. Ideas about what you need to do to be clean and avoid impurity vary enormously across different societies. Menstruation, sexual intercourse, incest, are often considered polluting, but there are exceptions.[13] So if we are looking for cross-cultural universals here, they are not so much a matter of the items held to be unclean, but the very notion of uncleanness itself. The power of that notion stems in part from its very opacity. Those who lay down, or who maintain, the rules separating the clean from the unclean thereby exercise a wide-ranging but covert control over many aspects of behaviour. However, when a whole caste is classified as impure, as in Hinduism, the use of the

---

[13] On ancient Greek ideas on menstruation, see Dean-Jones (1994) and King (1998), on Greek and Egyptian views on incest, see Hopkins (1980) and Scheidel (1997), and on pollution in general, Parker (1983).

notion to establish and perpetuate social boundaries in the interests of those at the top of the hierarchy is pretty clear.

Prestige in religious matters may derive from mastery of a sacred text or its interpretation, or come from perceived qualities of sagehood, holiness, sanctity that may attach to individuals. Charismatic leaders, the founders of new religions, may start as highly individualistic, but if their teaching is to catch on, that will depend on the formation of an elite around them, disciples, apostles, interpreters, sometimes more, sometimes less, hierarchical, selected, maybe, for loyalty as much as for learning and expected to prove their vocation. But once religion has become institutionalized with churches, temples, seminaries, religious schools, and once a canon of doctrines is established, the question that then arises is: how can any change ever be made to the accepted fundamental articles of faith or to the patterns of behaviour that orthodoxy stipulates?[14] How, when an elite is in control, whether of priests, of theologians, or just of elders, can innovation occur? Change may be more or less welcome in other domains. But in that of religion it is liable to pose a destabilizing threat, and the firmer the institutional basis of the religion, the greater that will tend to be.

To be sure, in many societies ethnography carried out over a period of years reveals that changes *do* take place, in beliefs and customs, whether or not this is explicitly recognized, and it sometimes clearly is, and not just when, as often nowadays, those changes reflect the influence of a colonial power.[15] But where, as often, the practices of social incorporation and the system of induction into the faith are strong, that will make them difficult to challenge. Rank outsiders are in no position to have any influence: their opinions or objections will count for nothing. Indeed they may even serve to confirm orthodoxy, as providing cautionary examples of what *not* to believe, how *not* to behave.

While polytheisms can accommodate a plurality of deities and modes of worship, and even tolerate alternative views of where the boundaries of the religious lie, a monotheistic religion confronted

---

[14] Cf. Whitehouse 1995, 2000. Ando 2008 raises the question in relation to early Christianity and the contrasts between it and pagan Roman religion, the former, according to Ando, a matter of faith, the latter of knowledge.

[15] As when a colonial power forbids traditional customs that it decides it cannot tolerate, whether it be polygamy or headhunting.

with other conceptions of God is far more liable to be forced on the defensive. The options it has to choose between vary. One militant reaction is to attempt to wipe out or convert their rivals, or at least to ban them from practising their faith. Alternatively they may simply ignore them, or more rarely they may show them at least a modicum of tolerance. It may have some difficulty in accounting to others for how it was that God came to privilege his chosen people, especially if this was an event located in historical time. But usually that choice is not one that is thought to need any explanation. In practice, Islam is able to accommodate, up to a point, the 'peoples of the book'. Judaism recognizes that all human beings are descended from Noah and so subject only to Noahide Laws. Christianity uses Purgatory as a half-way house between heaven and hell to which morally good persons who had the misfortune not to be baptized can be assigned. However, in the famous 'rites' controversy in the sixteenth and seventeenth centuries, the authorities at Rome had great difficulties in coming to terms with Chinese religion starting with the problem of whether the Chinese had any word adequately to express the concept of God. If their rituals were religion, they were false: in order to begin to accommodate them, they had to be classified as not religion at all but as secular, that is as merely civil, social, or moral.[16] Besides, by definition no monotheistic religion makes any compromises on the question of the one true God, and a realization that not everyone agrees with them may make the upholders of the one true faith more strident, rather than less, in their claims both as to its uniqueness and as to its truth.

But those within the circle of believers, on the periphery of the group or even at its centre, may attempt modification and reform. This may be just a reflection of rivalries internal to the group, the power struggle between those competing for prestige by claiming superior holiness or piety, a closer relationship with God, a divine revelation, an ability to perform miracles. Time and again, in the

---

[16] One of the main problems was whether Chinese converts to Christianity should be allowed to continue to engage in ancestor worship. Realizing how difficult it was in practice to persuade potential converts to give this up, the Jesuit missionaries based in China were generally in favour of accommodation. But at Rome, after several shifts in policy, those who rejected any compromise were eventually victorious, with the papal bull of Benedict XIV in 1742 that condemned indigenous Chinese rituals as idolatrous. See Mungello 1994, and cf. Gernet 1985 on the debates that the Chinese literati, for their part, held on the teachings of the Jesuits.

history of Christianity, and long before Luther indeed, the call has gone out to return to the original teachings and practices of Christ himself and to cut out the excrescences with which they had become overlaid. But preserving, in the long term, the simplicity that a sect advocates has generally proved more difficult than diagnosing the laxity that it exposes as a departure from the original faith.

Again, an apparent failure of a religion to deliver what it promised to the faithful—the land flowing with milk and honey, or some equivalent—may trigger dissent, doubt, criticism, though as I noted such failures may be subject to reinterpretation and put down to the shortcomings of the faithful rather than to the deceptions of the faith. Studies of millenarian cults show how extraordinarily resilient they may be in the face of facts that apparently refute their claims, arguing for example that such setbacks are sent by God precisely to test how strong the conviction of the faithful is.[17] In a remarkable modern case, studied by Festinger, Riecken, and Schachter 1956, when a prediction that the world would be destroyed on a particular date was disconfirmed, the rationalization that most members of the sect accepted was that the group itself had spread so much light that God had called off the cataclysm.

Religion, as I remarked, may be believed to have to qualify its stance in the light of advances made in philosophy and more especially in science, though in the face first of Copernicus and Galileo, then of Darwin, the Christian Church at first chose to deny those advances. But the alternative reaction I mentioned is now more common, namely to maintain that no such qualifications are necessary, on the grounds that there is no overlap between those three domains. Whatever philosophy or science may teach, the claim would be that they have no business trespassing on the province of religion, construed as a matter of a very special way of understanding the divine, namely by revelation.[18]

---

[17] The classic study of Melanesian cargo cults is Worsley 1957, cf. also Jarvie 1970, Whitehouse 1995, and more generally Wojcik 1997: ch. 6.

[18] Polkinghorne 2000: 41 cites the view that 'in eschatological discourse, science mostly poses some of the questions and looks to theology principally to provide the answers'. However, to that the riposte might be that questions posed by science have to be answered by science. Whatever satisfaction religion offers does not relate to the intellectual one of providing solutions to scientific problems.

The extraordinary hold that religion still has, in the twenty-first century, shows that positivist assumptions that it faced irreversible decline as other disciplines took over more and more of the task of making sense of experience were well wide of the mark. Evidently matters of common-sense conviction are not the only, nor the most important, consideration. The counter-intuitive elements in religious belief and practice are both a strength and a weakness. On the one hand, the totally exceptional nature of the godhead is one feature that increases the sense, among the faithful, that the religion is worth adhering to. On the other, that very exceptionality imposes a constant pressure on its credibility and constitutes an inherent potential source of vulnerability to challenge. Participation in belief has to become routinized for the evident paradoxes on which it depends not to cause severe cognitive dissonance (cf. Whitehouse 2000). Not all religions have elites to defend their position in the face of criticisms and objections—elites that maintain their own authority partly in virtue of their ability to counter such threats. But with or without elites to do the explaining, the paradox is that the very questionability of a set of beliefs can be turned into a source of unquestionability.

8

Science

PHILOSOPHY of science has debated just how science is to be defined for decades. The focus of my own interest here—as in my other chapters—is rather on a cross-cultural perspective, and the first problem I face is whether such a perspective is possible. On a conventional view, 'science' is a uniquely modern Western phenomenon. Challenging that view will lead me to open up wider issues to do with what stimulates or inhibits the systematic investigation of nature and to examine (as in my other studies) the positive and the negative roles of elites in those processes.

Let me once again sketch out my tactics. I shall first introduce the issue that I have just alluded to, namely whether it makes sense to talk of 'science' in other than a Western, indeed a modern, context. For this purpose I shall deploy a contrast similar to the one I used in relation to 'philosophy', namely between a narrower and a broader view of the subject. Both conceptions, in my view, have their strengths, but both also have their weaknesses. In particular, there are problems, I shall argue, that face the conventional, that is the narrower, view.

That will then lead me to raise the difficult question of how we are to understand radical innovation in the domain of scientific inquiries when it occurs, for example when an apparently brand new mode of investigation of natural phenomena is inaugurated. Are quite new cognitive capacities involved? How can that be? If we adopt the contrary view, that human cognitive capacities and potential are invariant throughout time and across all cultures, how do we account for the revolutions that are thought to have occurred in scientific investigation? Here it is essential to distinguish the different styles of scientific inquiry, as that idea has been developed first by Crombie, then by Hacking. Only if we do so, can we hope to see where each style innovates, and where it draws on widespread, if not universal, human faculties. One of the recurrent problems we face is the conflict between the bid to give a general characterization of science and the recognition (even on the conventional, narrow, view) of its considerable variety (cf. Dupré 1993, Dunbar 1995, Galison and Stump 1996, Haack 2007).

In my opening chapter on philosophy I remarked first on the tension between a restricted and a broader construal of the discipline, where the restricted conception defines it in terms of the technical analysis of certain well-demarcated subjects, while the broader one does so in terms of basic human cognitive capacities, for logical reasoning, for example, or for raising questions about how to behave, about what makes life worth living, about morality, in other words. Then a second observation that I made about philosophy was that there are considerable ongoing disagreements, in European and North American universities, on what the curriculum should comprise and how it should be studied.

Now as regards the second point, there is nowadays a greater measure of agreement about how to study chemistry or even fundamental particle physics, than there is about how to go about philosophy—though it is worth noting straight away how different the investigation of those two accepted representatives of the natural sciences is. I shall come back to this. But if we take our general word 'science' and what are considered its approximate equivalents in other European languages, there are certainly appreciable differences in what the terms in question are held to cover—just as I claimed was and still to some extent is the case with 'philosophy' and its European cognates. Latin *scientia* was a general term for systematic knowledge,[1] and that general construal still persists in French *science*, Italian *scienza*, and Spanish *ciencia*. In German too *Wissenschaft* has a similar range, while to refer to what we call the 'natural sciences' German specifies *Naturwissenschaften*. In one common English usage, however, 'science', without qualification, is taken to refer first

---

[1] That is also the case with the Chinese term *xue*, 'learning' (see Lloyd and Sivin 2002: 5) the term that was later adapted, but only in the 19th century, to translate the European words for 'science' and for 'philosophy', the former in combination with *ke*, the latter with *zhe*.

and foremost to just those 'natural sciences'. Of course psychology, anthropology, economics, and the 'social sciences' in general also claim to be (proper) science, giving rise to controversies within and outside the discipline about just how far, and on what grounds, such a claim can be maintained, with some keen to justify that claim while others have held it to be fundamentally misguided. Indeed in a positivist mode philosophers too considered that what they studied was 'moral science': as I remarked before, the examination that philosophy undergraduates sat at Cambridge to obtain their BA was until recently called the Moral Sciences Tripos. However, the dominance of the natural sciences as paradigmatic of science is a far more pronounced phenomenon in the English-speaking world than in other European countries.

That takes me back to the first point I mentioned, namely the contrast between a more restricted and a broader construal of science. On the more conventional construal, science has only been practised for the past 150 years or so, or at least only since the scientific revolution of the seventeenth century. It may not require the entire gamut of the sophisticated gadgetry of modern laboratories, but it depends on such concepts as the mathematization of physics and on quantitative analyses generally, on the use of hypotheses and postulates, and especially on the experimental method.[2] It is certainly not, then, a worldwide phenomenon to be found, to some extent at least, in any human society at any period.

But on a broader view, science can be said to exist wherever there is systematic understanding of a range of natural phenomena, whether or not that understanding is the result of the self-conscious application of a programme of research governed by an explicit 'scientific method'. On this view, the extremely detailed and complex plant and animal taxonomies reported for such societies as the Hanunóo of the Philippines will count as science (Conklin 1954), even though we are in no position to trace how that knowledge was first acquired nor how it came to be consolidated.[3] Lévi-Strauss (1966: ch. 1) cited that case among others to build up a picture of what he called 'the science of the

---

[2] What was discovered, in the 'scientific revolution', was how to discover, as some have put it, though the question of whether this was—just—a discovery, or should rather be treated as an invention, is one way of putting the issue this chapter addresses.

[3] It will be science then in the sense of knowledge acquired, not in the sense of an ongoing investigation.

concrete' or rather, in his original, 'la science du concret'—where we should bear in mind the wider range of the French term *science*. The Hanunóo identify no fewer than 1,625 plants by distinctive names: indeed 93 per cent of the total number of native plants are recognized by them as culturally significant. Similarly the thousands of insect forms present are grouped by the Hanunóo into 108 named categories, including thirteen for ants and termites.

The Hanunóo are far from unique in this. Among many other societies with similarly detailed classifications of flora and fauna are the Pinatubo Negritos studied by Robert Fox (1952). Fox commented, for example, on the distinctions drawn between different kinds of bats, according to habitat. 'The *tididín* lives on the dry leaves of palms, the *dikidík* on the underside of the leaves of the wild banana, the *litlít* in bamboo clumps, the *kolumbóy* in holes in trees, the *konanabá* in dark thickets, and so forth. In this manner, the Pinatubo Negrito can distinguish the habits of more than 15 species of bats', though Fox added: 'Of course, the classification of bats, as well as of insects, birds, animals, fish, and plants, is determined primarily by their actual physical differences and/or similarities' (Fox 1952: 187–8). The contrast between the richness of many folk classifications and the impoverishment of knowledge about animals and plants among modern urbanized Westerners, commented on by Ross (2002) and others, is striking. Asked to identify all the trees she knew, an honours student in a major American university came up with under ten kinds. When asked about plants, she said she could not think of any that were not trees. She claimed to know a lot about angiosperms, gymnosperms, and so on, but that was just 'biology': 'it was not really about plants and trees' (Atran, Medin, and Ross 2004: 395).

All of the examples in Lévi-Strauss's discussion of 'science of the concrete' were drawn from the ethnographic accounts of still existing societies. But we can add many of the achievements of ancient societies, not just in their classifications of natural kinds, but also, for example, in the matter of the understanding of the causes of eclipses and the ability to predict them, in Mesopotamia, China, and Greece. Moreover in those cases, unlike the Hanunóo one, we *can* say something about the histories of the developments in question, that is to say how the knowledge was built up and systematized. This will turn out to be a key issue for my inquiry and I shall return to it in due course. All humans desire to know, as Aristotle put it:[4] the survival of any group depends on a considerable knowledge of the ecology of its environment, and that may lay the basis of its claims to have science at least to some degree.

Let me now rehearse in rather more detail both the strengths and the weaknesses first of the narrow, then of the broader construal of science.

The overwhelming weight of modern specialist opinion in the philosophy and sociology of science undoubtedly favours what I call the narrow or more restricted view. It is true that both the question of identifying the defining characteristics of science in general, and that of demarcating good science from bad, have repeatedly eluded resolution and sometimes been confusingly run together. In nineteenth- and early twentieth-century positivism, science was confidently defined by its adherence to the hypothetico-deductive and experimental methods. But that was before the categorical contrast between observation and theory was undermined. When it was assumed that observation can yield indubitable facts, they could be appealed to as the test of whether a scientific theory was true or not. Superior scientific theories, on that view, are those that explained more facts, not just those that had been accounted for by earlier theories, but additional ones as well. Einstein thus improved on Newton who had in his day superseded Kepler and Copernicus. So progress in science could be defined by the extension of its power to give such explanations. Similarly theories that could not be matched against facts did not count as science at all. Science depended, then, on verifiability, though for that Popper, preoccupied with the problem of induction and conscious that no verification is complete, substituted falsifiability.

While such positivist views seemed to hold unchallenged sway for several decades, they were fatally undermined by the objections that were mounted to the very idea that an observation statement can be totally theory-free and so to the notion that unimpeachable foundations for the whole investigation can be secured. Philosophy of science has subsequently been marked by the ongoing debate between revised realist interpretations on the one hand, and relativist or instrumentalist ones on the other. The realist will not retreat entirely from the

---

[4] But that is not to say that they all manifest that desire equally: see further below.

claim that science deals, however indirectly, with entities that are, in some sense, there and that exist independently of the scientist theorizing about them. If you can spray them, as Hacking (1983) put it, they are real, by which he meant, not if you can act on them, but rather if you can get them to act on other things.

According to the latter, relativist/instrumentalist, view, the truth of a scientific theory is not settled by a direct correspondence to facts (for that is impossible), but rather first by its internal consistency, and secondly by its ability to generate hypotheses that can yield predictions. The hypotheses *can* thus be evaluated, not that there is any suggestion that they are true of the world, only that they are adequate for the purposes of making and testing predictions. On a view that has become increasingly influential the opinions of the scientific community are what count in determining the acceptability of a theory (Kusch 2002). On that view scientists themselves constitute the sole ultimate court of appeal as to what science is—and what counts as good science—and it is recognized that as the opinions of the scientific community change, we have to allow for changes also in how science is to be defined. Sociological explanations step in to supplement, or even replace, philosophical ones where the latter appear to have reached an impasse.

This is not the place to go further into the current *status quaestionis* as between realists and relativists of different types. The more important point, for my agenda here, is that those on both sides of the dispute are generally agreed that their explanandum is *modern* scientific practice. They disagree about the account to be offered as to its status and procedures of justification, but when, as usually, they focus *just* on modern science, they clearly tend towards what I called the restricted view of what science is. There may be difficulties in specifying the necessary and sufficient conditions for what is to count as science, but we recognize the scientists around us, in universities and research laboratories, well enough, even though, as I said, there are appreciable differences, as between different fields, in the ways they tackle the problems they investigate. If we take those differences into account, 'science', even on the narrow view, has to be acknowledged to be a polyvalent endeavour.

But on that, narrower, view, namely that science is just a modern phenomenon, one fundamental question that arises is how 'it' or 'they' (the different branches we recognize) originated. That cannot be sensibly investigated until we have a clear idea of *when* it—or they—can be said to have begun, but the answer to that remains contested, even by those who share an adherence to the restricted view. Some would associate the key breakthrough with the development of modern, laboratory-based, science. Others have focused on the importance of such institutions as the Royal Society and the Académie Royale. But those who popularized the whole idea that there *was* a 'scientific revolution', indeed just the one crucial one, placed that in the sixteenth and seventeenth centuries, with the work of Copernicus and Galileo especially (for example Butterfield 1949). Accepting that view of the decisive turning point in Western science, Needham spent much of his working life trying to answer the question of why such a revolution never took place in China.

While proponents of the more restricted view disagree about the key characterization, and timing, of the Great Divide, let alone its explanation, they are united by the assumption that there was one.[5] Some Great Divide theory can even be said to be constitutive of the narrower view, for it was only after that happened, that 'science' began: what happened before it, interesting as that may be, does not count as such. It lacked the experimental method, or the hypothetico-deductive one, or whatever other concepts or techniques are held to be essential to modern science.

But if some such view is accepted, what are the consequences? How can we begin to understand how it was that—suddenly, or over a period of time—humans, who had had (on this view) no science at all up until then, came to practise this mode, or modes, of inquiry? It is crucial here to get clear how strong a claim for innovation is being made, and in what regard. Did the breakthrough (however understood) depend on new cognitive capacities, or merely on the new deployment of already existing ones? Either way there are problems. If we take the first option, what sense can we make of the idea of acquiring new cognitive capacities, and were they just confined to the scientists in question or did they somehow become more generally available? On the latter option, if the capacities were always there,

---

[5] Among the more important of the contributions on this extensively debated topic are Gellner 1973, 1985 and Goody 1977. While the Great Divide has generally been located in the events of the 16th and 17th centuries, analogous major changes have sometimes been postulated in much earlier periods, as for instance in the now discarded view that Greek rationality constituted what Renan (1935: 243 ff.) liked to call a 'miracle'.

why were they not used? On that view the problem can be said to be one of what inhibited the development of science, and what removed the obstacles to its growth, and not simply what stimulated that development.

Let me set that problem to one side for the moment: we shall need to come back to it later to modify the terms in which it is posed. But now let me rehearse the pros and cons of the alternative, broader, view of science. On that view, 'science' does not just pick out the modern, Western, phenomenon, but can be found across the world and already in much earlier periods (cf. Lloyd 2004: ch. 2). If science is defined primarily in terms of the ambition to understand the world around us, that is widespread, if not universal. Of course what passes as understanding is often mistaken. But then even modern science makes mistakes. We cannot define science merely in terms of success, for that is always provisional. On the other hand, most would agree that we need more than mere curiosity, but also concerted efforts towards acquiring knowledge.

The great strength of the broader view is that it recognizes a universal potential for science and there is no question of needing to invoke some special new cognitive capacity to account for the rise of modern science. On the other hand, it is faced with its problems, too, notably the differential actualization of that potential, the varied performance of societies and groups at different times and places. Some do, but others do not, have the complex botanical taxonomies such as that reported for the Hanunóo. Some have a detailed understanding of the movements of the heavenly bodies, on which they produce theories based on records they have built up over considerable periods of time. But others make no such records and have no such interest. Several even claim that it is wrong-headed, or even impossible, to try to investigate how the world works. It is beyond our capacity to reach any full understanding, and besides (some have added) all we need to know is set down in a sacred text. We do not need research, as Tertullian put it,[6] when we have the gospel. At that point we have left any ambition to investigate phenomena and have thrown in our lot with revelation. Yet Tertullian's denial helps to underline, by contrast, the possibilities of the endeavours he rejected.

---

[6] Tertullian, *On Prescriptions against Heretics*, ch. 7.

Moreover that certainly shows that not everyone in every age has shown an interest in increasing understanding of the world around them.

If the narrower view has difficulty accounting for the Great Divide, one could argue that the broader one is also faced with an appreciably more complex set of problems of explaining the great variety in the actual pursuit of that ambition to understand the world that it assumes to be widespread across humankind. We appear to be confronted with the daunting task of analysing the different manifestations of concrete science across the world. Obviously to do that would involve the widest possible survey of the ethnographic and historical evidence. But at least we can make a start by tracking the growth and development of different skills and interests in different societies or in different groups within them.

For some people, we may imagine that the only plants that are worth knowing about are those that are edible or poisonous, the only animals they are concerned with fall into the categories of predator or prey. But far more often the classification of natural kinds comes to be elaborated in part because they are the bearers of symbolic meaning. When interests change and special ones come to be followed up, this may be because some group within the society realizes a possibility that had not been appreciated before. For some, we may suppose, the stars are no more interesting than clouds. But once constellations have been identified and their movements tracked, they can be used to tell the time at night—if indeed it is important to tell the time.

We can see those interests developing in practice in ancient societies. In both Mesopotamia and China observation of the heavens became a specialist study with considerable political importance. In both societies the fortunes of the ruler and of the state as a whole were thought to be directly linked to what happened in the heavens. In one sense this was straightforward. Those in authority needed to ensure the orderly conduct of agricultural activities: so it was essential that the calendar should not get out of step with the seasons, and increasingly accurate estimates came to be made of the lengths of the solar year and the lunar month—as they were elsewhere in the ancient world, for example in Greece. But any exceptional phenomenon in the heavens was a potential omen. There was a demand for people who could interpret what they meant, and this was met by specialists, in all three ancient civilizations, who certainly claimed that they could do so.

But then some of the phenomena in question were discovered to exhibit certain regularities, and it proved possible for those interpreters to predict them—to say, for example, when a planet would become visible again after a period of invisibility, or when a lunar, and even within limits a solar, eclipse would occur. The confidence and pride of the Assyrian and Babylonian scribes in their ability to do this are evident in their Letters and Reports to the Assyrian kings.[7] From the point of view of the development of science, what was important was that a number of highly obscure phenomena came to be seen to be intelligible and predictable. What may have started—what did start—as a study of portents came to be a source of a reliable understanding of the regularities underlying seemingly random events. Even if the chief motives of the scribes were to prove their expertise and put themselves in a position to be able to advise their kings about the future, the regularities they discovered enabled them indeed to claim an altogether new style of understanding of what had never been understood before. The interested parties they worked for may have been looking for ways and means to increase political control, by predicting the future, even anticipating the intentions of the gods. But what the scribes achieved was a breakthrough in knowledge and the development of a method that could deliver its subsequent growth.[8]

---

[7] There is now an extensive literature on the extant Letters and Reports that mainly date from the 8th and more especially the 7th century BCE: see e.g. Parpola 1970, 1983, 1993, Hunger 1992, and the overviews in Brown 2000 and Rochberg 2004. Lloyd and Sivin 2002 undertakes a similar review of early Chinese astronomy in comparison with early Greek studies in that area, and cf. above, Ch. 2.

[8] Similarly both ancient Greek and Chinese investigators notched up important advances in their studies of the heavens, though the nature of their achievements, and the sociopolitical framework within which they were made, both differ profoundly (cf. above, Ch. 2). As noted, Chinese observers were generally officials working for rulers to ensure that the calendar was in good order, that no unforeseen eclipses occurred, and so on, so the ruler could rest assured that his mandate from heaven was not going to be called into question. Greek astronomers, by contrast, were generally private individuals: much of the effort of many of them was expended on demonstrating in detail a thesis that had important moral implications, namely that the heavens are a *cosmos*, an orderly system. Ptolemy, for one, stated that the study of its regularities could bring order and beauty into our lives. In none of the ancient societies on which we are best informed was new understanding sought just for its own sake, and why it was pursued gives us, in each case, important clues concerning why what we may, on the broader view, call scientific research was undertaken.

They were less successful, to be sure, in establishing correlations within meteorological phenomena or in the behaviour of animals, though these were still considered to be significant omens too. But some ancient doctors built up similarly detailed knowledge of the progress of different types of diseases.[9] In that case too we may contrast (mere) observation and experience with a determined effort to collect and record data that could be referenced for later use. Admittedly the motives of those who did so, in China and in Greece, are complex. The recorded individual case histories were in some instances part of the doctors' justification of their own competence. In Greece, as I pointed out, some texts include warnings to fellow practitioners not to take on dangerous cases where the chance of fatality was high. Of course these investigators did not have in mind some eventual publication in a learned medical journal.[10] But that is not to deny their interest in what was recognized as research, that is in accumulating and transmitting detailed records of their own clinical practice.

On a minimalist view, the claim is that science everywhere depends on the extension and elaboration of capacities we all possess. How will that work out in practice and how far does it justify the broader view of what science is? Given that all normal human beings have the sense of sight, the capacity to observe is basic and universal: but what is observed will vary with the interests I have sketched out and will depend on interactions between observer and observed (Ingold 2000, Grasseni 2007, Henare et al. 2007). No observation, as I remarked before, is entirely free from preconceptions. But just as they vary, so too obviously will the subject-matter to which the observations are directed and the corresponding skills that are developed. One question that then arises is whether the observations are thought important enough to be recorded, and if so, by whom and in what medium. Is something like an archive accumulated, and does that lead to the establishment of more or less formal institutions to oversee the collection of data and its analysis and interpretation?

---

[9] See above, Ch. 4.

[10] However, those learned modern publications share one feature with some much earlier case histories, namely their justificatory purpose. In the modern case we should not ignore how they contribute to the RAE (Research Assessment Exercise) of the group concerned and are used to testify to the quality of their research.

Similar points are relevant to the topic of experimentation. Evidently no one can intervene to change the movements of the stars: but intervention is possible to yield more information about plants and animals, for instance, and again about metals and other minerals. There can be no society that does not use what we may call trial and error methods to extend their knowledge.[11] Speaking of the enormous advances made in pre-historic times in such fields as agriculture, pottery, weaving, and metallurgy, Lévi-Strauss (1966: 13–14) remarked that no one could think that such skills were the result of the 'fortuitous accumulation of a series of chance discoveries or believe them to have been revealed by the passive perception of certain natural phenomena'. On one view, then, the practice of experimentation may be seen as just a more systematic and controlled version of those methods.

The differentiation in performance that the broader view of science has to come to terms with can be put down, at least up to a point, to the degree of systematicity and self-consciousness with which those capacities are deployed and to the interests they are made to serve. There is, on this view, no radical difference in kind between a chance observation and observations that form part of a sustained and self-conscious programme, but there may be important differences in the results obtained. Working out, by trial and error, how to extract the poisons from certain plants for use in hunting animals, and again by trial and error how to make the blow-pipes to deliver the poisons, the right materials to use, and the right dimensions of the weapon, all require great skill (cf. Descola 1996). But when experimentation is made the subject of self-conscious analysis, it can be more systematically applied.[12] Similarly, in my discussion of reasoning, in relation to

---

[11] Fox's comments on the growth of knowledge concerning introduced exotic plants in the Philippines make the point very vividly. 'The speed with which the exotic flora is utilized, such as *tümtüm*, is undoubtedly influenced by the presence or absence of physical characteristics of the plants which do, or do not, meet established local prerequisites determining uses. For example, plants having bitter leaves or stems are commonly used in the Philippines for stomach disorders. If an introduced plant is found to have this characteristic, it will be quickly utilized. The fact that many Philippine groups, such as the Pinatubo Negritos, constantly experiment with plants hastens the process of the recognition of the potential usefulness, as defined by the culture, of the introduced flora' (Fox 1952: 212–13).

[12] In practice, however, as I argued in Lloyd 1991: ch. 4, the early history of experimentation in Greece shows that it was more often used in support of a theory—as an adjunct to non-interventionist observation—than to adjudicate between competing hypotheses.

the broader conception of 'philosophy', I distinguished between the general capacity to distinguish between good and bad reasoning, and what happens when logic is subject to formal analysis.

In all those instances, on the broad view of science, there are differences in the modes and contexts of use of certain faculties, though there is no occasion to consider that the underlying faculties themselves differ. The broad view, we said, also faces the problem of the great differences in the actual understanding of the world arrived at in different societies at different periods. But although each situation calls for its own careful and detailed analysis, the *shape* of the inquiry we need to undertake is clear up to a point. What observations were made, and how deliberate were they? How was new knowledge built up, and were there ways of recording and transmitting it? When new ideas were put forward, how were they received, and how did their proponents go about maximizing their acceptability? What were the interests that motivated the societies as a whole or groups within them? What view was taken of inquiry and research themselves? Were they supported by state institutions, or were they left to private individuals? If the former (as in Babylonia and China, for instance) what were the state's interests, and if the latter (as generally in Greece) what motivated those individuals? How far did the investigators, in either case, seek to restrict access to the new knowledge they had acquired? Did they try to control the next generation of investigators or open up their modes of research to all comers? What ideas were entertained concerning what was worth investigating, the subject-matter in other words, and how far did they see a potential for growth by extension or by extrapolation?

In the matter of the progress the ancients made in understanding, we have to be wary of any assumption that this was in any way linear or smooth. In our previous studies we have drawn attention to the possibly negative effects of what might seem progressive developments. The existence of an elite corps charged with responsibility for certain investigations might look like an unmixed blessing. The most sustained examples of data collection from antiquity, especially with regard to the study of the heavens, relate, we said, to the work of such elites, in Mesopotamia and China in particular. But once an elite has achieved a certain prestige and authority, its concern to maintain its position may lead it to be no longer a force for innovation, but rather one for secretiveness and stagnation. One recurrent factor in the history of the development of more sophisticated forms of science is that the very elements that stimulated the initial development may in time impede its further growth. As I have remarked before (cf. Lloyd 2002), there is what I have called the momentum effect, where the perceived success of one schema led to a certain resistance to other alternatives both within the domain in which it had originally proved its worth, and in other areas in which it was used as a model. In my study of mathematics here (Chapter 2) I argued similarly that one Greek tradition of axiomatization had certain negative effects as well as positive ones, not just within mathematics itself, but when attempts were made to apply it to other fields such as medicine and theology.

The broad view of science has, then, on the arguments I have advanced, some strengths and in not needing to invoke new cognitive capacities may be more economical than one version of its rival. Yet to many, the differences between Hanunóo botany and DNA analysis, and again between Mesopotamian or ancient Chinese or Greek astronomy and modern cosmology, are so huge that it seems absurd to use the same rubric 'science' to cover both. The more restricted view of science, which limits it to its more recent manifestations, does, however, run the risk of implying that there is a radical contrast, if not between two types of humans, at least between two kinds of societies, 'hot' and 'cold' ones as they have sometimes been called.[13] Yet it seems extravagant to speak of 'hot' societies as a whole, as if all their members were enthusiastic proponents of, or at least equally receptive to, the idea of increasing knowledge by scientific investigations.

To make progress on the thorny issue of the cognitive capacities in play, we need to discriminate more finely within the range of activities that science (on any construal) comprehends. Of course we have to pay attention to the points I have just made concerning skills, interests, and institutions. But we need to and can go further. Hacking (1982, 1992a), following Crombie, has insisted on the differences within styles of scientific thinking or reasoning, ranging from the postulational/demonstrative style exemplified already in Greek geometry to the laboratory style of modern times. Crombie's original

---

[13] Characterizing societies as a whole as 'hot' or 'cold' is open to the objection that it distracts attention from the fact that in *any* society the attitudes and ambitions of different individuals and groups differ appreciably.

six styles were a matter of (1) the postulational style established in the mathematical sciences, (2) the experimental exploration and measurement of more complex observable relations, (3) the hypothetical construction of analogical models, (4) the ordering of variety by comparison and taxonomy, (5) the statistical analysis of regularities of populations and the calculus of probabilities, and (6) the historical derivation of genetic development. But among the modifications that Hacking introduced,[14] he subdivided (1) into (1a) the geometrical style employing demonstrations and (1b) the algorithmic and combinatory style. Again (3) had to be subdivided into (3a) the Galilean style and (3b) the laboratory style of more recent times. In each case the style is defined partly in terms of the modes of reasoning it adopts and the concepts it uses, but partly also by the objects it studies. While his own interests centred mainly on science since Galileo, Hacking recognized, as I have just noted, precursors of the postulational style already in antiquity.

If we follow up these distinctions, that can help us to be more determinate both as to the novelty of each style and on where each draws on earlier ideas and techniques—and thereby to attempt at least a partial reconciliation between what I call the narrower and the broader construals of 'science'. Thus I have already suggested that the experimental method can be seen as an extension of widespread techniques of trial and error. Admittedly once experiment is defined as such, the method can be used far more systematically, more self-consciously and with greater rigour. Similarly the taxonomic style exemplified for instance by Linnaeus in early modern times can be represented as the more explicit development of widespread interests in classification, indeed maybe universal ones insofar as classifying is implicit in any use of language. Yet those interests are by no means uniform, and the modes of classification favoured certainly vary, as also do the criteria invoked. Not all proceed by way of a hierarchy of genera and species with the latter defined by a single differentia, for some are polythetic and to that extent may be non-hierarchical.

---

[14] Since those pioneering articles (1982, 1992a), which acknowledged a debt to Crombie's ideas, later published in Crombie 1994, Hacking has devoted a series of lectures delivered at the Collège de France to developing a sophisticated analysis of a revised set of styles of scientific thinking, with their different histories.

In such cases the idea of science as an extension of ordinary common-or-garden techniques has some plausibility. But going back to
the points that are cited to favour the narrower view of science, we
have also to allow that in the laboratory, for instance, we have
techniques and methods that have no precedent. It is obvious that
new instruments, once they are available, extend the range of the
investigable. Once the telescope and the microscope had been invented, then the moons of Jupiter, and micro-organisms, became
visible—though most would say that they had always been there.
But in many modern laboratory interventions new objects are actually
brought into existence. Indeed we can see that happening already in
the creation of a vacuum in Boyle's famous experiments with the air
pump (Shapin and Schaffer 1985). Latour especially has insisted on
the role of other agents besides individual scientists, that is non-
human factors, 'actants', in science, including, for example, the microbes that were at the centre of the debate between Pasteur and his
opponents (Latour 1988).

In the light of these considerations, how far does it seem possible to
identify areas of convergence, if also ones of continuing divergence,
between the various views of science we have been discussing? The
notion of styles is doubly useful, since it enables one to pay attention
first to the distinctiveness of each mode of investigation in question,
but also secondly to the degree of systematicity with which each is
conducted, that is to the question of how far any given style is adopted
self-consciously or its methods and procedures made explicit by those
who use it. It allows us to complexify the hypothesis of a Great Divide,
for there was not just the one revolutionary breakthrough, when *the*
scientific method, the one that all science has to exemplify, was
established. Rather there was a whole series of developments and
changes in styles, involving new techniques and concepts, in processes
of elaboration that continue at an ever-increasing pace today. Moreover whereas, on the Kuhnian model, paradigms supersede one another, styles of inquiry, as I would interpret them, are more often
complementary and cumulative, than alternatives, to one another.

Insofar as the aims of science, described in the most general terms,
are to achieve understanding, clearly that is common ground to
all the styles we encounter, and to both the narrower and the broader
view of 'science'. Equally obviously, degrees of explicitness and self-
consciousness vary, new subject-matter calls for new modes of inquiry

which may owe more or less to existing precedents, and indeed conversely, new techniques of investigation bring into existence new objects to be studied. Meanwhile the institutions within which the researchers work, and the perceived role of those researchers in society, are also subject to their changes and transformations, both as causes and as effects of the development of the sciences themselves.

The differences in the scientific styles that we can identify suggest that aspects of both the broader and the narrower views should be retained. The broader construal seems favoured when it is plausible to consider (as with observation, experiment, measurement, and classification) that a style represents the more explicit and sustained deployment of certain basic, if not universal, skills. That allows for some important continuities between modern and pre-modern investigations and avoids the need to postulate a radical break marked by the invention of brand new cognitive capacities. But where (as in statistical analysis and in the laboratory style) the key concepts and techniques are more obviously unprecedented, that serves as a reminder of the distinctiveness of some areas of modern scientific activity—the type of consideration that serves to support the narrower view. However, even on that view, there is still nothing like universal agreement about *how* restrictive that definition should be. Criticism of certain areas of the natural sciences, in geography for instance, as 'soft' continue to be made, even if few would go so far as to limit the sciences to the purely mathematical ones. But medicine, for example, certainly occupies an ambiguous position, depending on whether the focus is on the application of theories to the individual patient, or on the theories themselves. Equally the inclusion of any of the social sciences remains problematic.

Given the prestige of the category of science, the claim to title will always be hotly contested, among philosophers, historians, and anthropologists at least (cf. Cunningham and Wilson 1993). The actual practitioners, however, the physicists, biologists, cosmologists, will get on with the job, largely unconcerned with how to define what they are doing and secure in the sense of the more or less universal recognition their work now receives. However, philosophers and sociologists of science, as I noted, still dispute what exactly makes science science. Historians and anthropologists for their part have first the task of investigating what the sources they deal with yield by way of ideas and practices that bear on the question, and then they have to decide on what conclusions they suggest on the wider issues. Science in the modern world is in a unique position in that it has a more or less unchallenged, all but unchallengeable, status, at least as an intellectual discipline, even though the way it has been applied raises wide-ranging and indeed urgent problems. Yet reflections on its scope, its origins, and its history raise the considerable problems I have adumbrated in this chapter.

However, some aspects of the role of cadres are clear. As in the other learned disciplines we have discussed in this book, so too in science, once it becomes institutionalized,[15] that role is twofold. On the one hand, the more advanced the investigation, the more its practitioners will need to have been trained in the techniques on which it depends and to have served an apprenticeship in the institutions within which it is conducted. Showing signs of independence too soon, before that apprenticeship has been completed, runs the risk of rejection and thus forfeiting the opportunity eventually to work at the cutting edge of the field, a phenomenon that can be exemplified already in antiquity as well as in modern times.

On the other hand, for those with an established place within the elite, there is a delicate balance to be struck between innovation and conformity. Rivalry will undoubtedly serve to stimulate the former. But to be acceptable, innovation will need to be seen to conform, at least up to a point, to the patterns and ideals that, consciously or otherwise, the elite uses to define itself. Indeed nowadays those patterns and ideals may be specific to individual areas within science, to the branches into which it is divided, physics, chemistry, the earth sciences, the biological ones, and the rest. Pressure to conform will not just be general, but specific to specific groups of investigators, indeed sometimes to specific laboratories, though in setting up their norms, each group has to keep an eye on what others, their rivals in other institutions, are up to, and that may introduce a further element of competitiveness that may, but will not necessarily, prove to be a stimulus to innovation. Besides, on the question of which innovations

---

[15] However, on the broader view of science that I have proposed, cadres are not always the driving force, since observation and trial and error experimentation are not the prerogative of a limited elite. Pre-institutionalized science is not a learned discipline, but a widespread, if not universal, human activity.

will prove fruitful in the medium or longer term, the history of both ancient and modern science provides plenty of examples where mistakes were made not just by single experts, but by the consensus among them. I shall take up some of the further issues of the relationships between groups of disciplines and within them briefly in my concluding chapter.

Conclusion: Disciplines and Interdisciplinarity

THE eight different fields of human activity that I have surveyed are, as I remarked at the outset, a mixed bag, answering to different needs, whether practical or intellectual. The aim of this final chapter is twofold, first to attempt to summarize what we have learnt from the study of each discipline severally, in particular in the matter of the ways they are established, the roles of elites, and what stimulates or inhibits innovation, and secondly to consider their commonalities and their interrelations from an interdisciplinary perspective.

The definitional problems are all contentious issues, not least because each discipline prides itself on its value and importance. We might think that we could settle them by reference to what is laid down by qualified experts in well-established institutions of higher education in the West—not just universities, but also medical schools, art schools, seminaries—though there are generally many other professional practitioners besides those whose primary task is to teach. But I have argued that that is a mistake, for two kinds of reasons. First, there is nothing like universal agreement among the experts we might consult even just in the English-speaking world, while as soon as we examine what seem close equivalents for our terms in European languages, further discrepancies emerge, as I exemplified with *philosophie* and *science* in French.

Secondly, if we adopt a broader cross-cultural perspective, even greater divergences come to light. Even in the absence of obviously, if maybe deceptively, similar 'actors' categories, none of the basic activities that each discipline comprises is confined to Europe nor even just to 'advanced' industrialized societies across the world. That is sufficiently obvious in the cases of medicine, art, religion, and law, even though we have seen that the forms they take and the ways in which they are practised differ markedly.

But in the other four areas, too, history, mathematics, philosophy, and science, I have expressed doubts about an exclusive view that would limit the subject in each case to what we are used to in our modern institutions, even though the ways in which they are pursued there may be particularly complex and elaborate. A historical interest, for instance, is shown by any society that constructs and employs its conception of its own past whether to celebrate and commemorate it, to use it as a source of models for how to behave, or for any one of the various other functions that we find that records, oral or written, are put to. The practical applications of mathematics, in calculating quantities and magnitudes, are, for sure, good enough examples of extremely widespread skills, even though they may not lead on to the theoretical abstract study of problems in arithmetic, geometry, trigonometry, calculus, set theory, and the rest. Philosophy too, I argued, on the broad view, may be represented in any society where issues of right and wrong, or of the correctness of reasoning, are raised as explicit questions. So too even is science, wherever we find sustained manifestations of the ambitions to understand, explain, and predict phenomena that are the basic aims of even the most complex modern investigations.

So the first set of problems I have tackled, in each chapter, is quite how we should understand the core nature of the activity in question, and in each case I have mounted an argument for a wider, rather than, or at least as well as, a more restricted, Eurocentric, or academic, view. That does not necessarily turn the activity into a universal, cross-cultural one, though I have pointed out that medicine, mathematics, and law, for instance, all answer to more or less general human needs, and more controversially I reviewed the case for saying that basic cognitive capacities are in play in what, on a broad construal, can be called science, even though in its more advanced forms it certainly calls on distinctive techniques and concepts.

The wider non-Eurocentric view of the activities in question clearly allows for very diverse manifestations of each of them in different cultural circumstances. The historical record illustrates this very clearly, demonstrating how, in their early phases, philosophy, mathematics, history, science, even medicine, all took rather different forms. In our own society, too, we have intellectual leaders who continue to dispute the question of what the proper aims and methods of historiography, for instance, or of philosophy, should be, or the competing claims for various styles of pure or applied mathematics. As I pointed out in my discussion of art, self-styled connoisseurs have a particular commercial interest in having their ideas on the subject accepted. But if that last example exhibits particularly clearly the ongoing controversies between different experts on the demarcation of the activities and disciplines they practise, this is certainly not a phenomenon confined to modern times nor to complex societies. No one set of experts has a monopoly of the truth on how each field is to be defined: no more do I myself claim any privileged access to the correct answers, though I would maintain that the wider acceptances of the terms that I favour are among those that we should keep in view.

Elites of various kinds come to be formed when their members claim specialist knowledge in some particular field—knowledge that is not available to just anyone, even though in certain circumstances just anyone may challenge any such claim. But in the second finding I would insist on, the subsequent role of an elite may be quite ambivalent. On the one hand, for a field to be developed, pioneers are generally needed to show the way ahead, to exploit the possibilities of a new inquiry or activity, or of a new manner of conducting it. They may lead by example—as when an original historian or philosopher or mathematician branches out, focusing on new goals or ideals, or bringing new techniques to bear, or when a great painter or sculptor or architect inaugurates a new style. Or they may lead by precept, as in some artists' manifestos or in the writings of art critics who promote a particular school of painting. In each case the innovator may create a group of followers in whose hands the new concepts and practices come to be accepted as standard, though that is sometimes with the idea of using them as a basis for further innovation, sometimes on the very different assumption that the subject has now been established on a permanent basis and all that is left to do is to implement the programme, not attempt to introduce any more changes to it.

When groups of like-minded individuals show the way, the subject may become more professionalized, receive more backing from private or public resources, and create the institutions that help to ensure the further development of the field. That happened in dramatic fashion, for the first time in recorded history, when Mesopotamian scribes realized the new potentials of their studies of the heavens.

On the other hand, elites are not always engines for growth. One of the recurrent phenomena we have encountered to a greater or less degree in all our individual studies is that of an elite jealously guarding its privileges—even, it may claim, its mandate—in the matter of how the subject should be pursued. The effect of elite influence may sometimes be not to stimulate and provide a framework for further development, but rather to restrict it, not to encourage innovation, but to block it. By definition any elite has a limited membership. Whether new members are welcome or not varies with the elite. They may have to undergo long apprenticeships, pass rigorous tests, prove themselves in other ways, for example by convincing others of their moral respectability. The qualifications for membership may not always simply be under the exclusive control of the existing members, but will certainly be influenced by their views.

But the key question for the way the elite operates is this. Once accepted, will the new recruits be allowed their heads, and encouraged to innovate in their turn, or will they be expected to conform to the existing rules, and practise the subject in the ways already laid down? Are the methods and practices, the ethos of the discipline, if not also the doctrines and theories, thought to be fixed once for all? We found that claims for the eternity, even the divine sanction, of systems of law are common. In religion itself articles of faith may be held to have come direct from God or indirectly from a prophet or priests whose word cannot be challenged. In medicine a body of canonical texts may prescribe theories and practices from which serious deviation is not allowed on pain of sanctions, rejection, or exclusion.

The very rigour of the tests that new members of the elite are subjected to may increase the sense that they incorporate everything that there is to be learnt. In art, too, long apprenticeship may create a presupposition that the traditions handed on should and will continue unchanged, though in practice, as we have found, the next generation of practitioners often finds room for manoeuvre within the framework of the style they have been taught. Competition for appreciation and prestige may act as a powerful force for innovation whether or not that is heralded as such. Originality within an existing style or set of models may spill over into more radical further innovation in the styles and methods themselves.

But the knowledge that members of the elite alone possess may be thought of not just as specialized and esoteric, but as a corpus of jealously guarded secrets, not to be divulged to ordinary people not because they will not be able to follow, but because it is exclusive to the initiated. Those ordinary people may not even be aware of the learning available to the few but confined to them.

Incorporation into an elite follows patterns that we can detect in the general processes of socialization that take place in any society. No doubt it would be foolish to attempt to generalize unduly about these. But clearly the vast majority of young children growing up in any society will be encouraged to follow the behaviour patterns, and to adopt the practices and values, of their elders, though very different degrees of tolerance may be shown towards them if they do not. The possibilities of youthful dissent—attempted innovation in that sense—will vary not just with the society in question (whether hier-archical or not) but also with the position of the individual within it. The socially privileged may, consciously or unconsciously, adopt as their primary aim the maintenance of the differentials that mark them out, or more altruistically—or at least less self-centredly—may accept some responsibility for providing leadership.

Analogous choices face those whose privileges depend not on birth nor on inherited or acquired wealth, but on learning and education. Are the techniques of learning they cultivate essentially circum-scribed or are they themselves subject to revision and thus inherently unstable? The defenders of our universities will insist that although the *cursus honorum*, of BA, MA, and PhD, is fixed, the content of the courses is not. Yet the record reveals how conservative the curricula in even the most renowned universities, and even in the sciences, have, in general, been.[1] Established professors tend to insist that the next generation should be qualified and trained in precisely the ways they themselves were. They may further claim that of course they allow their juniors room to innovate. But when proposals for curriculum reform are presented, these are often resisted by those who see or imagine that their own expertise is in the process of being superseded.

But if learned elites are sometimes open to innovation, though often not, is there any way in which we can begin to explain why? In the case of religion innovation may be difficult to reconcile with a claim that the true faith has been revealed to its devotees, and in

---

[1] I discussed this aspect of the history of Western universities in particular in Lloyd 2004, ch. 10.

general the more that knowledge is represented as inspired, the less liable it may be to modification. Again when an elite feels the need to control access to its membership to preserve its monopoly status and indeed its economic position, it may be reluctant to accept that its knowledge claims are subject to revision.

One relevant factor that may be thought to have emerged from our various studies is the degree to which the elite in question may feel threatened by potential radical challenges to its *raison d'être*, and the extent of possible disagreement about the nature of the discipline itself—the type of issue I have aired in each of the chapters of this book. In medicine, for instance, where there is always a fundamental problem concerning what true well-being is, learned groups generally face competition, to a greater or less extent, from other practitioners offering alternative conceptions of the goal or of how to reach it. In religion, claims to a monopoly of the truth depend on faith and will strike outsiders as arbitrary. Even in the case of the law, the recurrent problem is the basis on which they can claim objectivity. How can an appeal to divine authority be justified, when the merely human authorship of many regulations is obvious? Yet if an elite's desire to inhibit innovation may sometimes reflect their sense of insecurity, it would be extravagant to suggest that there is a hard and fast correlation between these two phenomena—insecurity and conservativeness.

One exception that illustrates this is science, where Kuhn (1970) argued that intellectual insecurity, generated by the anomalies that an existing paradigm faces, may sometimes lead to crisis and so to innovation, where conversely 'normal' science tends to be more stable and conservative. So we must certainly take into account other factors, the tightness of the organization of the elite, and the extent to which openness and pluralism are at least part of the self-image it adopts.

Elites are often a notable force for the development of a subject-area: but in none of the fields we have considered is there a clear sense that they are immune to the negative effects of closure and restriction that I have identified. The positive influences include ensuring the transmission of knowledge and techniques, gaining support and prestige, monitoring the quality of results and especially—in such fields as science and medicine in particular—organizing cooperative observation and research, where the cooperation is perfectly compatible with a certain rivalry stimulating original work. But the negative ones are the observed tendencies to form closed shops, to resist change, to block innovation whether from outside or within their own membership, to authoritarianism as well as to conservativeness.

Thus far I have been reviewing some of the factors in play when a given activity is turned into a learned discipline, taught by qualified experts in established institutions of higher education. But what about the relations between them? Often a discipline defines itself not just internally, where members of an elite contrast themselves with amateurs or lay practitioners, but also externally, in contrast to other fields of investigation.

This is particularly obvious when one discipline claims hegemonic status, as I mentioned in my introduction. Religion has sometimes presented itself as such, but other disciplines also have. History has often represented itself as the chief source of instruction for statesmen, and exploiting the gap left by the impasse faced by metaphysical system-building, pictured itself as the queen of the humanities. But philosophy replies with an argument that it has the responsibility, and the prerogative, for defining what all the other subjects consist in. In late medieval European universities law, medicine, and theology were the subjects of higher degrees—qualifying those who obtained them to practise—while mathematics and logic figured among the lower, preparatory studies in the trivium and quadrivium. In China, similarly, there was a pecking order as between the less prestigious mathematics, medicine, and history on the one hand and, on the other, the canonical texts that formed the core curriculum of the Imperial Academy, even though the ultimate aim that those of 'broad learning' aspired to was an all-inclusive one, the mastery and embodiment of the *dao*. Nowadays in the West the prestige of science is immense, though its position has begun to be questioned mainly on the grounds of its association with the disastrous consequences of some applied technology, consequences that the scientists themselves often disown. Meanwhile questions to do with the hierarchy within the sciences, as between 'hard' and 'soft' ones, continue, as I said, to be fiercely disputed.

On the one hand, it may seem beyond question that there are clear if broad distinctions between the subject-matter of each of the eight activities we have been considering. It is on the basis of some such assumption that I have organized the discussion in my several chapters. There appear to be clear enough boundaries both in the data that each deals with, and in the end results sought. Historians study the past, do they not?, just as the mathematician studies numbers and shapes, the scientist natural phenomena, while medicine, art, and law aim to produce health, aesthetically pleasing objects, and rules to regulate interpersonal relations. Religion is devoted to worship but generally claims to secure salvation. As for philosophers, some see at least parts of their subject-matter, logic for instance, as distinctive, while others say or have said that philosophical understanding is essential for happiness.

On the other hand, several of these disciplines share certain methodological and epistemological concerns and aims, and indeed may present alternative views on how to secure them. The search for objectivity, truth, and efficacy are recurrent themes used to underpin the authority claims that tend to be the basis for elite status. The question that then arises is whether or how far the same criteria apply across different fields. Most (law, history, science, and medicine especially) are faced with the problems of evaluating evidence, but what counts as evidence varies. Most adhere to certain canons of argumentation, such as the avoidance of inconsistency. But how far and under what conditions analogical reasoning is permissible, and how individual case studies may be used as the basis for general inferences, are contestable. Mathematics in particular is concerned with truth preservation and with proof, though, as we saw, there have been and remain differences in the actual criteria invoked to judge stretches of mathematical reasoning. Medicine seeks results, cures, or at least improvements in patients' conditions, though it is precisely at the point where these are claimed that difficulties of verification arise and elements of subjectivity obtrude. Yet in some circumstances how the patient feels, and whether the therapy is believed to be appropriate, are the main or even the only questions that count. 'Efficacy' in those circumstances, as I said, may be reduced to a matter of 'felicity': 'felicity' may be the only mode of 'efficacy' sought or attainable.

Though art and religion may be exceptions, the common thread that links the rest is the aim of reaching objectively verifiable or at least defensible results—to demonstrate that the discipline does not just depend on the rhetorical skills of its proponents. As for art, implicitly or explicitly artists too hope to convince their audiences of the authenticity of their claims to produce aesthetically pleasing work. For religion, however, the truth revealed is, rather, a matter of faith, and divinely sanctioned, and when issues to do with consistency arise, a defence is sometimes mounted by way of the figurative nature of its discourse. Yet as I observed, there may be a high price to pay for insisting that the language used is not subject to the normal implicit logical rules, since any such move undermines its very intelligibility. At the same time some innovation in language use is generally involved in the development of most technical disciplines and debates on their proper conduct. Indeed the terms used for the discipline itself may in the process be subject to considerable shifts and modifications—as we saw with the changing fortunes of the expressions from which 'history' and 'mathematics' originate.

Thus there are evident overlaps between the goals of certain disciplines; nor are their subject-matters as hermetically sealed off from one another as we might initially assume.[2] As our discussion of medicine indicated, 'health' may be not just a matter of physical, but also of psychological and social, well-being, in some views not fully attainable other than in an equitable community. Again, the notions of purity and the impure straddle medicine, religion, even law. While the legal is often sharply distinguished from the moral, questions to do with morality inevitably come back into the picture when the justifiability of certain legal provisions is debated, and so philosophy, and even religion, may be implicated. Conversely, religion often serves to give the legal system sanctity. Again what kind of understanding of the world around us is to be sought, and what is considered essential for the true well-being of individuals, groups, even complete societies? These are matters on which philosophy, science, history, law, religion, and even mathematics may make distinctive, powerful, overlapping, but at points conflicting,

---

[2] The relations that art may have with religion, history, and science are particularly complex. As we have seen, art has often served the ideological or propaganda purposes of religion; it has often also been a powerful adjunct to historiography in its function of memorializing the past: and its role as an important tool of research in support of science and medicine has come to be increasingly recognized, as when a new field of investigation such as anatomy is opened up in part with the aid of visual representations that themselves draw on, and stand comparison with, the artistic traditions of the time. In this context, Daston and Galison (2007) have traced the changing relations between scientists ('naturalists') and artists ('illustrators') from the 17th century onwards in Europe, when the idea of truth to nature gradually gave way to one of mechanical objectivity. The first involved selection and judgement and the avoidance of the idiosyncrasies of individual specimens; the second eschewed any overt intervention on the part of the observer. Although the success of the end products—the often lavishly produced books—frequently owed more to the artist than to the naturalist, the latter still tended to look down on the former as their subordinates.

pronouncements. What is at stake is not just values, but models of what makes a life worth living.

Budding professionals, as they enter a discipline, have, to be sure, to immerse themselves in the way in which it is currently conducted, that is they have to meet the criteria their mentors and peers adopt for judging their mastery of the field. Current academic boundaries evidently serve a dual role, both liberating and constraining. They liberate in that they enable the student potentially to reach the frontiers of knowledge in the field. But they constrain in that specialization inevitably entails a narrowing in the focus of interest. Narrower and narrower specializations are a phenomenon of twenty-first-century science especially, where interdisciplinary or cross-disciplinary interests are frowned on as diluting the concentration on the specific problems at the cutting edge of research, when they are not condemned as evidence of hopeless superficiality.[3] Yet that tends to beg the questions of how the subject can and will progress and what benefit an individual may gain from engagement in its study. There is evidently no algorithm for successful innovation, but there are plenty of examples where that is achieved by bringing to bear ideas, models, and methods that originate in other neighbouring or even quite distant fields. However, those who seek to combine the insights of several disciplines thereby run the risk of being criticized by the elites of each. Interdisciplinarity itself has no such elite, which may make innovation easier but acceptability in existing academic circles more difficult. The double-bind is that for a subject to establish itself it needs firm boundaries and well-organized cadres to defend them. But for its ongoing success it needs, in science especially, to remain open to alternatives.

The investigation of how learned disciplines are constituted, such as I have undertaken here, thus brings to light some of the dangers of the tendency to increasing specialization, as well as some of its advantages. It is in the interests of existing elites to lay claims to the sole proper understanding of the discipline and the exclusively correct way

---

[3] Lip-service is sometimes paid to the advantages of a mastery of a variety of disciplines, and polymaths such as Leonardo and Newton are held up as models of human genius. But when it comes to implementing programmes of collaborative research, the complaint is still often made that each of the participants approaches the problems too much influenced by the particular ways they were taught to handle them in their original specializations.

of conducting it. But in none of the subjects we have investigated are the answers to those questions straightforward. Yet the complexities are often ignored or downplayed by those responsible for training the next generation of practitioners when they concentrate on ensuring the transmission of *their* conception of the subject and *their* way of doing it.

A recurrent theme in each of my individual chapters has been a pluralism of alternative conceptions, both of individual disciplines and of the boundaries and relations between them. A greater awareness of these can, and arguably should, serve as an antidote to a certain narrow-mindedness that is often endemic in an elite's conception of itself. More generally, we have, I should say, to guard against any assumption that the current taxonomy of the learned disciplines in Western universities in particular is sacrosanct. It is in the hope of contributing to such an understanding, and of increasing critical awareness of implicit or hidden Western hegemonic assumptions concerning the correctness of current disciplinary boundaries, that I have undertaken this series of studies.

The very variety of forms that the different inquiries we have studied have taken and continue to take is testimony to the human imagination, and yet also to the hazards of creativity, when new ideas, techniques, ambitions come to be hijacked by an exclusive group and the negative effects of the formation of an elite come to counterbalance or even outweigh the positive ones. But then who would expect the history of human endeavour to be one of uninterrupted progress? It is one rather of a constant, or as Kuhn (1977) called it essential, tension between innovation and authority, though the histories we have charted suggest that it is scarcely possible to secure the advantages of the one without the disadvantages associated with the other.

GLOSSARY OF KEY CHINESE
TERMS AND NAMES

Ban Gu	班固	(author of *Hanshu*)
bei	悖	rebellion
ben	本	trunk
bienao	鱉臑	pyramid with right triangular base and one lateral edge perpendicular to the base
boshi	博士	scholars of broad learning
bushi	卜筮	divination by turtle and milfoil (chapter of *Lun Heng*)
cha jin	察今	'scrutinizing the present' (chapter of *Lüshi chunqiu*)
Chunqiu	春秋	*Spring and Autumn Annals*
dao	道	the way
di li	地理	terrestrial organization
duan	端	source, principle
fa	法	law, order, standard
fa jia	法家	'School of Law'
Fu Xi	伏羲	(legendary culture hero)
gangji	綱紀	guiding principles
Gaozi	告子	(philosopher of fourth century BCE)
gong	宮	first pentatonic note
Gongsun Long	公孫龍	(philosopher of 'School of Names')
gou gu	句股	base and height of a right-angled triangle
Han Fei	韓非	(philosopher of 'School of Law')
Han Wu Di	漢武帝	('Martial Emperor' of Han dynasty)
Hong Fan	洪範	'Great Plan' section of *Shangshu*
hua	畫	'painting'
Hui Shi	惠施	(philosopher of 'School of Names')
jia	家	family, lineage
jian ai	兼愛	'concern for all'

Jie	桀	(legendary tyrant: last ruler of Xia dynasty)
jing	經	canon
junzi	君子	'gentleman'
kexue	科學	science
Kong Fuzi	孔夫子	Confucius, author of *Lun Yu* (*Analects*)
Laozi	老子	(legendary philosopher, reputed author of *Daodejing*)
lei	類	category
li$_1$	禮	rites, propriety, convention
li$_2$	戾	perversity
Li Chunfeng	李淳風	(seventh-century CE mathematician)
Li Shizhen	李時珍	(seventeenth-century collector of *materia medica*)
lifa	曆法	'calendar studies'
lipu	曆譜	'calendars and chronologies'
Li Si	李斯	(prime minister of state of Qin)
Liu An	劉安	(king of Huainan)
Liu Hui	劉徽	(third-century CE mathematician)
Liu Xiang	劉向	(Han bibliographer)
Liu Xin	劉歆	(Han bibliographer)
Lü Buwei	呂不韋	(compiler of *Lüshi chunqiu*)
luan	亂	disorder, chaos, anarchy
Mengzi	孟子	Mencius
ming jia	名家	'School of Names'
Mozi	墨子	(philosopher, founder of Mohists)
qi$_1$	氣	breath/energy
qi$_2$	齊	'homogenize'
qiandu	塹堵	right prism with right triangular base
qiguai	奇怪	'strange and wonderful things' (chapter of *Lun Heng*)
Qin Shi Huang Di	秦始皇帝	(first emperor)
ru	儒	literate elite
Shang	商	(pre-imperial dynasty)
shao	韶	music played in kingdom of Qi
Shennong	神農	(legendary culture hero)
shi$_1$	士	officials, gentlemen retainers
Shi$_2$	詩	*Odes*

*shi*₃	勢	efficacity
shizhi	實知	'true knowledge' (chapter of *Lun Heng*)
*shu*₁	數	'counting' 'art' 'fate'
*shu*₁ *shu*₂	數術	'calculations and methods'
*Shu*₃	書	*Documents* (cf. *Shangshu*)
Shun	舜	(legendary sage king)
shuonan	說難	'difficulties of persuasion' (chapter of *Hanfeizi*)
Sima Qian	司馬遷	(co-author of *Shiji*)
Sima Tan	司馬談	(co-author of *Shiji*)
suan	算	reckoning
*suan shu*₂	算術	art of reckoning, mathematics
tai shi	太史	grand scribe
tai shi ling	太史令	grand scribe
tian wen	天文	patterns in the heavens
tian xia	天下	the empire, 'all under heaven'
tong	同	'equalize'
tu	圖	'diagrams' 'charts'
Wang Chong	王充	(author of *Lun Heng*)
wu wei	無為	'no ado'
wu xing	五行	five phases
Xia	夏	(pre-imperial dynasty)
xie qi	邪氣	heteropathy, pathogenic *qi*₁
xue	學	learning
Xunzi	荀子	(third-century BCE philosopher)
yangma	陽馬	pyramid with rectangular base and one lateral edge perpendicular to the base
Yao	堯	(legendary sage king)
*Yi*₁	易	*Book of Changes* (cf. *Yijing*)
*yi*₂	義	right, righteousness
yin yang	陰陽	negative and positive principles
youshui	遊說	'wandering advisers'
Yu	禹	(legendary sage king)
yue ling	月令	monthly ordinances
Zhao Youqin	趙友欽	(thirteenth-century CE mathematician)
zhexue	哲學	philosophy
zhi qu	指趣	essential points
Zhou	紂	(legendary tyrant: last ruler of Shang dynasty)

zhou jun	州 郡	provinces and commanderies
Zhuangzi	莊子	(fourth-century BCE philosopher)
ziran	自 然	'self so' spontaneity
Zu Chongzhi	祖 沖 之	(fifth-century CE mathematician)

NOTES ON EDITIONS

For Greek and Latin texts I use the editions specified in the third edition of *The Oxford Classical Dictionary*, ed. S. Hornblower and A. Spawforth (Oxford, 1996).

For the Chinese dynastic histories (*Hanshu* 漢書, *Hou Hanshu* 後漢書, and *Shiji* 史記) I use the standard *Zhonghua shuju* editions. I use the Harvard-Yenching Institute series editions of *Mengzi* 孟子, *Mozi* 墨子, *Xunzi* 荀子 (where I adopt the chapter subdivisions in Knoblock 1988–94); the University of Hong Kong Institute of Chinese Studies series editions of *Daodejing* 道德經, *Guanzi* 管子, *Lunyu* 論語, *Shangjunshu* 商君書, and *Yijing* 易經; and for the mathematical texts, *Zhoubi suanjing* 周髀算經, *Jiuzhang suanshu* 九章算術, and the commentary of Liu Hui on the latter, I use the edition of Qian Baocong, *Suanjing shishu* (Beijing, 1963).

I cite other texts by the following editions:

Hanfeizi 韓非子 in the edition of Chen Qiyou (Shanghai, 1958).

Huainanzi 淮南子 in that of Liu Wendian (Shanghai, 1923).

Huangdi neijing 黃帝內經 in the edition of Ren Yingqiu (Beijing, 1986).

Lun Heng 論衡 in that of Liu Pansui (Beijing, 1957).

Lüshi chunqiu 呂氏春秋 in that of Chen Qiyou (Shanghai, 1984). using the section subdivisions in Knoblock and Riegel 2000.

Shangshu 商書 in that of Gu Jiegang (Beijing, 1936).

Suanshushu 算數書 from the *Zhangjiashan han mu zhu jian* edition (Beijing, 2001).

Zuozhuan 左傳 in the edition of Yang Bojun, 4 vols. (Beijing, 1981) cited by Duke and Year.

All modern works are cited by author's name and year of publication. Full details are to be found in the Bibliography that follows.

BIBLIOGRAPHY

AIKEN, N. E. (1998) *The Biological Origins of Art* (Westport, Conn.).

ANDO, C. (2008) *The Matter of the Gods: Religion and the Roman Empire* (Berkeley and Los Angeles).

ASCHER, M. (1991) *Ethnomathematics* (Pacific Grove, Calif.).

ASPER, M. (2009) 'The Two Cultures of Mathematics in Ancient Greece', in Robson and Stedall (2009), ch. 2.1: 107–32.

ATRAN, S. (2002) *In Gods we Trust* (Oxford).

ATRAN, S., MEDIN, D., and ROSS, N. (2004) 'Evolution and Devolution of Knowledge: A Tale of Two Biologies', *Journal of the Royal Anthropological Institute* 10: 395–420.

BARKER, A. D. (1984) *Greek Musical Writings, i* (Cambridge).

——(2000) *Scientific Method in Ptolemy's Harmonics* (Cambridge).

——(2007) *The Science of Harmonics in Classical Greece* (Cambridge).

BARROW, T. (1984) *An Illustrated Guide to Maori Art* (Auckland).

BARTH, F. (1975) *Ritual and Knowledge among the Baktaman of New Guinea* (Oslo).

BATES, D. G. (2000) 'Why Not Call Modern Medicine "Alternative"?', *Perspectives in Biology and Medicine* 43: 502–18.

BLACKING, J. (1987) *A Common-Sense View of All Music* (Cambridge).

BOAS, F. (1930) *The Religion of the Kwakiutl Indians*, pt. 2 (New York).

——(1955) *Primitive Art* (1st edn. 1927) 2nd edn. (New York).

BOLTON, J. D. P. (1962) *Aristeas of Proconnesus* (Oxford).

BOURDIEU, P. (1984) *Distinction: A Social Critique of the Judgement of Taste* (trans. R. Nice of *La Distinction: Critique sociale du jugement* (Paris 1979)) (London).

BOWEN, A. C. (2001) 'La scienza del cielo nel periodo pretolemaico', in S. Petruccioli (ed.), *Storia della scienza, i* (Rome: Enciclopedia Italiana), sect. 4, ch. 21: 806–39.

——(2002a) 'Simplicius and the Early History of Greek Planetary Theory', *Perspectives on Science* 10: 155–67.

——(2002b) 'The Art of the Commander and the Emergence of Predictive Astronomy', in C. J. Tuplin and T. E. Rihll (eds.), *Science and Mathematics in Ancient Greek Culture* (Oxford), 76–111.

——(2007) 'The Demarcation of Physical Theory and Astronomy by Geminus and Ptolemy', *Perspectives on Science* 15/3: 327–58.

BOYD, R., and RICHERSON, P. J. (2006) 'Solving the Puzzle of Human Cooperation', in S. C. Levinson and P. Jaisson (eds.), *Evolution and Culture* (Cambridge, Mass.), 105–32.

BOYER, P. (1994) *The Naturalness of Religious Ideas* (Berkeley and Los Angeles).

—— (2001) *Religion Explained* (New York).

BRAGUE, R. (2002) *Eccentric Culture* (trans. S. Lester of 2nd edn. of *Europe, la voie romaine* (Paris 1993)) (South Bend, Ind.).

—— (2007) *The Law of God* (trans. L. G. Cochrane of *La Loi de Dieu* (Paris 2005)) (Chicago).

BRAIN, P. (1986) *Galen on Blood-letting* (Cambridge).

BRAY, F., DOROFEEVA-LICHTMANN, V., and MÉTAILIÉ, G. (eds.) (2007) *Graphics and Text in the Production of Technical Knowledge in China: the Warp and the Weft* (Leiden).

BRONKHORST, J. (1999) 'Why Is There Philosophy in India?' (Royal Netherlands Academy of Arts and Sciences, Amsterdam).

—— (2001) 'Pāṇini and Euclid: Reflections on Indian Geometry', *Journal of Indian Philosophy* 29: 43–80.

—— (2002) 'Discipliné par le débat', in L. Bansat-Boudon and J. Scheid (eds.), *Le Disciple et ses maîtres* (Paris), 207–25.

—— (2007) 'Modes of Debate and Refutation of Adversaries in Classical and Medieval India: A Preliminary Investigation', *Antiquorum Philosophia* 1: 269–80.

—— (forthcoming) *Aux origines de la philosophie indienne: Esquisse d'une histoire de la philosophie indienne ancienne*.

BROOKE, J. H. (1991) *Science and Religion: Some Historical Perspectives* (Cambridge).

BROWN, D. (2000) *Mesopotamian Planetary Astronomy-Astrology* (Groningen).

BROWN, P. (2003) *The Rise of Western Christendom* (1st edn. 1996) 2nd edn. (Oxford).

BRUNSCHWIG, J. (1980) 'Du mouvement et de l'immobilité de la loi', *Revue internationale de philosophie* 133–4: 512–40.

—— (1996) 'Rule and Exception: On the Aristotelian Theory of Equity', in M. Frede and G. Striker (eds.), *Rationality in Greek Thought* (Oxford), 115–55.

BURKE, P. (2001) 'Overture: The New History: Its Past and its Future', in P. Burke (ed.), *New Perspectives in Historical Writing* (1st edn. 1991) 2nd edn. (Cambridge), 1–24.

BUTTERFIELD, H. (1949) *The Origins of Modern Science* (London).

CALAME, C. (1996) *Mythe et l'histoire dans l'antiquité grecque* (Lausanne).

—— (1999) 'The Rhetoric of *Muthos* and *Logos*: Forms of Figurative Discourse', in R. Buxton (ed.), *From Myth to Reason?* (Oxford), 119–43.

CAMPBELL, S. (2001) 'The Captivating Agency of Art', in Pinney and Thomas (2001), 117–35.

CARR, E. H. (2001) *What is History? With a New Introduction by R. J. Evans* (original edn. 1961) (Houndmills, Basingstoke).

CHEMLA, K., and GUO SHUCHUN (2004) *Les Neuf chapitres: Le Classique mathématique de la Chine ancienne et ses commentaires* (Paris).

CHENG, A. (ed.) (2005) 'Y a-t-il une philosophie chinoise? Un état de la question', *Extrême-Orient Extrême-Occident* 27.

CLUNAS, C. (1991) *Superfluous Things* (Cambridge).

——(1997) *Pictures and Visuality in Early Modern China* (London).

COHEN, D. (1995) *Law, Violence, and Community in Classical Athens* (Cambridge).

CONKLIN, H. C. (1954) 'The Relation of Hanunóo Culture to the Plant World', PhD diss., Yale University.

CROMBIE, A. C. (1994) *Styles of Scientific Thinking in the European Tradition*, 3 vols. (London).

CULLEN, C. (1996) *Astronomy and Mathematics in Ancient China: The Zhou bi suan jing* (Cambridge).

——(2001) *'Yi'an* (case statements): The Origins of a Genre of Chinese Medical Literature', in Hsu (2001), 297–323.

——(2004) *The Suan Shu Shu: Writings on Reckoning* (Needham Research Institute Working Papers, 1) (Cambridge).

CULPEPER, N. (1979) *Culpeper's Complete Herbal and English Physician* (1st pub. as *The English Physitian*, London 1652) (Hong Kong).

CUNNINGHAM, A., and WILSON, P. (1993) 'De-centring the "Big Picture": *The Origins of Modern Science* and the Modern Origins of Science', *British Journal for the History of Science* 26: 407–32.

CUOMO, S. (2001) *Ancient Mathematics* (London).

DARBO-PESCHANSKI, C. (2007) 'The Origins of Greek Historiography', in Marincola (2007), i. 27–38.

DASCAL, M. (2006) *G. W. Leibniz: The Art of Controversies* (Dordrecht).

DASTON, L., and GALISON, P. (2007) *Objectivity* (New York).

DAVIES, J. K. (1996) 'Deconstructing Gortyn: When Is a Code a Code?' in L. Foxhall and A. D. E. Lewis (eds.), *Greek Law in its Political Setting* (Oxford), 33–56.

DE CAMARGO, K. R. (2002) 'The Thought Style of Physicians: Strategies for Keeping Up with Medical Knowledge', *Social Studies of Science* 32: 827–55.

DEAN-JONES, L. A. (1994) *Women's Bodies in Classical Greek Science* (Oxford).

DEHAENE, S. (1997) *The Number Sense: How the Mind Creates Mathematics* (Oxford).

DELEUZE, G., and GUATTARI, F. (1991) *Qu'est-ce que la philosophie?* (Paris).

DESCOLA, P. (1996) *The Spears of Twilight* (trans. J. Lloyd of *Les Lances du crépuscule* (Paris 1993)) (London).

——(2005) *Par delà nature et culture* (Paris).

DETIENNE, M. (2008) *Comparing the Incomparable* (trans. J. Lloyd of *Comparer l'incomparable* (Paris 2000)) (Stanford, Calif.).

——(ed.) (2003) *Qui veut prendre la parole?* (Paris).

DEVEREUX, G. (1961a) 'Shamans as Neurotics', *American Anthropologist* 63: 1088–90.

——(1961b) *Mohave Ethnopsychiatry and Suicide: The Psychiatric Knowledge and the Psychic Disturbances of an Indian Tribe* (Bureau of American Ethnology, Bulletin 175, Smithsonian Institution, Washington DC).

DIAMOND, A. S. (1971) *Primitive Law Past and Present* (London).

DOROFEEVA-LICHTMANN, V. (1995) 'Conception of Terrestrial Organization in the *Shan hai jing*', *Bulletin de l'École Française d'Extrême Orient* 82: 57–110.

——(2001) 'I testi geografici ufficiali dalla dinastia Han alla dinastia Tang', in S. Petruccioli (ed.) *Storia della scienza* (Rome), vol. ii, sect. 16: 190–7.

DOUGLAS, M. (1966) *Purity and Danger* (London).

DRURY, N. (1996) *The Elements of Shamanism* (Shaftesbury).

DUNBAR, R. (1995) *The Trouble with Science* (London).

DUPRÉ, J. (1993) *The Disorder of Things* (Cambridge, Mass.).

DURKHEIM, E. (1976) *The Elementary Forms of the Religious Life* (trans. J. W. Swain of *Les Formes élémentaires de la vie religieuse* (Paris 1912)) 2nd edn. (London).

EAGLETON, T. (1990) *The Ideology of the Aesthetic* (Oxford).

ELIADE, M. (1954) *The Myth of the Eternal Return* (trans. W. R. Trask of *Le Mythe de l'éternel retour* (Paris 1949)) (New York).

——(1964) *Shamanism: Archaic Techniques of Ecstasy* (trans. W. R. Trask of *Le Chamanisme et les techniques archäiques de l'extase* (Paris 1951)) (New York).

EVANS, E. P. (1906) *The Criminal Prosecution and Capital Punishment of Animals* (London).

EVERETT, D. L. (2005) 'Cultural Constraints on Grammar and Cognition in Pirahã', *Current Anthropology* 46: 621–34.

FELDHERR, A., and HARDY, G. (eds.) (forthcoming) *The Oxford History of Historical Writing*, i. *Beginnings to 600 CE* (Oxford).

FESTINGER, L., RIECKEN, H. W., and SCHACHTER, S. (1956) *When Prophecy Fails: A Social and Psychological Study of a Modern Group that Predicted the Destruction of the World* (Minneapolis).

FEYERABEND, P. K. (1975) *Against Method* (London).

FINLEY, M. I. (1962) 'Athenian Demagogues', *Past and Present* 21: 3–24.

—— (1975) *The Use and Abuse of History* (London).

FORGE, A. (1967) 'The Abelam Artist', in M. Freedman, *Social Organization: Essays Presented to Raymond Firth* (London), 65–84.

FORNARA, C. W. (1983) *The Nature of History in Ancient Greece and Rome* (Berkeley and Los Angeles).

FORRESTER, J. (1996), 'If *p*, then what? Thinking in Cases', *History of the Human Sciences* 9/3: 1–25.

FOUCAULT, M. (1967) *Madness and Civilization* (trans. R. Howard of *Histoire de la folie* (Paris 1961)) (London).

—— (1973) *The Birth of the Clinic* (trans. A. M. Sheridan Smith of *La Naissance de la clinique* (Paris 1963)) (London).

—— (1977) *Discipline and Punish* (trans. A. Sheridan of *Surveiller et punir* (Paris 1975)) (London).

FOWLER, D. H. (1999) *The Mathematics of Plato's Academy*, 2nd edn. (Oxford).

—— (1996) 'Herodotos and His Contemporaries', *Journal of Hellenic Studies* 116: 62–87.

FOX, R. B. (1952) 'The Pinatubo Negritos: Their Useful Plants and Material Culture', *Philippine Journal of Science* 81: 173–391.

FREDE, M. (2004) 'Aristotle's Account of the Origins of Philosophy', *Rhizai* 1: 9–44.

FRIEDLANDER, S. (ed.) (1992) *Probing the Limits of Representation* (Cambridge, Mass.).

FURTH, C., ZEITLIN, J. T., and HSIUNG, P. C. (eds.) (2007) *Thinking with Cases* (Honolulu).

GALISON, P., and STUMP, D. J. (eds.) (1996) *The Disunity of Science* (Stanford, Calif.).

GALLAGHER, C., and GREENBLATT, S. (2000) *Practicing New Historicism* (Chicago).

GARNSEY, P. (2007) *Thinking about Property: From Antiquity to the Age of Revolution* (Cambridge).

GEERTZ, C. (1973) *The Interpretation of Cultures* (New York).

—— (1983) *Local Knowledge* (New York).

GELL, A. (1998) *Art and Agency: An Anthropological Theory* (Oxford).

—— (1999) *The Art of Anthropology* (London).

GELLNER, E. (1973) 'The Savage and the Modern Mind', in Horton and Finnegan (1973), 162–81.

—— (1985) *Relativism and the Social Sciences* (Cambridge).

GELMAN, R., and GALLISTEL, C. R. (1986) *The Child's Understanding of Number* (Cambridge, Mass.).

GERNET, J. (1985) *China and the Christian Impact* (trans. J. Lloyd of *Chine et christianisme* (Paris 1982)) (Cambridge).

GERNET, L. (1981) *The Anthropology of Ancient Greece* (trans. J. Hamilton and B. Nagy of *Anthropologie de la Grèce antique* (Paris 1968)) (Baltimore).

GINZBURG, C. (1992) 'Just One Witness', in Friedlander (1992), ch. 5: 82–96.

—— (1999) *History, Rhetoric and Proof* (Hanover).

GLUCKMAN, M. (1965) *Politics, Law and Ritual in Tribal Society* (Oxford).

—— (1967) *The Judicial Process among the Barotse of Northern Rhodesia* (1st edn. 1955) 2nd edn. (Manchester).

—— (1972) *The Ideas in Barotse Jurisprudence* (1st edn. 1965) 2nd edn. (Manchester).

GÓMEZ NOGALES, S. (1990) 'Ibn Ṭufayl, primer filósofo-novelista', in Martínez Lorca (1990b), 359–85.

GOOD, B. J. (1994) *Medicine, Rationality, and Experience* (Cambridge).

GOODMAN, N. (1976) *Languages of Art* (1st edn. 1969), 2nd edn. (Indianapolis).

GOODY, E. (1995) 'Social Intelligence and Prayer as Dialogue', in E. Goody (ed.), *Social Intelligence and Interaction* (Cambridge), 206–20.

GOODY, J. (1961) 'Religion and Ritual: the Definitional Problem', *British Journal of Sociology* 12: 142–64.

—— (1977) *The Domestication of the Savage Mind* (Cambridge).

GORDON, P. (2004) 'Numerical Cognition Without Words: Evidence from Amazonia', *Science* 306/5695: 496–9.

GRAFTON, A. (2007) *What was History?* (Cambridge).

GRAHAM, A. C. (1978) *Later Mohist Logic, Ethics and Science* (London).

—— (1989) *Disputers of the Tao* (La Salle, Ill.).

GRANET, M. (1934) *La Pensée chinoise* (Paris).

GRASSENI, C. (ed.) (2007) *Skilled Visions* (New York).

GREENWOOD, D. J. (1978) 'Culture by the Pound: An Anthropological Perspective on Tourism as Cultural Commoditization', in V. L. Smith (ed.), *Hosts and Guests: The Anthropology of Tourism* (Oxford), 129–38.

GREGORY, R. L. (1970) *The Intelligent Eye* (London).

GUTHRIE, S. E. (1993) *Faces in the Clouds: A New Theory of Religion* (Oxford).

HAACK, S. (2007) *Defending Science Within Reason*, 2nd edn. (Amherst, Mass.).

HACKING, I. (1982) 'Language, Truth and Reason', in Hollis and Lukes (1982) 48–66 (repr. in Hacking 2002: 159–77).

—— (1983) *Representing and Intervening* (Cambridge).

—— (1991) 'The Making and Molding of Child Abuse', *Critical Inquiry* 17: 253–88.

—— (1992a) '"Style" for Historians and Philosophers', *Studies in History and Philosophy of Science* 23: 1–20 (repr. in Hacking 2002: 178–99).

——(1992b) 'Multiple Personality Disorder and its Hosts', *History of the Human Sciences* 5/2: 3–31.

——(1995) 'The Looping Effects of Human Kinds', in D. Sperber, D. Premack, and A. J. Premack (eds.), *Causal Cognition* (Oxford), 351–83.

——(1996) 'The Disunities of the Sciences', in Galison and Stump (1996), 37–74.

——(2002) *Historical Ontology* (Cambridge, Mass.).

HADOT, P. (1990) 'Forms of Life and Forms of Discourse in Ancient Philosophy', *Critical Inquiry* 16: 483–505.

——(2002) *What Is Ancient Philosophy?* (trans. M. Chase of *Qu'est-ce que la philosophie antique?* (Paris 1995)) (Cambridge, Mass.).

HAIDT, J., and JOSEPH, C. (2004) 'Intuitive Ethics: How Innately Prepared Intuitions Generate Culturally Variable Virtues', *Daedalus* (Fall), 55–66.

HANSEN, M. H. (1983) *The Athenian Ecclesia* (Copenhagen).

HARPER, D. (1998) *Early Chinese Medical Literature: The Mawangdui Medical Manuscripts* (London).

HARRISON, P. (2002) *'Religion' and the Religions in the English Enlightenment* (1st pub. 1990), 2nd edn. (Cambridge).

HARTOG, F. (1988) *The Mirror of Herodotus* (trans. J. Lloyd of *Le Miroir d'Hérodote* (Paris 1980)) (Berkeley and Los Angeles).

——(2003) *Régimes d'historicité* (Paris).

——(2005) *Évidence de l'histoire* (Paris).

HASKELL, F. (1963) *Patrons and Painters: A Study in the Relations between Italian Art and Society in the Age of the Baroque* (London).

HAYES, P. J. (1990) 'The Naive Physics Manifesto', in M. Boden (ed.), *The Philosophy of Artificial Intelligence* (Oxford), 171–205 (originally published in D. Michie (ed.), *Expert Systems in the Micro-Electronic Age* (Edinburgh 1979), 242–70).

HENARE, A., HOLBRAAD, M., and WASTELL, S. (eds.) (2007) *Thinking Through Things* (London).

HERMAN, G. (1987) *Ritualised Friendship and the Greek City* (Cambridge).

HO PENG-YOKE (1991) 'Chinese Science: The Traditional Chinese View', *Bulletin of the School of Oriental and African Studies* 54: 506–19.

HÖLKESKAMP, K.-J. (2005) 'What's in a Code? Solon's Laws between Complexity, Compilation and Contingency', *Hermes* 133: 280–93.

HOLLIS, M., and LUKES, S. (eds.) (1982) *Rationality and Relativism* (Oxford).

HOPKINS, K. (1980) 'Brother–Sister Marriage in Roman Egypt', *Comparative Studies in Society and History* 22: 303–54.

HORNBLOWER, S. (ed.) (1994) *Greek Historiography* (Oxford).

HORTON, R. (1960) 'A Definition of Religion, and Its Uses', *Journal of the Royal Anthropological Institute of Great Britain and Ireland* 90: 201–26.

——(1965) *Kalabari Sculpture* (Lagos).

HORTON, R. (1970) 'African Traditional Thought and Western Science' (originally published in *Africa* 37: 50–71 and 155–87), in Wilson (1970), 131–71.

—— and FINNEGAN, R. (eds.) (1973) *Modes of Thought* (London).

HSU, E. (2002) *The Telling Touch* (Habilitationschrift, Sinology, University of Heidelberg).

—— (ed.) (2001) *Innovation in Chinese Medicine* (Cambridge).

—— and HØG, E. (eds.) (2002) *Countervailing Creativity: Patient Agency in the Globalisation of Asian Medicines* (Special Issue of *Anthropology and Medicine* 9/3) (Oxford).

—— and LOW, C. (eds.) (2007) *Wind, Life, Health: Anthropological and Historical Perspectives* (Special Issue of *Journal of the Royal Anthropological Institute*).

HUANG YI-LONG and CHANG CHIH-CH'ENG (1996) 'The Evolution and Decline of the Ancient Chinese Practice of Watching for the Ethers', *Chinese Science* 13: 82–106.

HUFFMAN, C. A. (2005) *Archytas of Tarentum* (Cambridge).

HUGHES-FREELAND, F. (1997) 'Art and Politics: From Javanese Court Dance to Indonesian Art', *Journal of the Royal Anthropological Institute* 3: 473–95.

HULSEWÉ, A. F. P. (1955) *Remnants of Han Law*, i. *Introductory Studies* (LEIDEN).

—— (1986) 'Ch'in and Han Law', in D. Twitchett and M. A. N. Loewe (eds.), *The Cambridge History of China* (Cambridge), i, ch. 9: 520–44.

HUMPHREY, C., and ONON, U. (1996) *Shamans and Elders: Experience, Knowledge, and Power among the Daur Mongols* (Oxford).

HUMPHREYS, S. C. (1985) 'Social Relations on Stage: Witnesses in Classical Athens', *History and Anthropology* 1: 313–69.

HUNGER, H. (1992) *Astrological Reports to Assyrian Kings* (State Archives of Assyria 8, Helsinki).

IMHAUSEN, A. (2009), 'Traditions and Myths in the Historiography of Egyptian Mathematics', in Robson and Stedall (2009), ch. 9.1: 781–800.

INGOLD, T. (2000) *The Perception of the Environment* (London).

—— (ed.) (1996) *Key Debates in Anthropology* (London).

JAMES, W. (1902) *The Varieties of Religious Experience* (London).

JARVIE, I. C. (1970) 'Explaining Cargo Cults', in Wilson (1970), 50–61.

JONES, A. R. (1999) *Astronomical Papyri from Oxyrhynchus* (Memoirs of the American Philosophical Society, 233, Philadelphia).

JULLIEN, F. (1995) *The Propensity of Things* (trans. J. Lloyd of *La Propension des choses* (Paris, 1992)) (New York).

KAUL, A. R. (2007) 'The Limits of Commodification in Traditional Irish Music Sessions', *Journal of the Royal Anthropological Institute* 13: 703–19.

KEANE, W. (2008) 'The Evidence of the Senses and the Materiality of Religion', *Journal of the Royal Anthropological Institute*, special issue: S110–S127.

KEEGAN, D. J. (1988) 'The "Huang-ti nei-ching": The Structure of the Compilation, the Significance of the Structure', unpublished PhD, University of California, Berkeley.

KING, H. (1998) *Hippocrates' Woman: Reading the Female Body in Ancient Greece* (London).

KLEINMAN, A. (1980) *Patients and Healers in the Context of Culture* (Berkeley and Los Angeles).

—— (1995) *Writing at the Margin: Discourse between Anthropology and Medicine* (Berkeley and Los Angeles).

—— and GOOD, B. (eds.) (1985) *Culture and Depression* (Berkeley and Los Angeles).

KLEINMAN, A., KUNSTADTER, P., ALEXANDER, E. R., and GALL, J. L. (eds.) (1975) *Medicine in Chinese Cultures* (Bethesda).

KNOBLOCK, J. (1988–94) *Xunzi: A Translation and Study of the Complete Works*, 3 vols. (Stanford, Calif.).

—— and RIEGEL, J. (2000) *The Annals of Lü Buwei* (Stanford, Calif.).

KNORR, W. R. (1986) *The Ancient Tradition of Geometric Problems* (Boston).

KOSELLECK, R. (1985) *Historia Magistra Vitae* (1st pub. in H. Braun and M. Riedel (eds.) *Natur und Geschichte: Karl Löwith zum 70 Geburtstag* (Stuttgart 1967), 825–38) in *Futures Past* (trans. K. Tribe of *Vergangene Zukunft* (Frankfurt 1985)) (Cambridge, Mass.), 21–38.

KROEBER, T. (1961) *Ishi* (Berkeley and Los Angeles).

KUHN, T. S. (1970) *The Structure of Scientific Revolutions* (1st pub. 1962) 2nd edn. (Chicago).

—— (1977) *The Essential Tension* (Chicago).

KURIYAMA, S. (1999) *The Expressiveness of the Body and the Divergence of Greek and Chinese Medicine* (New York).

KUSCH, M. (2002) *Knowledge by Agreement* (Oxford).

LAÍN ENTRALGO, P. (1970) *The Therapy of the Word in Classical Antiquity* (trans. L. J. Rather and J. M. Sharp of *La curación por la palabra en la Antigüedad clásica* (Madrid 1958)) (New Haven).

LANG, P. (ed.) (2004) *Reinventions: Essays on Hellenistic and Early Roman Science* (Kelowna).

LATOUR, B. (1988) *The Pasteurization of France* (trans. A. Sheridan and J. Law of *Les Microbes: Guerre et paix suivi de irréductions* (Paris 1984)) (Cambridge, Mass.).

LAYTON, R. (1991) *The Anthropology of Art* (1st edn. 1981) 2nd edn, (Cambridge).

LEACH, E. R. (1961) *Rethinking Anthopology* (London).

LESLIE, C. (ed.) (1976) *Asian Medical Systems: A Comparative Study* (Berkeley and Los Angeles).

LÉVI-STRAUSS, C. (1966) *The Savage Mind* (trans. of *La Pensée sauvage* (Paris 1962)) (London).

—— (1968) *Structural Anthropology* (trans. C. Jacobson and B. G. Schoepf of *Anthropologie structurale* (Paris 1958)) (London).

LEWIS, G. (1975) *Knowledge of Illness in a Sepik Society* (London).

LEWIS, M. E. (1999) *Writing and Authority in Early China* (Albany, NY).

LINDENBAUM, S., and LOCK, M. (eds.) (1993) *Knowledge, Power, and Practice: The Anthropology of Medicine and Everyday Life* (Berkeley and Los Angeles).

LITTLE, K. (1965) 'The Political Function of the Poro, Part I', *Africa* 35: 349–65.

—— (1966) 'The Political Function of the Poro, Part II', *Africa* 36: 62–72.

LLOYD, G. E. R. (1987) *The Revolutions of Wisdom* (Berkeley and Los Angeles).

—— (1990) *Demystifying Mentalities* (Cambridge).

—— (1991) *Methods and Problems in Greek Science* (Cambridge).

—— (2002) *The Ambitions of Curiosity* (Cambridge).

—— (2003) *In the Grip of Disease* (Oxford).

—— (2004) *Ancient Worlds, Modern Reflections* (Oxford).

—— (2005a) 'The Institutions of Censure: China, Greece and the Modern World', *Quaderni di storia* 62: 7–52.

—— (2005b) *The Delusions of Invulnerability* (London).

—— (2006) 'Mathematics as a Model of Method in Galen', in *Principles and Practices in Ancient Greek and Chinese Science* (Aldershot), ch. v.

—— and SIVIN, N. (2002) *The Way and the Word* (New Haven).

LOEWE, M. A. N. (2004) *The Men who Governed Han China* (Leiden).

—— (2006) *The Government of the Qin and Han Empires 221 BCE – 220 CE* (Indianapolis).

LUHRMANN, T. H. (2000) *Of Two Minds: The Growing Disorder in American Psychiatry* (New York).

MACDOWELL, D. M. (1978) *The Law in Classical Athens* (London).

MACINTYRE, A. (1970) 'Is Understanding Religion Compatible with Believing?' in Wilson (1970), 62–77.

MAJOR, J. S. (1993) *Heaven and Earth in Early Han Thought* (Albany, NY).

MALINOWSKI, B. (1925) 'Magic Science and Religion' in Needham (1925), 19–84.

MARCOVITCH, H. (ed.) (2005) *Black's Medical Dictionary*, 41st edn. (London).

MARINCOLA, J. (ed.) (2007) *A Companion to Greek and Roman Historiography*, 2 vols. (Oxford).

MARTÍNEZ LORCA, A. (1990a) 'La Filosofía en al-Andalus: Una aproximación histórica', in Martínez Lorca (1990b), 7–93.

—— (ed.) (1990b) *Ensayos sobre la Filosofía en el al-Andalus* (Barcelona).

MASUZAWA, T. (2005) *The Invention of World Religions* (Chicago).

MATILAL, B. K. (1971) *Epistemology, Logic and Grammar in Indian Philosophical Analysis*, Janua Linguarum Series Minor 111 (The Hague).

—— (1985) *Logic, Language and Reality* (Delhi).

MATTHEWS, G. B. (1984) *Dialogues with Children* (Cambridge, Mass.)

MÉTAILIÉ, G. (2001) 'The *Bencao gangmu* of Li Shizhen: An Innovation in Medical History?', in Hsu (2001), 221–61.

MITHEN, S. (1996) *The Prehistory of the Mind: A Search for the Origins of Art, Religion and Science* (London).

MOMIGLIANO, A. (1966) 'Time in Ancient Historiography', *History and Theory* 6: 1–23.

MUELLER, I. (2004) 'Remarks on Physics and Mathematical Astronomy and Optics in Epicurus, Sextus Empiricus, and Some Stoics', in Lang (2004), 57–87.

MUNGELLO, D. (ed.) (1994) *The Chinese Rites Controversy* (Nettetal).

NAPIER, A. D. (1992) *Foreign Bodies: Performance, Art, and Symbolic Anthropology* (Berkeley and Los Angeles).

NEEDHAM, J. (ed.) (1925) *Science Religion and Reality* (London).

NEEDHAM, J. (1954–) *Science and Civilisation in China* (24 vols. to date) (Cambridge).

NETZ, R. (1999) *The Shaping of Deduction in Greek Mathematics* (Cambridge).

—— (2009) *Ludic Proof* (Cambridge).

NICHTER, M. and LOCK, M. (eds.) (2002) *New Horizons in Medical Anthopology* (London).

NICOLAI, R. (2007) 'The Place of History in the Ancient World', in Marincola (2007), i. 13–26.

NUTTON, V. (2004) *Ancient Medicine* (London).

NYLAN, M. (2001) *The Five "Confucian" Classics* (New Haven).

OSBORNE, R. (1985) 'Law in Action in Classical Athens', *Journal of Hellenic Studies* 105: 40–58.

—— (1997) 'Law and Laws: How Do We Join Up the Dots?' in L. G. Mitchell and P. J. Rhodes (eds.), *The Development of the Polis in Archaic Greece* (London), 74–82.

OVERMYER, D. L., KEIGHTLEY, D. N., SHAUGHNESSY, E. L., COOK, C. A., and HARPER, D. (1995) 'Early Religious Traditions: The Neolithic Period Through the Han Dynasty, ca. 4000 B.C.E. to 220 C.E.', *The Journal of Asian Studies* 54/1: 124–60.

PARKER, R. (1983) *Miasma: Pollution and Purification in Early Greek Religion* (Oxford).

PARPOLA, S. (1970) *Letters from Assyrian Scholars to the Kings Esarhaddon and Assurbanipal* pt. 1 (Alter Orient und Altes Testament 5/1, Neukirchen).

——(1983) *Letters from Assyrian Scholars to the Kings Esarhaddon and Assurbanipal* pt. 2 (Alter Orient und Altes Testament 5/2, Neukirchen).

——(1993) *Letters from Assyrian and Babylonian Scholars* (State Archives of Assyria 10, Helsinki).

PIAGET, J. (1930) *The Child's Conception of Physical Causality* (trans. M. Gabain of *La Causalité physique chez l'enfant* (Paris 1927)) (London).

PINNEY, C., and THOMAS, N. (eds.) (2001) *Beyond Aesthetics* (Oxford).

POLKINGHORNE, J. (2000) 'Eschatology: Some Questions and Some Insights from Science', in *The End of the World and the Ends of God*, eds. J. Polkinghorne and M. Welker (Harrisburg), 29–41.

PRESS, G. A. (1982) *The Development of the Idea of History* (Kingston).

PRITCHARD, J. B. (1969) *Ancient Near Eastern Texts* (1st edn. 1955), 3rd edn. (Princeton).

PUETT, M. J. (2002) *To Become a God: Cosmology, Sacrifice, and Self-Divinization in Early China* (Cambridge, Mass.).

PYYSIÄINEN, I. (2001) *How Religion Works: Towards a New Cognitive Science of Religion* (Leiden).

——and ANTTONEN, V. (eds.) (2002) *Current Approaches in the Cognitive Science of Religion* (London).

REDING, J.-P. (1985) *Les Fondements philosophiques de la rhétorique chez les sophistes grecs et chez les sophistes chinois* (Bern).

RENAN, E. (1935) *The Memoirs of Ernest Renan* (trans. J. Lewis May of *Souvenirs d'enfance et de jeunesse* (Paris 1883)) (London).

RICHARDSON, M. E. J. (2000) *Hammurabi's Laws* (Sheffield).

RICOEUR, P. (2004) *Memory, History, Forgetting* (trans. K. Blamey and D. Pellauer of *La Mémoire, l'histoire, l'oubli* (Paris 2000)) (Chicago).

RIDDLE, J. M. (1985) *Dioscorides on Pharmacy and Medicine* (Austin).

ROBINET, I. (1997) *Taoism: Growth of a Religion* (trans. P. Brooks of *Histoire du Taoisme: Des origines au xive siècle* (Paris 1991)) (Stanford, Calif.).

ROBSON, E. (2009) 'Mathematics Education in an Old Babylonian Scribal School', in Robson and Stedall (2009), ch. 3.1: 199–227.

——and STEDALL, J. (eds.) (2009) *The Oxford Handbook of the History of Mathematics* (Oxford).

ROCHBERG, F. (2004) *The Heavenly Writing: Divination, Horoscopy, and Astronomy in Mesopotamian Culture* (Cambridge).

ROSEN, L. (1989) *The Anthropology of Justice* (Cambridge).

Ross, N. (2002) 'Cognitive Aspects of Intergenerational Change: Mental Models, Cultural Change, and Environmental Behavior among the Lacandon Maya of Southern Mexico', *Human Organization* 61: 125–38.

Rossi, C. (2009), 'Mixing, Building, and Feeding: Mathematics and Technology in Ancient Egypt', in Robson and Stedall (2009), ch. 5.1: 407–28.

Sackett, D. L., Scott Richardson, W., Rosenberg, W., and Haynes, R. B. (1997) *Evidence Based Medicine: How to Practice and Teach EBM* (Edinburgh).

Saito, K. (2009) 'Reading Ancient Greek Mathematics', in Robson and Stedall (2009), ch. 9.2: 801–26.

Saler, B. (2000) *Conceptualizing Religion* (New York).

Scarborough, J., and Nutton, V. (1982) 'The Preface of Dioscorides' *De Materia Medica*', *Transactions and Studies of the College of Physicians of Philadelphia* ser. 5, 4: 187–227.

Schacht, J. (1964) *An Introduction to Islamic Law* (Oxford).

Scheidel, W. (1997) 'Brother–Sister Marriage in Roman Egypt', *Journal of Biosocial Science* 29: 361–71.

Scoditti, G. M. G. (1990) *Kitawa: A Linguistic and Aesthetic Analysis of Visual Art in Melanesia* (Berlin).

Shapin, S., and Schaffer, S. (1985) *Leviathan and the Air Pump* (Princeton).

Shepherd, R. (2002) 'Commodification, Culture and Tourism', *Tourist Studies* 2: 183–201.

Shirokogoroff, S. M. (1935) *Psychomental Complex of the Tungus* (London).

Silverman, J. (1967) 'Shamanism and Acute Schizophrenia', *American Anthropologist* 69: 21–31.

Sivin, N. (1987) *Traditional Medicine in Contemporary China* (Ann Arbor).

——(1995a) 'Cosmos and Computation in Early Chinese Mathematical Astronomy', in *Researches and Reflections*, i. *Science in Ancient China* (Aldershot) ch. ii (original publication *T'oung Pao* 55 (1969): 1–73).

——(1995b) 'On the Word "Taoist" as a Source of Perplexity', in N. Sivin, *Researches and Reflections*, ii. *Medicine, Philosophy and Religion in Ancient China* (Aldershot), ch. vi (original publication *History of Religions* 17 (1978): 303–30).

Skorupski, J. (1976) *Symbol and Theory* (Cambridge).

Smith, B., and Casati, R. (1994) 'Naive Physics: An Essay in Ontology', *Philosophical Psychology* 7: 227–47.

Solso, R. L. (2004) *The Psychology of Art and the Evolution of the Conscious Brain* (Cambridge, Mass.).

Sperber, D. (1975) *Rethinking Symbolism* (trans. A. Morton of *Le Symbolisme en général* (Paris 1974)) (Cambridge).

——(1985) *On Anthropological Knowledge* (Cambridge).

Staden, H. von (1989) *Herophilus: The Art of Medicine in Early Alexandria* (Cambridge).

STRATHERN, A., and STRATHERN, M. (1971) *Self-Decoration in Mount Hagen* (London).

STRATHERN, M. (1979). 'The Self in Self-Decoration', *Oceania* 49: 241–57.

TAMBIAH, S. J. (1968) 'The Magical Power of Words', *Man*, NS 3: 175–208.

—— (1973) 'Form and Meaning of Magical Acts: A Point of View', in Horton and Finnegan (1973), 199–229.

—— (1990) *Magic, Science, Religion, and the Scope of Rationality* (Cambridge).

TAYLOR, L. (2008) '"They May Say Tourist, May Say Truly Painting": Aesthetic Evaluation and Meaning of Bark Paintings in Western Arnhem Land, Northern Australia', *Journal of the Royal Anthropological Institute* 14: 865–85.

THAPAR, R. (1996) *Time as a Metaphor of History: Early India* (Delhi).

THOMAS, K. (1971) *Religion and the Decline of Magic* (London).

THOMAS, N., and HUMPHREY, C. (eds.) (1994) *Shamanism, History, and the State* (Ann Arbor).

TODD, S. C. (1990) 'The Purpose of Evidence in Athenian Courts', in *Nomos*, eds. P. Cartledge, P. Millett, and S. Todd (Cambridge), 19–39.

TOOBY, J., and COSMIDES, L. (2001) 'Does Beauty Build Adapted Minds?', *SubStance* 30/1–2: 6–27.

TOUWAIDE, A. (1997) 'La Thérapeutique médicamenteuse de Dioscoride à Galien: Du *pharmaco-centrisme* au *médico-centrisme*', in A. Debru (ed.), *Galen on Pharmacology* (Leiden), 255–82.

TYBJERG, K. (2004) 'Hero of Alexandria's Mechanical Geometry', in Lang (2004), 29–56.

TYLOR, E. B. (1891) *Primitive Culture* (1st edn. 1871) 2nd edn., 2 vols. (London).

UNSCHULD, P. U. (1985) *Medicine in China: A History of Ideas* (Berkeley and Los Angeles).

—— (1986) *Medicine in China: A History of Pharmaceutics* (Berkeley and Los Angeles).

VANDERMEERSCH, L. (2007) 'La Conception chinoise de l'histoire', in A. Cheng (ed.), *La Pensée en Chine aujourd'hui* (Paris), 47–74.

VERNANT, J.-P. (1983) *Myth and Thought among the Greeks* (trans. of *Mythe et pensée chez les grecs* (Paris 1965)) (London).

VIDAL-NAQUET, P. (1977) 'Du bon usage de la trahison', in *Flavius Josèphe: La Guerre des Juifs*, P. Savinel (Paris), 9–115.

—— (1986) *The Black Hunter* (trans. A. Szegedy-Maszak of *Le Chasseur noir* (Paris 1981)) (Baltimore).

—— (2005) *Flavius Josèphe et la Guerre des juifs* (Paris).

VITEBSKY, P. (1995) *The Shaman* (London).

VITRAC, B. (2005) 'Les Classifications des sciences mathématiques en Grèce ancienne', *Archives de philosophie* 68: 269–301.

VIVEIROS DE CASTRO, E. (1998) 'Cosmological Deixis and Amerindian Perspectivism', *Journal of the Royal Anthropological Institute*, NS 4: 469–88.

VOLKOV, A. (1997) 'Zhao Youqin and his Calculation of π', *Historia Mathematica* 24: 301–31.

WAGNER, D. B. (1979) 'An Early Chinese Derivation of the Volume of a Pyramid: Liu Hui, Third Century AD', *Historia Mathematica* 6: 164–88.

WATSON, B. (2003) *Han Feizi: Basic Writings* (1st edn. 1964), 2nd edn. (New York).

WEBER, M. (1947) *From Max Weber: Essays in Sociology* (trans., ed., and introd. H. H. Gerth and C. Wright Mills) (London).

——(2001) *The Protestant Ethic and the Spirit of Capitalism* (trans. T. Parsons of *Protestantische Ethik und der Geist des Kapitalismus*) (1st edn. 1930), 2nd edn. A. Giddens (London).

WEINER, J. F. (ed.) (1994) *Aesthetics Is a Cross-Cultural Category* (Manchester).

WHITE, H. V. (1973) *Metahistory: The Historical Imagination in Nineteenth-Century Europe* (Baltimore).

——(1978) *Tropics of Discourse* (Baltimore).

——(1992) 'Historical Emplotment and the Problem of Truth', in Friedlander (1992), ch. 2: 37–53.

WHITEHOUSE, H. (1995) *Inside the Cult: Religious Innovation and Transmission in Papua New Guinea* (Oxford).

——(2000) *Arguments and Icons: Divergent Modes of Religiosity* (Oxford).

——(2004) *Modes of Religiosity: A Cognitive Theory of Religious Transmission* (Walnut Creek).

WILLETTS, R. F. (1967) *The Law Code of Gortyn* (Berlin).

WILLIAMS, B. A. O. (1981) 'Philosophy', in M. I. Finley (ed.), *The Legacy of Greece* (London), ch. 8: 202–55.

——(2002) *Truth and Truthfulness: An Essay in Genealogy* (Princeton).

WILSON, B. R. (ed.) (1970) *Rationality* (Oxford).

WINCH, P. (1970) 'Understanding a Primitive Society', in Wilson (1970), 78–110.

WITTGENSTEIN, L. (1966) *Lectures and Conversations on Aesthetics, Psychology and Religious Belief*, ed. C. Barrett (Oxford).

WOJCIK, D. (1997) *The End of the World as We Know It: Faith, Fatalism, and Apocalypse in America* (New York).

WORSLEY, P. (1957) *The Trumpet Shall Sound: A Study of 'Cargo' Cults in Melanesia* (London).

ZEMPLÉNI, A. (2003) 'Les Assemblées secrètes du Poro sénoufo (Nafara, Côte d'Ivoire)', in Detienne (2003), 107–44.

ZIMMERMANN, F. (1987) *The Jungle and the Aroma of Meats* (trans. J. Lloyd of *La Jungle et le fumet des viandes* (Paris 1982)) (Berkeley and Los Angeles).

ZYSK, K. G. (1991) *Asceticism and Healing in Ancient India: Medicine in the Buddhist Monastery* (Oxford).

——(2007) 'The Bodily Winds in Ancient India Revisited', in Hsu and Low (2007), 105–15.

INDEX